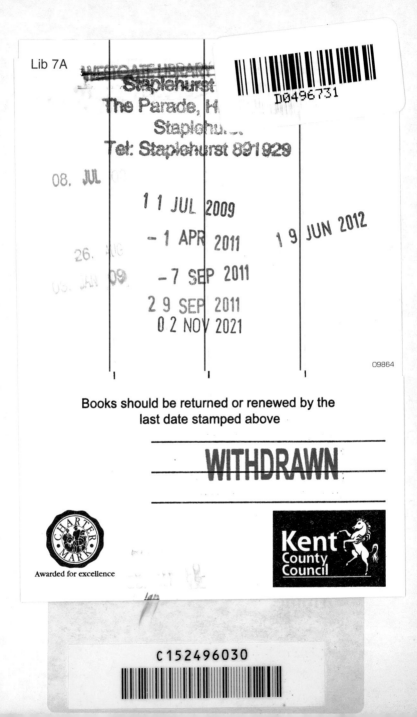

Dedicated to all those Everest climbers, sherpas and
porters – over 170 – who never came back.

'In great things it is enough to have tried.'

Erasmus

MOUNT EVEREST FOUNDATION

ROYAL GEOGRAPHICAL SOCIETY
(WITH THE INSTITUTE OF BRITISH GEOGRAPHERS)

Alpine
CLUB

Everest Exposed
The MEF Authorised History

GEORGE BAND

Collins

HarperCollinsPublishers Ltd.
77-85 Fulham Palace Road
London
W6 8JB

The Collins website address is: www.collins.co.uk

Collins is a registered trademark of HarperCollinsPublishers Ltd.

First published in 2003
First published in paperback in 2005

10 9 8 7 6 5 4 3 2 1

A catalogue record for this book is available from the British Library.

ISBN 0 00 719461 7

Typeset by Rowland Phototypesetting Ltd, Bury St Edmunds, Suffolk
Printed and bound in Great Britain by Clays Ltd, St Ives plc

Contents

List of Maps

RECORD OF FIRST ASCENTS 1953–1996
MOUNT EVEREST 8,848m

1953 BRITISH EXPEDITION
Route No. 1

First ascent via Khumbu Glacier and South Col, 29.5.53

Leader: John Hunt; **Deputy Leader:** Charles Evans; **Other Climbers:** George Band, Thomas Bourdillon, Alfred Gregory, Edmund Hillary, George Lowe, Wilfrid Noyce, Griffith Pugh, Tom Stobart, Michael Ward, Michael Westmacott, Charles Wylie. **Sirdar:** Tenzing Norgay with 34 Sherpas.

First ascent of the world's highest mountain by Edmund Hillary and Tenzing Norgay.

1960 CHINESE EXPEDITION
Route No. 2

First ascent via North Col, east edge of North-west Face and North-east Ridge, 25.5.60. The North Col was approached via the East Rongbuk Glacier and its East Face.

Leader: Shih Chan-chun; **Other Climbers:** Wang Fu-chou, Chu Yin-hua, Konbu (Gonpa) and Liu Lien-man.

All four of this team reached the summit. This was essentially the same route attempted several times by British expeditions in the 1920s and 1930s.

1963 US EXPEDITION
Route No. 3

First ascent via West Ridge, then traverse of the North-west Face to complete via the Hornbein Coloir and the final 250m of the West Ridge, 22.5.63

Leader: Norman Dyhrenfurth with 18 other climbers; **Sirdar:** Pasang Phutar with 32 Sherpas.

This large expedition, which made the third ascent of the mountain, operated as two separate teams above the Western Cwm. Hornbein and Unsoeld reached the summit via the West Ridge late in the evening of 22.5.63. The South Col route was climbed by Whittaker and Sherpa Nawang Gombu on 1 May, and Bishop and Jerstad repeated this climb on 22 May. All six climbers descended by the South Col route, Horbein and Unsoeld thus making the first traverse of Everest.

1975 BRITISH EXPEDITION
Route No. 4

First ascent of the South-west Face, 24.9.75

Leader: Christian Bonington with 18 other climbers; **Sirdar:** Pertemba with 33 Sherpas.

This 2,200m face was first climbed by Haston and Scott Boardman, Sherpa Pertemba and Mick Burke repeated the ascent on 26 Sept. Mick Burke, a member of this second group, disappeared, although his descending partners passed him, climbing upward, very near the top.

1979 YUGOSLAV EXPEDITION
Route No. 5

First ascent of the entire West Ridge, via the Khumbu Glacier and the Lho La, 13 and 15.5.79

Leader: Tone 7karja with 24 other climbers; **Sirdar:** Ang Phu with 20 Sherpas.

Andrej 7tremfelj and Zaplotnik reached the summit on 13 May and Belak, Bozi and Sherpa Ang Phu topped on 15 May. All descended via the Hornbein Couloir. Ang Phu fell and was killed while descending.

1980 JAPANESE EXPEDITION
Route No. 6

The entire North-west Face and Hornbein Couloir, 19.5.80

Expedition Leader: Hyoriko Watanabe; **Climbing Leader:** Hideki Miyashita and 24 climbers and 56 Sherpas.

The new route was climbed by Takashi Ozaki and Tsuneo Shigehiro. A 12-member team climbed the North Col route on 3 May.

1980 POLISH EXPEDITION

First ascent of the Main Couloir just east of Everest's South Pillar, 19.5.80

Leader: Andrzej Zawada with 10 other climbers.

The ascent was completed by Andrzej Czok and Jerzy Kukuczka.

1980 MESSNER SOLO

Route No. 8

First solo, oxygenless ascent, via the East Rongbuk Glacier, North Col and North-west Face by Reinhold Messner, 29.8.80.

This extraordinary feat was accomplished in 3 days from a base camp at the head of the East Rongbuk Glacier, where Messner's only non-climbing companion remained throughout. No route preparation and no assistance of any sort.

1982 SOVIET EXPEDITION

Route No. 9

First ascent of the Western Buttress of the South-west Face to 8,500m on the West Ridge, which was then followed to the summit, 4, 8 and 9.5.82.

Leader: Evgeny Tamm with 19 other climbers; **Sirdar:** Pemba Norbu with 10 Sherpas.

The summit was first reached by Myslovski and Balyberdin. Next came Bershov, Khrishchaty and Valiev on 8 May followed by Golodov, Khomutov and Puchkov on 9 May. This is the most continuously difficult route yet climbed on Everest; as yet unrepeated.

1983 US EXPEDITION

Route No. 10

First ascent of Kangshung Face, 8.10.83

Leader: James Morrisey with 13 other climbers.

The summit was reached by Buhler, Momb and Reichardt, followed by Cassell, Lowe and Reid the following day.

This ascent via the main central buttress of the East Face of Everest involved a very difficult technical rock headwall right at the beginning of the climb (up to 6,500m). This lower section had been reconnoitred in 1981, by Reichardt's first party to investigate the Kangshung side of Everest thoroughly.

1984 AUSTRALIAN EXPEDITION

Route No. 11

First ascent of the Great Couloir of Everest's North-west Face, 3.10.84

Leader: Geoffrey Bartram with just 4 other climbers: Lincoln Hall, Andrew Henderson, Tim McCartney-Snape and Greg Mortimer.

The summit was reached by McCartney-Snape and Mortimer. Oxygen not used. This was the first ascent of the entire Great Couloir which was approached directly from the valley of the Main Rongbuk Glacier.

1984 US EXPEDITION

Route No. 12

First ascent across Upper North-west Face, 20.10.84

Leader: Louis Whittaker with 8 other climbers.

This party approached the peak via both the East and Main Rongbuk Glaciers. Although considerable exploration was done of the lower North-west Face, the only person who reached the summit was Philip Ershler, who climbed diagonally across the North-west Face from above the North Col to the Great Couloir and then to the top via the Australian Route.

1988 INTERNATIONAL EXPEDITION

Route No. 13

First ascent via the South Buttress of the Kangshung Face, 12.5.88

Leader: Robert Anderson with just 3 other climbers: Paul Teare, Stephen Venables and Edward Webster.

Venables, climbing alone and without oxygen above the South Col, reached the summit and bivouacked during his descent to their South Col camp. This climb, like route No. 10, encountered major technical difficulties (mainly on ice) in its lower part, up to 6,650m.

1988 BRITISH ALPINE CLIMBING GROUP   Route No. 14

First Ascent of the Great North-east Ridge (up to 8,400m) 6.8.88

Leader: Brummie Stokes with 11 other climbers.

This long and exposed ridge, approached via the East Rongbuk Glacier, was climbed to an altitude of well over 8,000m by Peter Boardman and Joseph Tasker on 17.5.82. Both climbers disappeared while negotiating the Pinnacles. In 1988, Russell Brice (NZ) and Harry Taylor (GB) got past the Pinnacles, but did not attempt the summit, still a mile away and 400m higher. They descended via the regular North Col route.

A large Japanese team of 13 climbers and 31 Sherpas finally completed the route, 2 Japanese and 4 Sherpas reaching the summit on 11.5.95.

1996 KRASNOYARSK EXPEDITION   Route No. 15

A bold line (not shown on the map) directly up a couloir to the east of the North Ridge, Zakharov's Couloir, 20.5.93

Leader: Nikolai Zakharov with 14 other climbers.

Kohanov, Semikolenov and Kugnetzov reached the summit; the team descending safely in zero visibility by the North Col route.

LHOTSE 8,501m
1956 SWISS EXPEDITION   Route No. 21

Leader: Albert Eggler with 8 other climbers; **Sirdar:** Pasang Dawa Lama, later Dawa Tensing, with 22 Sherpas.

The first ascent to the summit of Lhotse was made on 18.5.56 by Fritz Luchsinger and Ernst Reiss, via the Great Couloir which splits its North-west Face, climbing directly out of the Western Cwm. They were members of the expedition which made the second ascent of Everest on 23 and 24.5.56.

NUPTSE 7,861m
1961 BRITISH EXPEDITION   Route No. 31

Leader: Joseph Walmsley with 8 other climbers; **Sirdar:** Ang Tsering with the Sherpas Nawa Dorje, Pemba, Tashi and Nima Tensing.

The first ascent was made from the south, via the Nuptse Glacier and the Central Ridge, 16 and 17.5.61. The summit was reached by Dennis Davis and Tashi on 16 May and by Bonington, Brown, Swallow and Pemba on 17 May.

1979 INTERNATIONAL EXPEDITION   Route No. 32

Climbers: Georges Bettembourg, Michael Covington, Brian Hall, Alan Rouse, Douglas Scott. An Alpine-style 3-day climb directly up the prominent spur of the North Face from the Western Cwm. Bettembourg (French); Rouse, Hall and Scott (British) all reached the summit on 19.10.79.

Foreword

BY SIR EDMUND HILLARY, KG ONZ KBE

George Band was the youngest member of our 1953 Mount Everest expedition but he was already a skilled mountaineer with wide experience and an excellent sense of humour. He proved his outstanding ability two years later when he reached the summit of the world's third highest peak, Kangchenjunga.

George not only continued making first ascents on other remote and difficult peaks but played a very important role in the administration of mountaineering worldwide. Few people have had his breadth of knowledge of world mountaineering in general and he is the ideal person to write the book in celebration of the 50th Anniversary of the first ascent of Mount Everest.

Author's Note

In the Preface to the only other book I have written, 50 years ago, I apologised for there being so many rotten mountaineering books on the market; they were written, I said, so hurriedly between one expedition and the next. Now to add to the pile, there is yet another book about Everest. One could truly say there were quite enough already, but there has never been one quite like this. It was Myles Archibald of HarperCollins who suggested to me that there should be a new book to celebrate the 50th Anniversary of the first ascent of Everest, and that as the youngest member of that climbing team, I should be the ideal one to pen my personal recollections of that great adventure. During the expedition, as we team members lay in our sleeping bags after supper recalling the events of the day, or memories of previous exciting climbs, we realised that between us we had ample material for a book or two, be it 'Everest Exposed', or 'The Hunt Manual of Man Management', but neither of these works saw the light of day – until now.

One has to see our climb in 1953 in its context as the culmination of a series of attempts each profiting from the experiences – both the successes and the misfortunes – of our predecessors. We were the lucky ones for whom at last it went all right. But that was all 50 years ago, and one could hardly end the story there. I felt I had to pay tribute to all those drawn by the magnetism of the mountain to explore other possible routes, and different ways to climb them, or just to have the thrill of repeating the original ascent.

So in preparing this book in a limited time, both in writing and in selecting the illustrations, I am extremely grateful to all those who have helped me. Fortunately, I have a good Everest library myself so I have gone back to the original expedition accounts where possible, as listed in the Bibliography, but I owe a special debt to three previous writers on Everest: Walt Unsworth, the late Bill Murray and Peter Gillman. Their exhaustive research and selection of the best quotations from the earlier accounts has saved me an immense amount of time and I strongly recommend their books for those who wish to read further. My thanks are also due to the authors and publishers whose works I have quoted in order to add greater authenticity to my account.

The illustrations up to and including 1953 have come partly from The Alpine Club, thanks to Sue Lawford, but mostly from the archives of the Royal Geographical Society, which are now being catalogued in a special Everest Archive under expert guidance, thanks to Joanna Wright. The 20,000 images were originally the property of the Mount Everest Committee, later named the Joint Himalayan Committee (of The Alpine Club and the Royal Geographical Society) by agreement with the expedition members who took the photographs. The ownership passed to the Mount Everest Foundation when it was created after 1953. As the Foundation had no premises of its own, it was agreed in 1974 that the Royal Geographical Society would take care of the images in their own archives. The images taken after 1953 are mostly privately owned and it has been my pleasure to make worldwide contact with the original photographers and thank them for their generous co-operation in making them available, often free of charge.

Sadly, the leader of our 1953 expedition, Lord Hunt, KT CBE DSO, died in November 1998, but our distinguished team member, Sir Edmund Hillary, KG ONZ KBE, has kindly contributed a foreword and I am honoured that the Mount Everest Foundation, The Alpine Club and the Royal Geographical Society (with the Institute of British Geographers) have granted the book official status by endorsing it with their imprimaturs. The Alpine Club even had to get one made specially! At times I wondered whether the three bodies would ever manage to sign their separate contracts with HarperCollins before publication date but they did so. Finally, I thank Myles Archibald, Helen Brocklehurst and their colleagues at HarperCollins; my personal assistant, June Perry, for her computing skills, proof reading and for generally helping me to meet deadlines; and my dear wife, Susan, for her forbearance, not forgetting our Gordon Setter bitch, Jannu, and demanding puppy, Meagaidh.

Hartley Wintney, May 2004

Perspective

I was in the London Underground recently, when a young girl took the vacant seat beside me. She wore a T-shirt, picturing a rare Ibisbill on her breast, that sent my mind racing back to September 1998 when I had first seen this striking bird with its red down-curved bill searching a shingle bank beside a mountain stream. I was in Tibet at some 12,000ft (3,650m), north of Everest, leading the first British purely trekking party, as opposed to a mountaineering expedition, to visit the totally deserted but incredibly spectacular approach up the Kama Valley to the eastern or Kangshung Face of Everest. In 1921, Mallory described it as one of the most beautiful valleys in the world. It astonished me that with some 15,000 trekkers and climbers annually visiting the south side of Everest in Nepal, and hundreds being driven in trucks to the desolate northern Base Camp above the Rongbuk Monastery in Tibet, this eastern side should have kept its secrets. There, I have let the cat out of the bag!

It is now over 80 years since the first expedition went to explore the approaches to Mount Everest, followed by a series of gallant failures, and 50 years have elapsed since our expedition team, brilliantly led by John Hunt, had the skill and good fortune for Ed Hillary and Tenzing Norgay to reach the summit at 11.30am, 29 May 1953. I was invited to write this account (Oh dear – yet another Everest book!) specially to celebrate the 50th Anniversary and to pay tribute to all those earlier expeditions whose members, by their hard-won experience and repeated determination, helped to pave the way.

The funding and organising of these expeditions was arranged by the Mount Everest Committee (later the Joint Himalayan Committee) composed of members of The Alpine Club and the Royal Geographical Society. By means of donations in cash or kind (including delicacies from Fortnum & Mason for the earlier expeditions!) and subsequent books, films and lectures, each expedition was able to pay off its debts. Then with ultimate success in 1953, we hit the jackpot. John Hunt's book *The Ascent of Everest*, written in an astonishing 30 days, outsold the Bible initially and the Everest film, premiered before the Queen on 21 October 1953 at the Warner Theatre, Leicester Square, together with the popular lectures delivered in all of the major cities by members of the team, helped to raise £100,000 within a year – a considerable sum in those days. This was used to create a charitable trust fund to encourage and support the exploration of the world's mountain regions, including education and scientific research. I was told that our Committee intended to name it the 'Everest Trust', but then discovered there was already a body with that name producing calculating machines for dog racing, so they called it the Mount Everest Foundation, which then took over the role and assets of the Joint Himalayan Committee.

We climbers assumed that with Everest 1953 costing some £20,000, which was the price of three Rolls-Royces at the time, the fund would probably be dissipated within 10 to 15 years, but the management committee invested the capital prudently and mostly only distributed the annual dividends to provide priming support for expeditions. There were a few exceptions. Charles Evans' successful 1955 expedition to Kangchenjunga, the world's third highest peak, cost £13,652 and was totally funded by the Foundation. It was the only other of the 14, 8,000m peaks, apart from Everest, to be first climbed by a British team.

I was a lucky recipient, sharing the Foundation's very first grant of £1,000 made to the Cambridge University Rakaposhi Expedition in 1954, and this met about a third of our costs. Grants to expeditions were mostly in the range of £300–£1,500. Almost more important than the grant was the recommendation of the screening committee who interviewed potential expedition leaders to ensure that their team had the competence to undertake their chosen objective, which had to be a new peak, or route, or high-quality exploration or research – not just repeating a known climb. Armed with the Foundation's 'seal of approval' the embryo expedition could more easily seek additional funds and donations to cover the balance remaining after the members' own contributions.

Each year the Foundation pays out in total some £30,000 to about 30 expeditions. Since its inception, it has dispensed £700,000 to over 1,400 expeditions to other greater mountain ranges in all parts of the world: Greenland, USA, Bolivia and India are currently the most popular destinations. This support is the envy of climbers in other countries. Over the years, it has also had a snowball effect in training and providing experience for future leaders. A participant on his or her first successful expedition will soon want to apply for a grant to launch and lead their own group.

The purpose of this book is not only to celebrate the 50th Anniversary of the first ascent of Everest but to create an awareness of the Mount Everest Foundation, and to take the opportunity to replenish its coffers so that it can continue with careful husbandry to dispense grants to expeditions indefinitely. It is ironic that with so many ranges and mountains left to explore, there is an absurd concentration of expensive, often 'commercial' expeditions repeating standard routes on Everest and a handful of other popular peaks when the money could be so much more productively spent on new ventures. For example, Pakistan Tourism's 1997 Annual Report records a total of 57 expeditions, 38, or two-thirds of them, just to their five 8,000m peaks. Plodding up prepared steps while holding on to a fixed rope is not real mountaineering.

This book bears the imprimaturs of the Mount Everest Foundation,

The Alpine Club and the Royal Geographical Society. The illustrations come mostly from the archives of the two parent bodies and the royalties, after costs, will go to the Foundation. It has been a fascinating task to research and select the best images from all the expeditions; not only the key historical photographs but many rarely seen before, including the astonishing panoramas taken by an unknown photographer in 1922 which have languished for 70 years virtually unseen in the basement of The Alpine Club. One of them reminds me of those school photographs taken by a rotating camera where the youngest boy is made to run behind the group from one end to the other and so appear twice in the same picture!

Another great spin-off from Everest 1953 has been a personal initiative by Sir Edmund Hillary, whose life was totally transformed after his summit climb. One October evening in Nepal during a 1960 expedition searching for the yeti, a group were huddled around a smoky fire on the Tolam Bau Glacier when the conversation turned idly to the future welfare of the Sherpas. 'What will happen to you all in the future?' Ed asked their sirdar, Urkein. He thought for a moment and then replied: 'In the mountains, we are as strong as you – maybe stronger – but our children lack education. Our children have eyes but they cannot see. What we need more than anything is a school in Khumjung village.' Hillary felt he owed a debt to the Sherpas and promised them a school. He was as good as his word, raising funds, purchasing materials, and 40 years later, always in response to the Sherpas' petitions, coupled with their own efforts, there are now 26 modestly maintained school buildings, two hospitals and 13 health centres. To highlight the effects of deforestation, almost 100,000 young trees are nurtured each year and more than one million have been planted in protected sites. Hillary has supported the Sherpas' community life and Buddhist culture, providing accident and disaster relief, notably helping in the rebuilding of Thyangboche Monastery after it was partially destroyed by fire on 19 January 1989. The Himalayan Trust's present emphasis is on primary and secondary teacher training, which is strongly supported by the UK branch, chaired by George Lowe, Ed's fellow New Zealander on Everest, from whom I took over as chairman in September 2003. We have even succeeded in obtaining a grant for this work from the National Lottery Charities Board. Hillary and his worldwide supporters in the Trust have more than repaid the debt to the Sherpas.

Now we turn to the early days of Everest, culminating, after years of setback, in the success of 1953. Ed Hillary's son, Peter, who summitted Everest for the second time in May 2002, is justly proud of his father. He says: 'I have met older people who still shed tears when they tell me what the feat meant to them.'

OI

Early Days and the 1921 Reconnaissance

'Sir, I have discovered the highest mountain in the world.'   Radhanath Sikhdar

The classic story is that one day in 1852 the Bengali chief 'computer', Radhanath Sikhdar, rushed into the office of Sir Andrew Waugh, the Surveyor General of India in Dehra Dun, and exclaimed, 'Sir, I have discovered the highest mountain in the world.'

Prior to that date, the accolade had been held by Kangchenjunga, lying on the frontier of Nepal and Sikkim, and dominating the north-western horizon as seen from the famous hill station of Darjeeling, only 44 miles (70km) away, where people who could afford it would go from the stifling summer heat of Calcutta for a break in the cool refreshing mountain air. A popular activity was to rise before dawn and climb to the top of Tiger Hill to see the first rays of the sun hit the jumble of Himalayan giants in Nepal, which was then a closed country. If it were a really clear morning you could see or at least imagine one far distant summit over 100 miles (160km) away, briefly illuminated before the sun hit Kangchenjunga itself.

It was in 1849 that the Great Trigonometrical Survey of India, under the direction of Sir George Everest, began to include the mountains of Nepal. As they were so far away, and the local names were not known, they were allocated Roman numerals and Everest was called Peak XV. Observations from six different stations, averaging 111 miles (179km) away, were used to compute the height which averaged 29,000ft (8,839m). A large number of corrections need to be applied, apart from deciding what is your reference datum and the geoid employed. Sea level on Earth is not measured as the surface of a sphere but the surface of a rotating spheroid (i.e. gravitational pull affecting the measurement). The Equator is 6.8 miles (11km) further from the centre of the Earth than are the Poles. One has also to allow for the gravitational attraction of Everest and its neighbours affecting the deflection of a plumb-line, but the largest correction of all is for atmospheric refraction. A later series of measurements making allowance for refraction, but still not for deviations due to gravity, averaged out at 29,141ft (8,882m) and this height was in vogue for some years, although the Survey of India preferred to maintain 29,002ft (8,840m) on their maps.

Not until after Everest was climbed in 1953, was a modern and more accurate assessment made of 29,028ft (8,848m) so Hillary and Tenzing had to climb an extra 26ft (8m)! The last word was introduced in the 1990s by Bradford Washburn, lifelong Director of the Boston Museum of Science, who in the era of satellite communication and geographical positioning systems (GPS), made the definitive mapping of Everest almost a personal crusade; he enlisted the most expert Swiss cartographers and received permission from the Nepalese and Chinese authorities to fly over the mountain in a Learjet. I recall Washburn showing me, beside a relief model of Everest at the Royal Geographical Society, how his latest 1:5,000-scale transparency with 5m contour intervals fitted over the most accurate map showing features of the mountain. One could virtually select the most nearly level places for campsites on the North-East Ridge.

Brad Washburn and his co-workers have been exceptionally generous in allowing me to reproduce portions of their maps and photographs: the 1:5,000-scale contour map, which shows everything from the South

Col to the North Col for the first time, made in collaboration with Swissphoto Surveys of Zurich; also the vertical photograph of the top of Everest taken for him from a Learjet, with National Geographic Society funding, from an altitude of 39,000ft (11,890m) on 20 December 1984 by Swissphoto Surveys.

The most generally available version of their beautifully crafted map of the Everest region is at a scale of 1:50,000 with 40m (13ft) contour intervals. A special version of this map at a scale of 1:25,000 is included as Plate 1 and is overprinted with all the routes achieved on the Everest, Lhotse and Nuptse massif at the date of its 1991 publication. On Everest itself it shows 14 routes, excluding only the full ascent of the North-East Ridge by the Japanese in May 1995, and the Zakharov's Couloir on the secondary North Face, climbed by the Russians in May 1996.

My geologist friend Mike Searle tells me that new space geodesy using GPS measures distances from the centre of the Earth's mass and can now provide accuracies of +/- 1cm in the horizontal and +/- 2cm in the vertical direction measuring to the spheroid. Washburn's final analysis resulted in a new height of 29,035ft that rounds off nicely to 8,850m. With small metal reference discs now firmly bolted to the bed rock and permanently located at various points on the mountain, including one at the South Col at 25,888.5ft (7,890.8m), future measurements will be able to detect whether, as suspected, Everest is drifting ever so slightly to the north-east at 6cm per year and surreptitiously creeping upward in keeping with the continuing uplift of the Himalayas over geological time, which is thought to be rising in places at 1–3cm per year.

Radhanath Sikhdar would have marvelled at such accuracy. In fact, he was transferred from Dehra Dun to the Surveyor General's office in Calcutta in 1849 so was not involved in 1852 in computing the heights of Peak XV and other neighbouring peaks. The chief computer in Dehra Dun at that time was an Anglo-Indian, John B.N. Hennessy, who had read Mathematics at Jesus College, Cambridge. In fact, as Walt Unsworth and others point out, the discovery and confirmation of the height of Everest was the corporate work of field surveyors and computers and not the work of any one man. It is possible that Sikhdar had made preliminary calculations and Hennessy had revised them. The work had not been completed until 1856, so they and several others can all share in the credit.

It was Sir Andrew Waugh who suggested naming the mountain after his immediate predecessor, Sir George Everest, who had initiated the Great Trigonometrical Survey. This name was adopted by the Royal Geographical Society in 1865. How fortunate that it was such an appropriate-sounding epithet. A similar approach to naming the second highest peak after a later Surveyor General, Colonel Henry Haversham Godwin Austen, had not been so successful and the world has reverted to the original survey designation, K2; the 'K' standing for Karakoram.

A local name for a newly designated peak is usually sought, but from the Nepal side so little was known about the mountains that for many years Peak XV was confused with another striking peak called 'Gaurisankar', some 36 miles (58km) away. Locals usually refer to a range rather than a single peak, which may have no special significance to them. It is only from the Tibetan side that Everest stands out as a single dominating mountain, particularly as seen by the Buddhist monks of the Rongbuk Monastery at its foot. They had known it for many years as 'Chomolungma', as it is now usually spelt in English. Indeed, in 1733, D'Anville of Paris had published a map of Tibet correctly marking the mountain's position and name based on the work of French Capuchin friars who had lived in Lhasa from 1707 to 1733 and who returned through western Tibet. 'Chomolungma' may be translated as 'Goddess Mother of the World', making it a very appropriate name, although another derivation used in official papers from Lhasa, which referred to the general district rather than the peak, may be translated as the 'Bird Country of the South'. Chomolungma is now the name regularly adopted by Chinese mountaineers. Not to be outdone, the Government of Nepal have recently introduced the alternative name 'Sagarmatha' for the mountain, but this is not catching on although it is used for the name of the National Park created in the 1970s on the southern side of Everest.

Himalayan Climbing Begins

It must be a coincidence that just one year after the survey of India completed the computation work on the height of Everest in 1856, The Alpine Club was founded in London. Although Mont Blanc had been climbed in 1786, it wasn't until the 1850s that mountaineering in Europe came to be regarded as a sport. Gradually the great Alpine peaks succumbed and British climbers began to look further afield – Freshfield to the Caucasus; Whymper and Conway to the Andes.

The first tentative steps in Himalayan climbing were taken in 1879 by the Hungarian Von Dechy and in 1883 by William Woodman Graham, but in 1892 Martin Conway organised a more elaborate expedition to the Karakoram, west of the Himalayas. One look at K2 was enough for the time being, but he did establish a new height record on reaching the summit of Pioneer Peak, 22,600ft (6,888m), a subsidiary of Balthoro Kangri. One of his companions was a lieutenant from the 5th Gurkhas, the Hon. Charles Granville Bruce, who was later to play a leading role in early Everest exploration. Conway's reports to The Times stimulated great interest which inevitably turned conversation towards Everest and whether it could possibly be climbed. Back in 1885, writing in his book *Above the Snowline*, Clinton Dent had said: 'I do not for a moment say that it would be wise to ascend Mount Everest, but I believe most firmly that it is humanly possible to do so; and, further, I feel sure that even in our own time perhaps, the truth of these views will receive material collaboration.'

The year following Conway's expedition, Bruce was in Chitral, with Francis Younghusband, and made the first direct proposal that they should try to climb Everest. Younghusband, then Political Officer in

Chitral, had already made a name for himself. After a mission in Manchuria, instead of returning to his regiment in India the conventional way by sea, he sought and gained the Viceroy's permission to cross the unexplored wastes of the Gobi Desert – the first westerner to do so since Marco Polo.

Pursuing the shortest route across the mountains into India, he then traversed the 19,000ft (5,790m) Mustagh Pass into the Shaksgam Valley. It was his first encounter with a glacier without boots, ropes, ice axes or crampons. Fortunately, it had not occurred to his local guide, Wali, to turn back, so Younghusband followed in his steps: 'I freely confess that I myself could never have attempted the ascent and that I – an Englishman – was afraid to go first.' Younghusband was awarded the Gold Medal of the Royal Geographical Society in 1890 for his journey and in 1904 was sent on a special mission to Lhasa in Tibet.

During this mission, two of his officers, Major Ryder and Captain Rawling, actually approached within 60 miles (96km) of Everest from the north and thought it might be climbed from that side. But could anyone survive at such altitudes? After Conway, climbers had gradually been raising the Himalayan altitude record. Dr and Mrs Bullock Workman, Kellas, Longstaff and Meade had all exceeded 23,000ft (7,010m) on various peaks and, in 1909, the Duke of Abruzzi, accompanied by his Alpine guides, the brothers Brocherel, reached 24,600ft (7,498m) on Bride Peak in Kashmir.

Alexander Mitchell Kellas, a lecturer in Chemistry, became very interested in the physiology of extreme altitude and, in particular, the challenge of climbing Mount Everest. In 1920, he wrote a remarkable paper that languished unpublished in The Alpine Club for 80 years until resuscitated by Dr John B. West in 2001 on the 80th anniversary of Kellas's death. Kellas reached the remarkable conclusion that 'Mount Everest could be ascended by a man of excellent physical and mental constitution in first rate training without adventitious aids (supplementary oxygen) if the physical difficulties are not too great, and with the use of oxygen, even if the mountain may be classed as difficult from the climbing point of view'. It took 58 years for Rheinhold Messner and Peter Habeler to bear out the first part of this prediction.

While at Cambridge in 1950, I also vividly remember Tom Longstaff speaking to the Mountaineering Club about his first ascent of Trisul in 1907, followed by an attempted climb on Gurla Mandata, 25,355ft (7,728m), in Tibet. He showed a slide illustrating his high point and then announced: 'We were swept down 2,000ft by an avalanche to here. Next slide, please,' banging the butt of his billiard cue pointer on the ground for emphasis. 'We then spent the night in this snow hole here.' Bang. 'Next slide, please.' He was a little man, still with traces of his original red hair, and I felt he had quite a resemblance, both physically and in character, to Francis Younghusband, who was named in Patrick French's biography as 'The Last Great Imperial Adventurer'.

Hopes of access to Mount Everest from the south through Nepal were discouraged by treaty obligations and also because the climb was suspected to be more difficult than from the north. The idea of an approach through Tibet was encouraged by the Viceroy, Lord Curzon, and it had occurred to Bruce, Longstaff and A.L. Mumm that the Golden Jubilee of The Alpine Club in 1907 could not be better celebrated than by an attempt on Everest; but a later Viceroy, Lord Morley, would have nothing to do with the project.

Access to Everest

World War I then put a stop to further exploration, but, as soon as it was over, interest revived. In March 1919, Captain J.B.L. Noel lectured to the Royal Geographical Society about a journey he had made in disguise towards Everest in 1913. Planning his route from the writing of one of the 'pundits' or Indian native surveyors, Sarat Chandra Das, he got within 40 miles (64km) of the mountain before being turned back by soldiers. 'Some day,' Noel concluded his lecture, 'the political difficulties will be overcome and a fully equipped expedition must explore and map Mount Everest.'

Captain J.P. Farrar, then President of The Alpine Club, took this as a proposal to attempt the mountain and replied that he had young mountaineers ready to take up the challenge. Younghusband countered: 'It must be done.' Within days, the Secretary of State for India was asked to receive a deputation from the two bodies and, in June 1920, Lieutenant Colonel Howard-Bury was invited to proceed to India, explain the proposal and ask the Government to obtain from the Dalai Lama permission to enter Tibet for the purpose of exploring and climbing Mount Everest. This task fell to Charles Bell, the political agent in Sikkim who happened to be in Lhasa and who was on very friendly terms with His Holiness. But it was not all that straightforward. Howard-Bury was 37 years old, an old Etonian, and had commanded the 60th Rifles during the war, earning a DSO and no fewer than six 'mentions in dispatches'. John Hunt, the leader of our 1953 expedition, draws some striking parallels in a memoir about Howard-Bury:

He was born in the same year as my father, 1881. They must have both passed through Sandhurst as cadets at the same time. He served in my regiment, the King's Royal Rifle Corps. Like my father, he was taken prisoner in Flanders, but unlike him, Howard-Bury survived the War. Like me, he served as an Intelligence Officer and shared with me a bent for foreign languages. As his part in obtaining the vital clearance for the expedition reveals, he was an able negotiator and something of a diplomat. Howard-Bury was a man of many parts.

Unlike John Hunt, he was not a member of The Alpine Club, nor was he really a mountaineer, but he had travelled in the Tien Shan and other parts of Central Asia on trophy hunting and botanical expeditions when stationed in India. He was once given a bear cub and also a collection of singing larks that he brought safely home to his estate, Belvedere House, near Mullingar in Ireland. As the bear grew, his master's favourite keep-fit exercise used to be a friendly wrestling match with his 7 foot (2.1m) friend. Visitors to the house must have been considerably taken aback when it learned how to open the door!

Howard-Bury was comfortably well off and agreed to undertake the Indian mission at his own expense, which I can imagine was a good reason for choosing him, and which was fortunate for the Committee back in England because it took him four months. Another burning topic which was being discussed between the India Office in London and the Government in India was whether certain modest arms should be sent to the Tibetans, and that needed to be settled first. Bell was also a very slow and cautious person, but he was eventually instructed and agreed to ask the Dalai Lama who, after several interviews, gave his consent. At the same time, records Bell, 'he handed me a little brown strip of parchment-like paper made in Tibet. On this was written in cursive Tibetan script what may be translated as follows: "To the west of the Five Treasuries of Great Snow, in the jurisdiction of White Glass Fort near Rocky Valley Inner Monastery, is the Bird Country of the South (Lho Cha-mo Lung)."' What could have been the Dalai Lama's thoughts about these strangers, wishing to climb the highest mountain in the world, of entering the abode of the gods? What conceivable object could they have? Bell was pleading a strange cause, but over many years he had never done any harm to Tibet. The Dalai Lama's consent was undoubtedly a gesture of friendship to a man whom he trusted.

Permission Granted

The great news was received in London on 20 December 1920. The Royal Geographical Society and The Alpine Club set up a special joint committee, the Mount Everest Committee, to put it into effect, and so in the words of Walt Unsworth, which I can confirm only slightly tongue in cheek, 'began a mild love-hate relationship between the two organisations which has endured to the present day'.

The Committee first met on 12 January 1921 and included Sir Francis Younghusband, Colonel E.M. Jack, Edward Somers-Cocks from the Geographical Society, and Norman Collie, Captain Farrar and C.F. Meade from The Alpine Club. The day-to-day duties fell to Arthur Hinks, the Professional Secretary of the Royal Geographical Society, a post he held from 1915 to 1945. Hinks was a formidable character, a mathematician and an authority on map projections. He was very hard working but also a difficult and abrasive person. He had a deep hatred of publicity which did not help when it came to raising funds. The Committee envisaged a two-year effort, a thorough reconnaissance in 1921 and a serious attempt the following year, the two together expected to cost about £10,000. The costs for 1921, between £3,000 and £4,000, were raised by private subscription mostly from members of The Alpine Club and fellows of the Geographical Society, plus a few wealthy individuals; King George V gave £100. To cover the following year, much to Hinks's disgust, contracts for expedition telegrams went to The Times and the Philadelphia Ledger and photographs to the Graphic.

General Bruce was considered for the leadership but he had just taken up a new appointment with the Glamorganshire Territorial Association and was not available, so the choice fell on Colonel Howard-Bury who had done such a good job in securing the permit and was an experienced Central Asian traveller. Hopefully Bruce would be available for the climb in 1922. The Committee stated that 'the main object this year is reconnaissance. This does not debar the mountain party climbing as high as possible on a favourable route, but attempts on a particular route must not be prolonged to hinder the completion of the reconnaissance.'

The 1921 Team

The climbing team was limited to four: two veterans, Harold Raeburn and A.M. Kellas, and two younger men who might spearhead the next year's assault, George Leigh Mallory and George Finch; but, at the time, the latter was unwell and failed his medical and was replaced at short notice by G.H. Bullock. Raeburn was an outstanding Scottish climber with a record of guideless climbing in the Alps and had been to 21,000ft (6,400m) on Kangchenjunga in 1920, but was already 56 years old. Kellas at 53 years old had accumulated considerable high-altitude Himalayan experience since his first visit in 1907, having made first ascents of Pauhunri, 23,180ft (7,065m), and Chomiomo, 22,430ft (6,837m), reached the summit plateau of Kangchenjau, 22,700ft (6,919m), and gone to 23,400ft (7,130m) on Kamet. Unusually, Kellas had mostly climbed accompanied only by local porters or coolies, as they were then called, but had come to realize that, with only a little training, the best of them could be trusted as strong, intelligent, loyal and cheerful companions. Whereas Mallory considered Raeburn to be difficult and dictatorial, he was intrigued by Kellas, describing him as 'very slight in build, short, thin, stooping and narrow chested. His head ... made grotesque by veritable gig-lamps of spectacles and a long pointed moustache'.

Mallory was 35 years old, a schoolmaster at Charterhouse, and had already established himself at Geoffrey Winthrop Young's Easter house-parties in North Wales as one of the best rock climbers around. 'He swung up rock with a long thigh, lifted knee and a ripple of irresistible movement,' wrote Young. Mallory soloed one new route on Lliwedd, the Slab Climb, reputedly to recover a pipe left behind on a grassy ledge called 'The Bowling Green'. At Winchester, he was influenced by a master, R.L.G. Irving, who was a keen Alpinist. At Cambridge, where his statuesque good looks and athleticism ensured his popularity, he overwhelmed the homosexual Lytton Strachey. After taking his degree, he was undecided what to do and drifted into school teaching. Even when invited by Farrar to go to Everest he thought of refusing, but Young persuaded him to go – the expedition would help his career if he decided to become a writer – so he accepted without visible emotion. It was a low key beginning for one whose name was to become inseparably linked with Everest. Mallory's partner, G.H. Bullock, was 24 years old and had also been a climbing protégé of Irving's at Winchester. He was now in the Consular Service but managed to get extended leave. He was a friendly character who seemed to be the only one who got on well with everyone. He had 'an ability to sleep under any conditions', said Howard-Bury – a valuable asset at high altitude to help recover from fatigue and keep going for days on end.

The party was completed by two scientists, Dr A.F.R. Wollaston as medical officer and naturalist and Dr A.M. Heron as geologist, and two surveyors, who were paid for by the Survey of India and selected from their staff: Majors H.T. Morshead and E.O. Wheeler. They were astute choices, being good mountaineers as well. Henry Morshead was 39, and in 1913 – travelling unofficially with F.M. Bailey and with slender resources – had shown that the Tsangpo in Tibet and the Brahmaputra in India were one and the same river, almost encircling the previously undiscovered isolated peak of Namche Barwa, 25,445ft (7,756m), at the eastern end of the Himalayan chain. He had been on Kamet with Kellas in 1920 and was later acknowledged by Norton as a tough character: 'His shirt open at the chest to the dreadful Tibetan wind – a heart breaking man to live with.' Inexplicably, he was murdered in Burma, 10 years later whilst out on an early morning ride, his horse returning riderless with the saddle covered in blood.

I had a friendly but reluctant encounter with his son, Nigel, many years later. We were in the same basic training intake during National Service, and as part of the toughening-up process, we were matched to box three minutes against each other. The Commanding Officer had addressed us all: 'You may not have much skill and you may get hurt but I want you to get in the ring and show you 'ave got guts. And I don't mind if there's some blood!' I found it utterly distasteful but went in, flailed my long arms around and, to my astonishment, was judged the winner! Only later did I learn that because of my poor eyesight I could have been medically excused from taking part. We met again in happier circumstances when he kindly came to the artistes' suite to say 'hallo' after I had given a 1953 Everest lecture at the Royal Festival Hall. The other surveyor, Oliver Wheeler, was 31 and had only been with the survey for two years but was chosen because of his experience in the new technique of photo-survey, which he had learned in his native Canada where he had accompanied his father on many expeditions in the Rockies.

Raeburn was invited to lead the climbing party – with an average age of 44 years – and it seemed that very little equipment was specially designed. They just took the best generally available. Each member was given £50 – later increased to £100 if necessary – to choose their clothing and boots, but Howard-Bury and Wollaston paid for their own.

The Approach through Sikkim

The expedition assembled in Darjeeling early in May 1921. As Nepal was closed to Europeans, it was necessary to travel north through Sikkim into Tibet making a long, circuitous approach across the desolate Tibetan Highlands to reach Everest from the north. Ironically, the best of their porters came from villages in the north-east corner of Nepal only a few miles to the south of Everest. These were the Sherpas, who originally settled in these deserted steep-sided valleys some 300 years previously, having crossed the high passes from Tibet. As Kellas had found, they could carry heavy loads to great heights. They were issued with extra-warm clothing and eiderdown sleeping bags for use at the higher camps, and boots specially made on a Sherpa last, as often, wrote Howard-Bury, their feet were almost as broad as they were long.

Two local men of some position and standing were engaged to act as interpreters: Gyalzen Kazi, a land owner from Gangtok, and Chhetan Wangdi, who had been a captain in the Tibetan Army and had served with the Indian Army in Egypt. One hundred mules had been engaged to carry 160lb (73kg) each, and 40 porters to carry loads. For convenience at limited camping grounds in Sikkim, they were split into two parties and left Darjeeling a day apart on 18 and 19 May. Morshead had left five days earlier with a survey party going directly up the valley of the Teesta – the river and its tributaries that drain the whole of Sikkim – then across the Serpo La to Kampa Dzong in Tibet. Their aim was to tie in the Indian Survey with the new survey they would carry out in Tibet. The others took a longer but easier route over the Jelap La to the Chumbi Valley and then across west to join up in Kampa Dzong.

They carried with them a special passport provided by the Government in Lhasa under the seal of the Prime Minister of Tibet, translated as follows:

To the Jongpens and Headmen of Pharijong, Ting-ke, Khamba and Kharta.

You are to bear in mind that a party of Sahibs are coming to see the Chha-mo-lung-ma mountain and they will evince great friendship towards the Tibetans. On the request of the Great Minister Bell a passport has been issued requiring you and all officials and subjects of the Tibetan Government to supply transport, e.g. riding ponies, pack animals and coolies as required by the Sahibs, the rates for which should be fixed to mutual satisfaction. Any other assistance that the Sahibs may require either by day or by night, on the march or during halts, should be faithfully given, and their requirements about transport or anything else should be promptly attended to. All the people of the country, wherever the Sahibs may happen to come, should render all necessary assistance in the best possible way, in order to maintain friendly relations between the British and Tibetan Governments.

Despatched during the Iron-Bird Year.
Seal of the Prime Minister.

It rained heavily the night before they started but, although it cleared, the hillsides were wreathed in soft grey mists and every moss-hung branch and tree dripped steadily with moisture all day long. The route descended rapidly 4,000ft (1,220m) through tea plantations and then a further 2,000ft (610m) of Sal forest into the hot steamy gorge of the Teesta River. Brilliant butterflies flitted across the path. Typical days of 12 miles (19km) or so followed, combined with 2,000–3,000ft of ascent and descent across forested ridges and past luxuriant gardens with scarlet hibiscus, purple bougainvillea and datura hedges laden with white trumpet-shaped blooms. They would meet other mules descending from Tibet with bales of wool which would return with sheets of copper, manufactured goods, grain and rice bought in exchange. Many of their mules were unfit for heavy work in the mountains and had to be sent back and exchanged for stronger hill ponies. As they began the climb towards Tibet, they were enveloped in mist but had occasional glimpses of pink, white or yellow rhododendrons on the hillsides. At length, passing banks of old winter snow, they reached the Jelap Pass at 14,390ft (4,386m). A big heap of stones decorated with strings of Buddhist prayer flags marked the frontier. On the other side, they emerged from the mist and rain to glimpses of clear blue sky. They had arrived in Tibet.

Into Tibet

They descended into the Chumbi Valley where the annual rainfall was only a quarter of that in Sikkim, with an almost European climate and vegetation, with forests of dark silver fir lightened with colourful rhododendrons and wild roses. This was one of the richest valleys in Tibet. At 9,400ft (2,865m), apples and pears, barley, wheat and potatoes all grew well, and in the villages there was a feeling of prosperity and peace.

They turned aside to visit a new monastery building at Galinka, with a great gilt image of Buddha. In a side room was a huge prayer wheel, 12ft (3.7m) high and 6ft (1.8m) in diameter, inscribed with the traditional prayer, 'Om Mani Padme Hum' (Hail to the Jewel in the Lotus). Inside it, said the monks, were one and a half million prayers which went up to heaven with every revolution, which also rang a bell.

On they went to Phari at 14,300ft (4,360m); a dirty, cold and windy village dominated by a stone fort and lying under the shadow of a great mountain, Chomolhari, 23,930ft (7,294m), straddling the frontier with Bhutan. Transport was becoming more complex, as half the pack animals were going right through to Kampa Dzong and the other half were being changed at every stage – one of the typical complications of travelling in Tibet. They also had trouble with some of their porters, and the cooks' lack of hygiene made all the Sahibs ill, in particular Dr Kellas who had not been very fit at the start and now had to be carried in a wicker armchair. One evening, a cook heated up some tinned fish in hot water without opening the tin first. When he started to open it in the rarefied air, it exploded violently and covered everyone in the kitchen with fragments of fish. Howard-Bury then explained to the porters that the stores were very dangerous and, if stolen, were liable to explode and hurt them!

At the Tang La, 15,200ft (4,634m), they crossed the main Himalayan watershed, after which the climate became much drier. The going was now easier over gentle passes, crossing a valley containing flocks of sheep and yaks, and then a barren stony plain over which the wind blew keenly. Howard-Bury shot a gazelle, which was good eating, and later a full-grown *Ovis ammon*, a big-horned sheep, giving several days' food for the porters. Nearby was a nunnery with 30 nuns, all with shorn heads but wearing curious wool headdresses instead.

The Death of Kellas

On 4 June, they arrived at the great fortress of Kampa Dzong where Morshead's party had already arrived. Suddenly, a man ran up excitedly to say that Dr Kellas had died on the way. Wollaston duly confirmed that it was a case of heart failure due to Kellas's weak condition, having over-exerted himself on expeditions earlier in the year. His death was a great loss to the expedition, as only he knew much about the effect of supplementary oxygen on performance and acclimatisation. He was buried there on a beautiful site looking across the broad Tibetan Plains towards those great peaks, Pauhunri, Kangchenjau and Chomiomo, that he, the only European, had climbed with his Sherpas. There was even a first distant view of the summit of Everest 100 miles (160km) or more to the west. Mallory wrote to Geoffrey Winthrop Young:

> I shan't easily forget the four boys, his own trained mountain men, children of nature seated in wonder on a great stone near the grave while Bury read out the passage from Corinthians.

Raeburn was also not feeling well and it was decided that he should return with Wollaston to Sikkim to recuperate. So without even reaching Everest, the senior half of the climbing team was gone as well as all three doctors. On the mountain itself, therefore, all would depend on Mallory and Bullock. Fortunately, the surveyors, Morshead and Wheeler, were still in good heart.

The next place of importance was the town of Shekar Dzongs situated on a rocky sharp-pointed mountain 'Like an enlarged St Michael's Mount,' said Bury. The whole town turned out, curious to see their first Europeans. Next day, 18 June, Howard-Bury and Morshead called on the chief official or Jongpen, who wisely lived at the bottom of the hill rather than in his official residence ¾ of the way up. He served the traditional Tibetan tea and sweets but then followed it with a meal of macaroni and meat seasoned with chillies, then junket in china bowls. He had some very fine tea cups carved from agate and hornblende schist with finely chased silver covers. Up the hill was the big monastery of Shekar Chöte, with a huge gilt figure of Buddha 50ft (15m) high and smaller ones decorated with turquoise and other precious stones. The monks had never seen photographs or a camera before but were able to persuade the aged and highly venerated Head Lama to come outside and be photographed seated on a raised dais and wearing golden brocades, with Chinese silk hangings draped behind him. The fame of the photograph spread and a print became a welcome present. One stage further was Tingri, reached on 19 June, in the middle of a great plain with a chain of snowy peaks over 25,000ft (7,620m) high to the south extending westward from Everest. This was to be the expedition's first base for the reconnaissance of the north and north-western approaches to Everest. The trip had taken a month from Darjeeling.

The First Views of Everest

Actually, the reconnaissance had begun at Kampa Dzong, the day after Kellas's death. On the way to Shiling, they had climbed up perhaps a thousand feet, above the rugged fort, turned and saw, in Mallory's words:

> There was no mistaking the two great peaks in the West; that to the left must be Makalu, grey, severe and yet distinctly graceful, and the other away to the right – who could doubt its identity? It was a prodigious white fang excrescent from the jaw of the world ... We were satisfied that the highest of mountains would not disappoint us.

As they went west from Kampa Dzong, they lost sight of Everest because their route lay in a gorge to the north of the mountains where the Yaru River cuts through to join the mighty Arun River which, in turn, cuts right through the Himalayas. On 11 June, unable to contain their curiosity, Mallory and Bullock climbed steeply to a rocky crest over-looking the gorge: 'The only visible snow mountains were in Sikkim. Kangchenjunga was clear and eminent; we had never seen it so fine before; it now seemed singularly strong and monumental, like the leonine face of some splendid musician with a glory of white hair.' It was cloudy in the direction of Everest, but in the middle distance their attention was drawn to a rocky spike or aiguille. Then a rift opened out in the clouds behind. Mallory wrote:

At first we had merely a fleeting glimpse of some mountain evidently much more distant; then a larger and clearer view revealed a recognizable form; it was Makalu appearing just where it should be according to our calculations with map and compass.

We were now able to make out almost exactly where Everest should be; but the clouds were dark in that direction. We gazed at them intently through field glasses as though by some miracle we might pierce the veil. Presently the miracle happened. We caught the gleam of snow behind the grey mists. A whole group of mountains began to appear in gigantic fragments. Mountain shapes are often fantastic seen through a mist; these were like the wildest creation of a dream. A preposterous triangular lump rose out of the depths; its edge came leaping up at an angle of about 70° and ended nowhere. To the left a black serrated crest was hanging in the sky incredibly. Gradually, very gradually, we saw the great mountain sides and glaciers and arêtes, now one fragment and now another through the floating rifts, until far higher in the sky than imagination had dared to suggest the white summit of Everest appeared. And in this series of partial glimpses we had seen a whole; we were able to piece together the fragments, to interpret the dream.

They were seeing Everest 57 miles (90km) away to the south-west. Mallory continued:

A long arête was thrust out towards us. Some little distance below the summit the arête came down to a black shoulder, which we conjectured would be an insuperable obstacle. To the right of this we saw the sky line in profile and judged it not impossibly steep. The edge was probably a true arête because it appeared to be joined by a col to a sharp peak to the North. From the direction of this col a valley came down to the East and evidently drained into the Arun. This was one fact of supreme importance which was now established and we noticed that it agreed with what was shown on the map; the map in fact went up in our esteem and we were inclined hereafter to believe in its veracity until we established the contrary. Another fact was even more remarkable. We knew something more about the great peak near Everest which we had seen from Kampa Dzong; we knew now that it was not

> a separate mountain; in a sense it was part of Everest, or rather Everest was
> not one mountain but two; this great black mountain to the South was connected
> with Everest by a continuous arête and divided from it only by a snow col which
> must itself be 27,000ft high. The black cliffs of this mountain, which faced us, were
> continuous with the icy East Face of Everest itself.

Mallory and Bullock had, in fact, identified the ridge leading up from the 'North Col' which would later be their attempted route of ascent. The great black mountain would later be called Lhotse, meaning 'south peak' in Tibetan, joined to Everest by the saddle later known as the 'South Col'. No later view gave them so much information as on that single occasion. The confidence in their rudimentary map increased, even though it was later to be dashed!

From Tingri, their task was to examine the north and north-western sides of Everest, but first they had to find the mountain. They split up into groups: Morshead surveying around Tingri; Wheeler and Heron moving south towards the Khumbu La, or Nangpa La, the main pass leading to Nepal. Wollaston stayed in Tingri collecting botanical specimens and doctoring – two porters had enteritis and one sadly died within a few days. Howard-Bury spent time visiting the various parties.

Exploring from Rongbuk

Mallory and Bullock left on 23 June and took 16 porters, a sirdar, Gyalzen, and a cook, Dukpa. They were all issued with climbing boots, nailed with clinkers during the march, ice axes and a suit of underwear. Now separated from their interpreters, Mallory regretted that his 150 words of Tibetan written in a notebook would hardly suffice for conversation. They followed the valley of the Dzahar Chu to Chobuk and then turned south to Rongbuk. Going through a gorge, they breasted a rise, crowned with two chortens, and paused in astonishment. The stupendous North Face of Everest rose dramatically before them, revealed for the first time. Mallory wrote:

> The Rongbuk Valley is well constructed to show off the peak at its head; for about 20 miles it is extraordinarily straight and in that distance rises only 4,000 feet, the glacier, which is 10 miles long, no more steeply than the rest. In consequence of this arrangement one has only to be raised very slightly above the bed of the valley to see it almost as flat way up to the very head of the glacier from which the cliffs of Everest spring. To the place where Everest stands one looks along rather than up. The glacier is prostrate; not a part of the mountain; not even a pediment; merely a floor footing the high walls. At the end of the valley and above the glacier Everest rises not so much a peak as a prodigious mountain-mass. There is no complication for the eye. The highest of the world's great mountains, it seems, has to make but a single gesture of magnificence to be lord of all, vast in unchallenged and isolated supremacy. To the discerning eye other mountains are visible, giants between 23,000 and 26,000 feet high. Not one of their slenderer heads even reaches their chief's shoulder; beside Everest they escape notice – such is the pre-eminence of the greatest.

From this viewpoint, the mountain was structurally simple. One steep face of 10,000ft (3,050m) bounded by ridges on either side: the long West Ridge and, on the left, a North-East Ridge falling 1,500ft (457m) to the shoulder already seen from Shiling. A northerly ridge descends from the shoulder, rising again to a north peak – later called Changtse – which forms the east wall of the Rongbuk Glacier. They pitched their base camp at 16,500ft (5,030m) near the snout of the Rongbuk Glacier, which was to serve them for a month. Neither of them had experience of big mountains outside the Alps. There the glaciers are most usually highways for the climber. What would they be like here? On their first day, they made an Alpine start at 3.15am. The lower part of the glacier was covered with stones but higher up it became a white stream with pinnacles of ice – not seracs such as one meets on an Alpine icefall, but firmly based, conical and quite regular; the result not of movement but of differential melting or sublimation. The largest were about 50ft (15m) high, a fairy world of spires from which they were divided by a boundary moat. To cross from one side of the glacier to the other took two hours. Sometimes they could follow convenient troughs for considerable distances but could never be certain where they were leading. At other times, they would be scrambling up a chimney or slithering down one, cutting round the floor of a tower or traversing an icy crest. Mounting a stony shoulder at 18,500ft (5,640m) they could see the glacier stretching away to the west, rising more steeply until it was lost in cloud. Returning by a different route, a stream which they had crossed without difficulty in the morning was now a swollen torrent. It was crossed with a rush – each choosing his own way for a wetting – in a race against the gathering darkness. They reached camp at 8.15pm, tired perhaps, but not exhausted. Afterwards, analysing their performance at altitude, they were surprised that coming down was so laborious and gradually realised that it was best to adopt a conscious method of breathing deeply (or hyperventilating, as the doctors would say) for coming down as for going up. They also experienced the enervating effect of the midday sun when they were surrounded by ice, a despairing feeling of glacier latitude, which seemed worse when compared with the effort of moving along the rocky moraine at the side.

Through a series of daily expeditions, their concept of Everest and the glaciers and lower summits to the north and west was coming into focus. 'This idea resembled the beginning of an artist's painting, a mere rough design at the start, but growing by steps of clearer definition in one part and another towards the precise completion of a whole,' wrote Mallory. They were also training their porters in mountain craft: to tread safely on snow and ice; to climb easy rocks and in particular the use of ice axe and ropes for the day when they would launch an assault on Everest itself.

In poor weather, they saw enough of the broken glacier leading steeply up to the gap between Everest and the North Peak – the Chang La or North Col, as they began to call it – to determine that they should also reconnoitre the other side in the hope of finding an easier way up. In one long day, they climbed a peak, later established at 22,520ft (6,864m), which they thought would be a good viewpoint. From it, they confirmed an impression that the North Peak had a long east ridge forming the side of whatever valley connected to the Arun River in this direction. Also that the upper parts of Everest's face were not impossibly steep and could be approached by the ridge leading from the North Col up to the North-East Shoulder. To the west they could establish a chain of summits forming the border with Nepal and connecting to the two great tri-angulated peaks of Gyachung Kang, 25,990ft (7,922m), and Cho Oyu, 26,906ft (8,201m).

On 8 July, they moved camp into the western extension of the Rongbuk Glacier, from where, following the medial moraine to a rocky feature known as the Island, they began to unravel the topographical mysteries surrounding the West Peak, later called Nuptse. They could see it was connected by a long, terrible arête to the South Peak, Lhotse, whose eastern side they had seen from Shiling. By following the glacier round to the south and then climbing a col on the frontier ridge, they hoped to traverse into the basin gap between the West Ridge of Everest and the West Peak, a feature which Mallory had already christened in Welsh terminology as the Western Cwm. On the first attempt, the clouds descended and completely obscured their view. But on 19 July they looked across into the Western Cwm at last, terribly forbidding under the shadow of Everest. It was a great disappointment. There was a 1,500ft (450m) drop down to the glacier, a hopeless precipice. The glacier itself issuing from the Cwm was terribly steep and broken and could only be tackled from a base in Nepal. So they ruled out an approach from the western side and this part of the reconnaissance ended.

So far as finding a way up the mountain, Mallory modestly asserted that little enough had been accomplished. They had been persevering in difficult monsoon conditions and yet it was enough to realize that progress on Everest could only be made along comparatively easy ground, not along the full length of its colossal ridges. The northern arête was of a gentler character, where the apparently horizontal strata and steep walls of rock merged into a comparatively smooth and continuous, bluntly rounded edge. But could they gain access to it from the eastern side of the North Col?

Mentally, after a short rest, they were now ready to join Howard-Bury in setting up a new base in Kharta to the east of Everest when, on 22 July, Mallory received a disastrous note from Bury. All Mallory's photographs taken with the quarter-plate camera had failed – for the good reason that the plates had been inserted back to front! It sadly confirmed the impression of many people that Mallory was 'a very innocent traveller' inclined to 'forget his boots on all occasions' or, as described by Tom Longstaff, 'a very good stout hearted baby, but quite unfit to be placed in charge of anything, including himself'. Poor Mallory, I feel for him. There was nothing for it but to return to the Island on the West Rongbuk Glacier, wait desperately for the grey clouds to lift and repeat his photographs. Moments later, the clouds rolled back and he saw no more. This diversion meant they did not have time to explore a stream emerging from a narrow valley which joined the Rongbuk from the east, 10 miles (16km) from Everest. Had they done so, they would have discovered the elusive East Rongbuk Glacier, which runs parallel to the Rongbuk, starting from the slopes of Everest itself. Into it drains the huge basin to the east of the North Col, which does not after all, as they and their map had assumed, drain directly eastward into the Arun River. It seemed unbelievable to Mallory that such a large area of ice could possibly give rise to such a small glacial stream where it joined the Rongbuk. It was left to Wheeler to make this discovery in the course of his photographic survey and to realise that this would be the obvious route to approach the North Col from the east.

Exploring from Kharta

While Mallory and Bullock were up the Rongbuk Valley exploring the northern and western approaches to Everest, Howard-Bury decided to make a quick reconnaissance to decide the best place for their next base camp to explore the eastern approach. This was most likely to be somewhere in the Kharta Valley. Howard-Bury and Heron left Tingri on 5 July. They crossed a range of rocky peaks by a pass called the Doya La at 17,000ft (5,180m), which acts as a barrier against the approach of the monsoon clouds. To the north, the country is mostly dry and arid, but to the south there is a rich and varied vegetation and the air feels soft and moist. They followed the valley of the Chongphu Chu until it debouched into the main Arun Valley, from which the Arun River is called the Bhong-chu until it reaches Nepal. As the great river had cut down through the rising Himalaya, it had created river terraces on either side and these were now cultivated with barley, peas and mustard, creating a blaze of yellow. After descending this valley for 3 miles (5km), they turned up a side valley to the west, down which flowed a very large and unfordable glacier stream. Three miles up was a settlement called Kharta Shika, where the Governor of the whole Kharta District lived. He pitched a Chinese tent for them in his garden and provided an excellent meal of macaroni with hot chillies. It rained steadily throughout the night – unfortunately the tent leaked like a sieve – but it was the first heavy monsoon rain they had had. The locals felt Howard-Bury and Heron had brought this rain for their crops and were very grateful. They were able to rent a well-situated house with a pleasant garden of poplars and willows for their future base for a negotiated rent of one Trangka (1½ pence) a day. It was the first time in the valley anyone had rented a house so there were no agents to push up prices! It would serve as a storeroom and photographic darkroom and they would camp in the garden at an agreeable 12,000ft (3,660m). Just below them flowed the Arun, here 100yd (90m) wide. A mile lower, it entered great gorges for 20 miles (32km), dropping from 12,000ft to 7,500ft (2,290m) or over 200ft/mile (43m/km). The sun shone brightly and they seemed to be in a dry zone between two storm systems to the north and south.

Their mission was accomplished and they returned to Tingri, but Howard-Bury was so delighted with the area that he resolved to go back to spend more time exploring the lower valleys while the climbers were on the high mountains. The first opportunity came on 30 July when, back in the Kharta Valley, he climbed the Samchung Pass, 15,000ft (4,570m), to the south and descended into a high-level glen reminding him of Killarney, where he counted 14 small lakes with colours of turquoise, blue-grey to black. On the slopes were rhododendrons, mountain ash, birch, willows, spiraea and juniper. In addition to eight varieties of gentian, there was the wonderful Himalayan blue poppy, Meconopsis baileyi, and another he had never seen before of a deep claret colour with 15–20 flowers on each stem growing up to 3ft (90cm) high. A second pass, the Chog La, 16,100ft (4,910m), enabled him to look over into the lower Kama Valley, but clouds and rain descended so he had to wait for another occasion for a view. The chance came in August. There are two other passes leading from Kharta to the Kama Valley: the Shao La, 16,500ft (5,030m)and the Langma La, 17,550ft (5,350m). Opposite, on the other side of the valley are the immense cliffs of Chomolonzo backed by Makalu towering up to nearly 26,000ft (7,925km), which from this viewpoint appears much more striking and higher than Everest to the west. Howard-Bury with his two Sherpa porters, Nyima and Ang Tenze, realised one ambition by crossing the Kangshung Glacier and climbing up to the frontier ridge between Makalu and Everest at about 21,500ft (6,550m), from which he could look into forbidden Nepal, where range upon range of snowy mountains receded into the distance. Indeed Ang Tenze, who came from the Khumbu Valley in Nepal, thought he could recognise some of the tops (most probably Ama Dablam?). From here Howard-Bury could also see about 3,000ft (900m) of the southern side of the summit pyramid of Everest for the first time. He was impressed by its steepness, and, even if it were possible to enter through Nepal, it seemed improbable that a practicable route lay up that face of the mountain. He was looking, in fact, at the final part of the first ascent route of 1953 from the South Col.

The Enchanting Kama Valley

On 23 August, Howard-Bury and Wollaston set out to explore the lower Kama Valley. Beyond the valley of the 14 lakes, they came to Sakeding (Pleasant Terrace), deserted after a 'pestilence sent by a local demon'. Below the village, they entered a forest with the finest junipers yet seen; trees up to 90ft (27m) high, many with trunks 18–20ft (5.5–6m) in circumference, the branches hung with grey lichens. These gave way to silver firs of great age where numerous crested tits and bullfinches flitted from branch to branch. They crossed the Kama River and at 10,200ft (3,110m) found a space to camp. As the tents were pitched, they found the foliage to be alive with leeches, but there was no better place. To quote Howard-Bury:

> All that evening we were busy picking leeches off our clothes, legs, hands or heads. They climbed up the sides of the tents and dropped down into our food, our cups and on to our plates. Wollaston invented the best way of killing them, which was by cutting them in two with a pair of scissors. Our interpreter remonstrated with him, as he said this method increased the number of leeches, thinking that both ends of them would grow.

Next day, they descended through the forest towards the Arun River, the silver fir giving way to spruce, some over 150ft (45m) in height without a branch below half height.

> Our only halts on the way down, and they were pretty frequent, were to pick off the leeches from our clothes. We took them off by tens at a time; they were very hungry,

and varied in size from great striped horse-leeches to tiny ones as thin as a pin and able to penetrate anywhere.

At their side, the Kama Chu hurled itself in a succession of waterfalls and swirling cauldrons to the junction with the Arun, at only 7,500ft (2,280m) above sea level. There is no path through the Arun Gorge. One has to climb up to a pass, the curiously named Popti La, 14,000ft (4,270m), through which all local traffic passes; the Tibetans bartering salt for Nepalese rice, dyes and vegetables.

I do not apologise for this short diversion from the high mountains; I too was so enchanted by Howard-Bury's description of the Kama Valley that I resolved to visit it myself. In September 1998, this dream was realised when I led a trekking party into its upper reaches, but time precluded a descent to the Arun. I must go again. Howard-Bury had written: 'This valley is so inaccessible that I am glad to think that these glorious forests can never be exploited commercially.'

'Never' was a rash word. We saw the beginnings of a tractor road up the hillside leading from Kharta to the Kama Valley constructed by a commercial logging company. But pressure from the World Wildlife Fund, I believe, thankfully led to its abandonment. Some logging is still allowed, even with the creation of the Chomolungma Nature Reserve. Luckily, the trees are being felled with handsaws and hauled out by porters, a slow process that should prevent major deforestation. Howard-Bury concluded his visit with the words:

We now turned our backs upon the Kama Valley with much regret. We had explored many of the Himalayan valleys, but none seemed to me to be comparable with this, either for the beauty of its Alpine scenery, or for its wonderful vegetation. We shall not easily forget the smiling pastures carpeted with gentians and every variety of Alpine flower that rise to the very verge of icebound and snow-covered tracts, where mighty glaciers descend among the forests which clothe the lower slopes.

Everest from the East

The new base at Karta suited the climbers as well as the other expedition members. Mallory and Bullock revelled in four clear days of idleness and reorganisation before they set off again on 2 August. They had noted the glacier stream coming from the direction of Everest to the west which flowed into the Arun above its gorge, leading into Nepal. The obvious plan was to follow up this stream. The headman was asked to direct them to Chomolungma. To their surprise, he soon pointed them up a delightful green-sided valley, covered with rhododendron and juniper but with no glacier stream. They camped beside a little blue lake on a flat shelf at 17,000ft (5,180m). Next day, they followed a track over a pass called the Langma La, feeling mystified that they were going too far south rather than west. There were, it appeared, two Chomolungmas! The first must be Makalu, so they asked to be guided to the furthest. They descended, crossed a rickety bridge and wound through lovely meadows and dwarf rhododendrons until they reached a glacier. Towards midday, the weather cleared and disclosed gigantic precipices across the glacier – the bastions of Makulu – so this valley must come up on the north side of Makalu all the way to Everest. They had entered the upper part of the Kama Valley. They camped on broad meadows above and beside the Kangshung Glacier at a place called Pethang Ringmo, where yaks were grazing and their herders had pitched tents, with the promise of good butter and cream. Saxifrages, gentians and primulas were dotted amongst the short grass. Next morning the clouds began to lift at the head of the valley. Everest itself appeared – the great North-East Ridge to the right; to the left the crest of the south peak, some 28,000ft (8,530m), and its prodigious south-east shoulder that joined the frontier ridge extending to Makalu. In this great cirque lay the Kangshung Glacier, cradled by three of the five highest summits in the world. They could hardly regret the deviation from their intended route. However, they were now on the wrong side of a watershed formed by the continuation of Everest's North-East Ridge separating them from the North Col. To get a clearer view, they determined to climb to a col on the watershed, Karpo La at almost 20,000ft (6,100m), and, if possible, scale the conspicuous snowy summit, Khartse, 21,300ft (6,490m), to its west. From that point, they could also better judge the steepness of the great East Face. Its upper part was one immense hanging glacier, so the rocky buttresses below would always be exposed to falling ice. Even were it possible to climb them, they led to no convenient platform. 'In short,' summarised Mallory, 'other men, less wise, might attempt this way if they would, but, emphatically, it was not for us.'

They could now also see on the far side of the watershed a glacier flowing east. Was this in the valley they had seen from the hill above Shiling? They were still separated from Everest by a spur turning northwards from the foot of the North-East Ridge, and the North Col remained hidden. The North-East Ridge ruled itself out as a possible line of attack: a sharp and steep crest culminating in the great rock towers of the North-East Shoulder.

The next step was to return over the Langma La and follow the Kharta stream to its glacier. So far, Mallory and Bullock had remained in good health and the majority of their porters had acclimatised well, but now Mallory had developed a bad headache and fever. He needed several days to recover. They were approaching the climax or anticlimax of the whole reconnaissance and he could not bear to be left out. Meantime, Bullock went ahead. Mallory sat in the sun, writing a dismal letter home when, unexpectedly, Morshead arrived and, better still, bearing medicine from Wollaston. As night fell, a porter ran down the slope bearing a chit from Bullock:

> I can see up the glacier ahead of me and it ends in another high pass. I shall get to the pass tomorrow morning if I can, and ought to see our glacier over it. But it looks, after all, as though the most unlikely solution is the right one and the glacier goes out into the Rongbuk Valley.

How could the little stream they had seen drain so large an area of ice?

The upper Kharta Valley had forked, Bullock taking the northern fork. Mallory, now feeling better and certainly not wishing to be upstaged by Bullock, set forth with Morshead to explore the southern fork. It led to the glacier they had looked down on from the Karpo La; at the head of it was a high snow col and beyond that the tip of Changtse was just visible. Could this be a sufficiently good approach? They decided to set up a camp so that they could reach the pass, later known as the Lhakpa La (Windy Gap), at an early hour in order to leave time to descend to the glacier on the other side.

To the Lhakpa La

They were in place on 17 August, and set off next morning – a critical day. The snow on the glacier up to the pass was deep and soft. They wore snow shoes. The final slope, about 700ft (210m), required greater effort than ever before. After every series of steps, 40 dwindling to 30 or 20 as their strength ebbed, they would pause a minute or so for the most furious sort of breathing. It was 1.15pm when they reached the col, so despite their early start, the clouds were down and they had no hope of a clear view, nor could they determine which way the glacier flowed on the other side of the pass. But they could see below them a broad bay, only occasionally broken by large crevasses, with an easy descent to it of some 800ft (240m) or more. There were some fleeting glimpses of the wall under the Chang La; probably steep but not much more than 500ft (150m). Mallory was prepared to bet his bottom dollar that they could get up it from this side. But was the best route to it from their new base at Kharta, or from the old base at Rongbuk, via the untrodden East Rongbuk Glacier whose junction into the main Rongbuk Valley had been discovered by Wheeler?

The soft snow up to the Lhakpa La and the loss of height in descending on the other side were disadvantages, but hopefully come

September and the end of the monsoon, which they believed to be the best time for climbing, the snow conditions would improve. As they turned to descend, Mallory mused that food and fuel were much more plentiful in Kharta: luxuries such as fresh vegetables and eggs; rhododendron and juniper wood rather than dried yak dung for fuel. He was very content to stay with the way they had found. It was 2am before they got back to their lower camp in the dim misty moonlight, 23 hours after their early start. Next day, 20 August, they descended to join the others in Kharta for 10 days of well-deserved rest and recuperation before the assault.

In their remaining time during September, their objective was to arrange sufficient camps and supplies to be able to cross over the Lhakpa La, descend to and cross the East Rongbuk Glacier, to the foot of the Chang La. Then to ascend the Chang La and, from a camp on the col, climb as far as possible up the North-East Ridge. It took many days to arrange the supplies and get them moved up to the Lhakpa La. They marshalled 23 porters, the maximum number being determined by the supply of boots. The other Sahibs, Howard-Bury, Wollaston, Morshead, Wheeler and Heron all arrived to back up the climbing party as best they could. Even Raeburn had recovered sufficiently to return, 'whom we rejoiced to see again' said Mallory, in the official account, although he wrote to Geoffrey Winthrop Young: 'Raeburn turned up a week ago looking extraordinarily old and grizzled and being no less old than he looks. When he is not being a bore I feel moved to pity, but that is not often. He takes no part luckily.'

At last the weather cleared, and on 20 September, Mallory and Morshead set out with 15 porters from their Advanced Base, on the same moonlit glacier as a month ago, with the snow now crisp and firm underfoot. But with sunrise, their confidence ebbed. They started to break through the crust and already the party was showing signs of fatigue. At length, 11 loads reached the pass and two more were only 800ft (240m) lower. When the tracks had frozen hard overnight, other loads could be brought up more easily. They set up camp on the Lhakpa La at 22,000ft (6,710m). Now they had a clearer view of the Chang La – more formidable than they had realised. 'A wall 1,000ft high unpleasantly broken by insuperable bergschrunds.' Clearly, before setting up a camp on the Chang La, they needed a strong party of climbers just to reach it. Mallory decided that only Bullock and Wheeler should accompany him. But the months of continued exertion at high altitudes were beginning to take their toll on both the expedition members and their porters. 'For my own part,' admitted Mallory, 'I had been excessively and unaccountably tired in coming up to the col; I observed no great sparkle of energy or enthusiasm among my companions.'

To the Chang La or North Col

Fierce squalls of wind shook their tents during the night. Mallory felt suffocated in his Mummery tent, which he was sharing with Morshead, and wrote: 'I congratulated myself on an act of mutilation in cutting two large slits in its roof.' If he had done that in one of today's lightweight mountain tents, the gusts would doubtless have shredded the fabric to pieces! They then slept well, but their porters did not. Those who had been sick had not recovered, and only ten were persuaded to continue. Howard-Bury, Wollaston and Morshead, therefore, returned so as not to burden the party. The descent to the East Rongbuk Glacier Basin was about 1,200ft (360m), not just 800ft (240m) as they had thought earlier. After a late start, they made it a short day and pitched tents on the open snow up towards the col. Another night of fierce squalls discouraged an early start until an hour after sunrise. They took the three strongest porters and, after cutting round the bergschrund, used them to help break the trail, first slanting up right and then a long upward traverse left. Only the last steep part gave concern, where the snow was deep and disagreeable. They reached the North Col by 11.30am. Having slept well, Mallory was now finding his best form and felt good for climbing another 2,000ft (610m). But what lay ahead? Looking up, the rounded edge of the North Ridge seemed straightforward for a long way. But as they came over the col, the wind hit them with gale force. Snow blown across the North Face was battering the ridge with unmitigated fury. They struggled up a few steps but it was folly to go on. The wind had settled the question. They were too weak a party to play a waiting game at this altitude. They still had to reserve enough energy to return safely over the Lhakpa La. As they did so, the real weakness of the party became only too apparent, but none of the three climbers felt any doubt or regret about their decision.

One Possible Route?

It was 30 September when the reconnaissance finished at Kharta. What had the expedition accomplished? The climbers had investigated the north, west and east sides of the mountain and found only one possible route to the summit. Bad weather and furious north-westerly gales had prevented them going any higher than the Chang La – the North Col – at 23,000ft (7,010m). They were told the rainy season had begun some three weeks later than usual, had been much heavier than most years in Tibet, and had lasted until nearly the end of September. After that, gales make climbing at heights above 23,000ft physically impossible and it becomes progressively colder. They concluded that the best time to climb the mountain was before the monsoon breaks in late May or early June. This would now be the objective of the 1922 expedition, whose leadership had already been promised to Brigadier-General C.G. Bruce. Howard-Bury was not too optimistic about their chances of success although he certainly expected them to beat the Duke of Abruzzi's height record of 24,600ft (7,498m) and maybe reach 25,000ft or even 26,000ft (7,925m). In addition, Morshead, Wheeler and their four survey assistants had mapped a huge tract of country lying between the Himalayas and the Brahmaputra River – 12,000 square miles (3.1Mha) of original survey and

600 square miles (155,000ha) of detailed photo-survey in the environs of Everest. Heron's geological survey of over 8,000 square miles (2.07Mha) and Wollaston's collections of birds, beasts, insects and flowers had added much new to science. In fact, as Norman Collie, The Alpine Club President, paid tribute:

> The Expedition has, therefore, accomplished all that was expected of it, and has brought back material of the greatest interest from a part of the world about which almost nothing was known, and into which Europeans had never been.

Let Mallory have the last word:

> In all it may be said that one factor beyond all others is required for success. Too many chances are against the climbers; too many contingencies may turn against them. Anything like a breakdown of the transport will be fatal; soft snow on the mountain will be an impregnable defence; a big wind will send back the strongest; even so small a matter as a boot fitting a shade too tight may endanger one man's foot and involve the whole party in retreat. The good fortune, and the greatest good fortune of all the mountaineers, some constant spirit of kindness in Mount Everest itself, the forgetfulness for long enough of its more cruel moods; for we must remember that the highest of mountains is capable of severity, a severity so awful and so fatal that the wiser sort of men do well to think and tremble even on the threshold of their high endeavour.

General Bruce's 1922 Expedition

'The benign bulldog . . .' 'Big, benevolent and bawdy.'   W. H. Murray & W. Unsworth

General Bruce had already been nominated as leader of the 1922 expedition before Howard-Bury's party had left India. This might seem rather tough on Howard-Bury, when, under his leadership, the 1921 Reconnaissance had accomplished so much in totally unknown territory. However, the object of the 1922 expedition was now to climb the mountain by the route which had been discovered. As Howard-Bury was not an experienced mountaineer, it was acknowledged by the Mount Everest Committee that Bruce was a better man for this purpose, particularly as he had experience of Alpine and Himalayan conditions accumulated over 30 years, going back to the 1892 expedition with Martin Conway in the Karakoram.

Bruce, a professional soldier with the Gurkhas, was clearly a great character and natural leader of men, described by Murray as a 'benign bulldog' and by Unsworth as 'big, benevolent and bawdy'. His Gurkha soldiers loved him and he knew how to handle them. He was among the first to recognise that the best of these tough Nepalese hill-men could be invaluable in helping to establish camps at high altitudes. As Sir Francis Younghusband wrote: 'For organizing this corps of porters, for dealing with the Tibetans, and lastly, for keeping together the climbers from England, who were mostly quite unknown to each other, but who all knew of General Bruce and his mountaineering achievements in the Himalaya, General Bruce was an ideal chief.'

He was now 56. He carried a few scars, having been wounded in Gallipoli, and the doctors expressed some concern about his medical condition, but one friend, Claude Wilson, both a climber and doctor, wrote to him: 'I hope you'll keep fit, but I take it there will be someone second-in-command . . . of course, with all care, you might knock up like Raeburn did – though I don't think you'll die like poor Kellas.'

I heard one story about Bruce when he was invited to a Climbers' Club Dinner in North Wales, and met the legendary Welsh rock climber Menlove Edwards in the climbers' hut at Helyg. They both had indoor party tricks to demonstrate their exceptional arm strength. Bruce could stand with his back in a roughcast corner, arms slightly bent but pointing down with palms flat against each wall. By exerting tremendous pressure with his palms, he could lift his whole body off the ground, an inch or two, and remain suspended. Simultaneously, Edwards showed how he could undergrasp a single square-cut wooden beam supporting the ceiling, with just his fingers, hands a few inches apart, and also hoist himself off the ground. 'The first one to let go is a clot!' shouted Bruce. It is not recorded who won!

It was accepted that Bruce would not go high on the mountain, so Lieutenant-Colonel E.L. Strutt was selected as his deputy. Strutt, a former High Commissioner in Danzig, was a very experienced Alpine climber in the traditional mould who, when he became President of The Alpine Club in the 1930s, made a point of strongly condemning the use of pitons and wedges being introduced by continental climbers in the Alps to overcome the hardest climbs. He was nominally to be chief at the mountain base, but did not get on all that well with Bruce, as two more disparate characters could hardly be imagined.

The Team of Eight

The choice of the actual climbing team was really the most important decision. Mallory had argued for a team of eight, and that they should be in position on the mountain well before the monsoon in order to have a reasonable chance, otherwise it was barely worth trying in 1922 and they should wait a year. He didn't even seem particularly eager to go. But the Committee had decided on a team of six and was already committed to an attempt in 1922.

George Ingle Finch, who was passed over in 1921 for being unfit, was now fully recovered. He was 34, an excellent climber who had done some difficult first ascents in Corsica with his brother, Maxwell. As a scientist – he was a lecturer in Chemistry at Imperial College – he was interested in the physiological aspects of climbing at high altitude and was a strong advocate for the use of oxygen. Brought up in Australia, he had also lived in Switzerland and spoke German well. However, his broader Antipodean and European outlook meant that he didn't fit naturally into the current British climbing establishment and was a little suspect. The same could not be said of Major E.F. Norton, an artillery officer, well known in India for his skill and interest in pig-sticking. He was a very reliable and skilled mountaineer, also a keen birdwatcher and competent artist. Dr Howard Somervell, who came from a Kendal family, was perhaps even more gifted and versatile. He was also a talented artist and a musician. At Cambridge, he received a double first in Natural Sciences and went on to become a surgeon. He and Mallory got on splendidly together, discussing literature in their tent or reading Shakespeare to each other. A.W. Wakefield was another doctor from Kendal, then practising in Canada, and had established a Lakeland record for the number of summits traversed in 24 hours. His run of 59 miles (95km) and 23,500ft (7,163m) of ascents in 22 hours was set in 1905 and lasted until broken by Eustace Thomas in 1920. At 45 years of age, Wakefield was incredibly fit but sadly seemed unable to acclimatise well on Everest. Even today, there is no specific series of physical or medical tests devised to determine in advance whether or not a person will perform well at high altitude.

Yet another doctor, Tom Longstaff, was chosen to act as medical officer and naturalist. He had held the height record by climbing Trisul in 1907, and had greater and more varied mountaineering experience than all the others, but was content to come along just for the ride. He wrote in his superb autobiography, *This My Voyage*:

> To experience all this is worth the penalty of being condemned to try to climb the monster; for monster it is, this relic of primordial chaos, the home of devils, not of gods. Everest is a forbidding mountain. It has an athlete's grace of form but the brutal mass of the all-in wrestler, murderous and threatening. Technically, I cannot agree that it is an easy peak.

After the debacle with Mallory and his back-to-front photographic plates in 1921, it was realised how important it was to bring back a high-quality photographic and film record, if only to help pay off expedition expenses. Captain J.B. Noel was selected as full-time photographer. He was the man who had travelled to within 40 miles (64km) of Everest in disguise in 1913 and who, by his lecture at the Royal Geographical Society in 1919, had provided the impetus for the first expedition.

Between the two expeditions, Mallory had given some 30 lectures up and down the country. To Younghusband he wrote: 'The public interest is immense. A crowd was turned away from the Free Trade Hall in Manchester which holds about 3,000.' This struck a chord with me because I gave my first public Everest lecture, jointly with Ed Hillary, in the same hall on 26 September 1953 to a full house followed by rapturous applause. In fact, we gave both a matinée and evening lecture with just time in between for tea and cucumber sandwiches with the Lord Mayor and the Bishop. The Lord Mayor, Alderman A. Moss, said that afterwards he would like to invite 'a few intimate friends to meet us'. It was a reception for 200. I could hardly sleep that night, my head was in such a whirl!

Other members of the expedition recruited in India were Colin G. Crawford of the Indian Civil Service, Major Morshead of the Indian Survey, now joining as a climber, and two officers from Gurkha regiments to serve as transport officers: Captain Geoffrey Bruce (the General's nephew) and Captain John Morris. The Government of India had wanted to include the geologist Dr Heron again, but he had upset the Tibetans in 1921 by digging holes in the ground which they feared would release demons and pestilence, so he was left behind. By including Crawford and Morshead, the General had cleverly increased the climbing team up to the eight considered necessary by Mallory.

As Mallory had also pointed out, there was very little time for preparation so, while the team was being selected, an equipment committee led by Farrar and Meade were working hard. As a variation to the Norfolk jacket, Finch, an innovative scientist, had personally designed one from balloon cloth, quilted with eiderdown, very similar to today's duvet jackets, which worked well, but the concept was not taken up by the committee. The food was also given greater attention than in 1921; cooks were more carefully chosen and delicacies such as tinned 'quails in truffles' and crystallised ginger provided by Fortnum & Mason, to tempt jaded appetites at high altitude. In 1953 we took five 'Luxury Boxes' for this purpose, but were not quite so sybaritic: taking only one bottle each of rum and brandy instead of five cases of champagne!

Do We Need Oxygen?

The most important debate was over whether to take supplementary oxygen equipment. The atmospheric pressure at 29,000ft (8,840m) is only one-third of that at sea level and nobody knew whether an acclimatised person could survive at that altitude. Professor Dreyer at Oxford, who had done work on this subject for the RAF, was consulted and said, 'I do not think you will get up without it, but if you do succeed without it you may not get down again.' There was the added potential danger that if oxygen supply was suddenly cut off at high altitude due to equipment failure, the climber might have become so reliant upon it that he would collapse. One would have to design the lightest possible equipment so that the advantage would outweigh the extra weight to be carried. Kellas had experimented with two types: one which carried the oxygen in steel cylinders under pressure and the other which generated it from chemical reaction on sodium peroxide. The latter proved too heavy and had unpleasant side effects and so was discarded. The chosen apparatus, designed by the Air Ministry, had four steel bottles in a pack frame, each bottle 5¾lb (2.6kg) when full, together with tubes, regulator valves and a face mask, the total weight being 32lb (14.5kg). It was agreed that oxygen was not necessary below 23,000ft (7,010m) – the height of the North Col – but some, such as Mallory, preferred not to use it at all, even regarding it as unsporting or cheating. Two camps developed. Those for were Collie, Farrar, Finch and Somervell, those against, Mallory, Longstaff and Hinks. Debate became acrimonious. Finch wrote:

> Instead of the aim being to climb Mount Everest with every resource at our disposal, the opponents of oxygen … had so successfully worked upon the minds of the members of the expedition as to induce them to entertain a fresh objective, namely to see how far they could climb without oxygen. It were pleasant to think that the writer who could thus acclaim possible failure and, in advocating a new objective, destroy the singleness of purpose of the expedition, was not a mountaineer.

Hinks never forgave him.

An important consequence of committing to use oxygen above 23,000ft is that it greatly increases the total load to be carried all the way to and up the mountain – by as much as 50 per cent. This requires more pack animals, more high-altitude porters and, therefore, a greater pyramid of support, leading in turn to greater costs. It is not surprising that the General was soon cabling Hinks for more money, but at least his skilled leadership was creating an harmonious team.

The Pilgrimage to Everest

The first party left Darjeeling on 26 March. They hired a young Tibetan interpreter, Karma Paul, who served them well, being very good with local officials, and he was retained by successive Everest expeditions. In all, there were 60 porters and 300 baggage animals (20 ponies, 80 mules and donkeys and 200 yaks and bullocks). Finch recounted:

> On the first night out from Phari we camped in the open. On the second, the nuns of the Buddhist convent of Ta-tsang afforded us hospitality. Crawford and I passed the night in the roofless temple chamber. Some of the nuns spread out my sleeping bag on the altar, and there I slept, awakened occasionally by the cold. A brilliant moon shone down and lit up my weird abode. The desiccated remains of a magnificent billy-goat hanging above the altar grinned down at me, and prayer wheels surrounded me on every side.

From Shekar Dzong, they took a short cut over the Pang La (the 'Grass Pass') to Chobuk and Rongbuk, which they reached on 30 April. It was a tedious journey, made more so by the bitter cold and the incessant Tibetan wind which made good windproof clothing a necessity. Finch may have been more comfortable in his home-made duvet than the General in his raincoat. 'I had a very efficient Mackintosh which covered everything,' wrote Bruce, 'but even then I suffered very considerably from the cold.'

Rongbuk means 'The valley of steep ravines', and 5 miles (8km) up it they came upon the monastery. Bruce paid his respects to the Head Lama, who was a remarkable person. 'He was a large, well-made man of about 60, full of dignity, with a most intelligent and wise face and an extraordinarily attractive smile.' Through Karma Paul, the Lama asked about the object of the expedition and Bruce, finding the question perhaps easier to answer than in Britain, was inspired to say that 'we regarded the whole Expedition, and especially our attempt to reach the summit of Everest, as a pilgrimage'. By also saying that he had sworn never to touch butter until he had arrived at the summit of Everest, he was able to decline the traditional Tibetan tea made with butter and salt, which he detested, and have his made specially with milk or sugar. In my opinion, the mistake is to regard it as tea; if you think of it as a hot but weak beef consommé it is not nearly so bad! The Upper Rongbuk Valley was considered an extremely sacred place. Bruce agreed there was to be no shooting of wildlife and indeed no animals were allowed to be killed in it, so that all fresh meat had to be killed lower down and brought up to the expedition's camp. The Lama then blessed the expedition team and gave them his best wishes for success. They chose a site at 16,500ft (5,030m) at the snout of the Rongbuk Glacier, a little protected from the prevailing west wind, and made it their Base Camp. It was 1 May. At last the climb could begin – a race against the monsoon.

East Rongbuk Glacier to North Col

Strutt, Norton, Longstaff and Morshead comprised a reconnaissance party as nobody had previously travelled the length of the East Rongbuk Glacier to below the North Col. As many local Tibetan 'coolies' as could be diverted from their spring ploughing were hired to carry loads to save the expedition's own porters for work higher up the mountain. Some of the Sherpas' relations even came over to help from Sola Khumbu in Nepal, by crossing the 19,000ft (5,790m) Nangpa La. Regular supplies of yak dung were required for fuel, as there was virtually no wood for burning. Strutt's party returned on 9 May, having planned the advance up the East Rongbuk. Camp I at 17,800ft (5,425m) took about three hours for a laden animal; Camp II at 19,800ft (6,035m) a further four hours up the glacier; and Camp III at 21,000ft (6,400m) on moraine at the edge of the glacier below the North Col.

On 10 May, Mallory and Somervell left Base Camp to establish Camp IV on the North Col and make a first attempt on the mountain. It was decided, possibly to Mallory's secret delight, that this should be without oxygen, as a lot of the equipment needed servicing after the overland journey and there were not enough porters at this stage to carry up all the bottles needed. On 13 May, Mallory and Somervell took a porter, Dasno, to reconnoitre a route to the North Col which would be feasible for porters. The snow and ice conditions had changed from the previous year, but they were able to ascend a crack which gave access to the sloping ramp. This could be protected by a fixed rope attached to wooden stakes driven into the hard snow which in places revealed unstable powder snow beneath. A great crevasse barred their way to the lowest point of the Col but they were able to work their way around it, and leave a tent there on a ledge. They returned to Camp III where they were joined on the 15th by Strutt, Morshead, Norton and Crawford. Crawford was feeling the effects of altitude and descended almost immediately.

The storm clouds over in Nepal were beginning to presage the onset of the monsoon, so they decided to make an immediate attack on the mountain. They made two carries to stock the North Col so that five small tents could hold four climbers and nine Sherpas. Strutt had reached his limit and descended, so this left Mallory, Somervell, Norton and Morshead for the first assault. This was the highest altitude at which anyone had ever camped. They had no precedent to draw upon and simply learned by their mistakes. All water had to be melted from snow and ice, and they had brought slow-burning alcohol and meta-fuel cookers instead of the heavier, more powerful but grimy primuses left at Camp III. Mallory used his leather boots as a pillow so that the slight warmth would prevent their freezing hard. Their breakfast – tinned spaghetti in tomato sauce – was frozen solid; they should have kept it warm in their sleeping bags. Supper at Camp IV and above would be pea soup, a 'hoosh' – a stew of mutton or beef or both from a tin – concocted by Morshead, some ham, or cheese, then cocoa and lashings of tea.

Mallory's plan was to place Camp V at 26,000ft (7,925m) with the help of the porters, and from there the four climbers would make a dash for the summit, a further 3,000ft (900m). Next morning, five porters were unwell, leaving only four to carry the four 20lb (9kg) loads, without any reserve as Mallory had planned. The wind – a breeze at first – grew perceptibly stronger until they were bracing themselves against a gale. Abandoning the rocks, they steered a slanting course to the left over snow. As it became steeper and icier, Mallory cut steps. Crampons would have been ideal here, but they had decided not to bring them above Camp IV, arguing in self-justification that the tight straps around the boots would have restricted circulation and led to frostbite. When the sun disappeared behind cloud, it grew intensely cold. They had to take shelter on the lee side of the ridge. The aneroid showed 25,000ft (7,620m), so they had climbed 2,000ft (610m) in 3½ hours. It would be folly to continue so they stopped at the first place they could find to pitch their two tents. The porters were sent back to Camp IV and the climbers settled down in their double sleeping bags for the night. They were now camping higher than anyone had ever been before.

A Brave Attempt

Next morning a mist lifted and the day seemed fair. They set off at 8am roped up in pairs: Norton and Mallory; Somervell and Morshead. Very soon Morshead had to turn back, knowing he was holding them up, and returned to the tent. Somervell tied onto the other two. During the night, some 4–8in (10–20cm) of snow had fallen. They were climbing at about 400ft (120m) per hour. Even if they maintained that rate, it would be ten hours to the summit. They would still be struggling upwards after night had fallen. 'We were prepared,' wrote Mallory, 'to leave to braver men to climb Mount Everest by night.' They realised they were only making a gesture. They agreed to turn back at 2.30pm. Their aneroid read 26,800ft, later confirmed by theodolite as 26,985ft (8,225m), and they were some 400ft (120m) below the North-East Shoulder. They were higher than neighbouring Cho Oyu, 26,906ft (8,201m). Only five peaks in the world were taller – no climber had ever been so high before. They got back to their tents at 4pm in 1½ hours – four times faster than their upward rate. As there were still three hours of daylight, they decided to descend to Camp IV. But Morshead was still weak and suffering from frostbite. He had not been wearing enough clothing. They made a single rope of four; Norton or Mallory in the lead to share the step cutting, Somervell descending last as anchor man. The fresh snow had covered their upward steps and they may have taken too low a line. Suddenly, at the head of a snowy slope, Morshead slipped. Somervell, taken unawares, was jerked from his steps, as was Norton. As the three men slid past him, Mallory was just able to drive the pick of his axe into the snow and hitch the rope around the head of it. Luckily the weight of the three men did not come upon the rope with a single jerk. With Mallory pressing his whole weight on the pick, the belay held. They were shaken by the incident so near to catastrophe and now proceeded with the utmost caution.

Morshead was deteriorating and needed constant rests. They crawled down the mountain in gathering darkness towards the North Col. Somervell produced a candle lantern from his rucksack to guide them through the confusing maze of crevasses to a recognisable landmark, a 15ft (4.5m) ice cliff, down which they jumped. A final steep slope remained, but their fixed rope was buried; by chance they found it and reached the tents with a 'Thank God' at 11.30pm. In such circumstances, a climber's first desire is for a drink. But where were the cooking pots? The porters had taken them down to Camp III in error! Norton concocted a sickly mush of strawberry jam, tinned milk and snow, which they could barely swallow and they collapsed into their double sleeping bags. Next morning, starting at 6am, they staggered down to Camp III, having to make fresh tracks and to cut new steps so that porters could come up to retrieve their sleeping bags. Mallory ignominiously slid the last 8oft (24m) down the ice to meet Finch, poised with his camera. The others came out to meet them and by noon they were in Camp III once more, with Noel turning the handle of his movie camera.

The supply of tea was inexhaustible. Somervell drank 17 mugfuls! Morshead's exhaustion was probably due to dehydration as much as anything. They only began to realise how badly he had been frostbitten as Wakefield bound up the black swollen fingers. General Bruce recorded:

> It was a tremendous effort, unparalleled in the history of mountain exploration, but it gave immense confidence to all that the mountain was not unconquerable. If on the first occasion such a gigantic height could be reached, we were pretty certain that later, with the experience so gained, and with the weather in the climbers' favour instead of the horrible conditions under which this climb was undertaken, the mountain would in time yield to assault.

Finch and Bruce to 27,300ft (8,321m) on Oxygen

While this first attempt was in progress, Finch and Bruce had been organising the oxygen equipment. It had not travelled well across Tibet; joints were leaking and gauges were out of order. To use it, the oxygen was compressed in four steel cylinders to a pressure of 120 atmospheres, carried in a backpack, and connected through copper tubes to a reducing valve and then by rubber tubing to a face mask. A full set weighed 32lb (14.5kg). The masks proved uncomfortable; the valves were too stiff to allow enough air to be inhaled, which caused a feeling of suffocation. Finch rejected them and designed a simpler solution, inserting a glass T-piece in the rubber tube and connecting a toy football bladder – bought in Darjeeling for this purpose. The climber simply put the end of the tube in his mouth to breathe, biting on it to stop the flow of the oxygen. When he exhaled, the bladder expanded and then collapsed in time with the climber's breathing. On trials at Camp III, it worked perfectly, soon becoming an easy and automatic process.

The equipment needed further testing. Finch had enrolled the Gurkha Tejbir Bura to help him and on a trial run to the North Col, during which they had met the first assault party coming down, they reached the Col in three hours and were down in 50 mins highly satisfied, including taking 36 photographs en route. So on 24 May, Noel, Tejbir, Geoffrey Bruce and Finch set off for a determined attack. Next day, with 12 porters, they departed from the North Col camp towards the North-East Shoulder. Despite the 32lb weight of the oxygen sets, they were able to overtake the lightly laden porters, who were not using oxygen, and were for the first time beginning to take a lively interest in the apparatus. Finch later wrote:

> Geoffrey Bruce was called upon to explain its workings. He told them that I could climb well in the Alps because the 'English air' about those mountains suited me. But Himalayan air disagreed with me, and I had, therefore, brought out a supply of the more vigorous air. Just to show them how strong 'English air' is, I turned a stream of oxygen from my apparatus on the glowing end of a cigarette, which thereupon flared up and spluttered with a brilliant white light. A better audience for this perhaps most beautiful of all laboratory experiments, carried out at 23,000ft above sea-level, could not have been desired.

Bruce, Finch and Tejbir camped at 25,500ft (7,770m), as high as they felt justifiable, so that their porters could return safely before the weather broke. Camped on the crest of the ridge, it was a violent night; terrific gusts tore at their tent, the canvas cracking like machine-gun fire. Sleep was impossible. Occasional forays outside to tighten the guy ropes confirmed they could neither advance nor retreat unless the gale subsided. They decided to risk a second night, and at 6pm were delighted when some porters brought up Thermos flasks of hot tea and beef tea, but they were unable to keep warm. Inspired, Finch thought of trying the effect of oxygen, so they could breathe at a low rate throughout the night. It was magic! Life and warmth returned to their limbs, and they could sleep. It saved their lives that night.

Finch also made a curious discovery, finding that smoking was beneficial at very high altitude. It forced one to take rather deeper breaths to combat the lack of air and feeling of suffocation experienced trying to breathe normally at altitude. Apparently, the carbon dioxide dissolved in the blood at lower altitudes stimulates the nerve centre controlling one's involuntary breathing. At high altitude, being forced to breathe greater quantities of air, much of this carbon dioxide is washed out of the blood. Some constituent of the cigarette smoke seemed to restore this stimulating function, lasting for about three hours.

Finch had taken his boots to bed, but Bruce and Tejbir's were frozen solid and it took them an hour next morning to mould them into shape over lighted candles. They set off at 6.30am as the first rays of sun struck the tent, Bruce and Finch each carrying 40lb (18kg), and Tejbir 50lb (23kg), including two extra cylinders. They planned to send him back at the North-east Shoulder, but he collapsed at 26,000ft (7,925m) and could go no further, so they sent him back, fortunately over easy ground.

Finch and Bruce continued unroped to 26,500ft (8,070m) when the steadily increasing wind forced them to leave the exposed ridge and traverse across the northern face, hoping to find some shelter. The angle steepened, and the smooth shelving slabs, like the slates on a roof, had few good footholds. Unbelievably, Bruce was on his first real mountaineering expedition, but he followed Finch confidently. Over occasional crusty snow or scree, they reached 27,000ft (8,230m) and then started to climb diagonally towards a point on the North-East Ridge midway between shoulder and summit. As each oxygen cylinder was exhausted, they stopped to change to a full one, and threw the empties down the precipice where at each impact the steel clanged 'like a church bell. There goes another 5lb off our backs,' they laughed.

At 27,300ft (8,321m) – now above Cho Uyo – Bruce's oxygen failed suddenly and he was gasping for breath. Finch connected him to his own set and was able to diagnose the fault – a broken glass tube – and replace it. They were on a little ledge, just below the belt of rocks surmounting what was later known as the Yellow Band, contrasting with the otherwise greenish-black slates. They had climbed higher than anyone before, but the summit was still 1,700ft (520m) above. Weak and exhausted, and fearful of any further failure of the oxygen, they decided to retreat, roped together. It was midday. They plunged down through thick mists driven by the west wind. During the long descent they became increasingly tired, but they were revived at Camp IV with tea and spaghetti provided by Noel, who had already spent three nights there, and who nursed them down to Camp III. They arrived at 5.30pm, having descended over 6,000ft (1,830m), and were quite finished. But Finch had not lost his appetite: four quails truffled in pâté de foie gras, followed by nine sausages, left him asking for more – provided by a tin of toffees crooked in his elbow as he drifted off in his sleeping bag. Finch had practically escaped frostbite, but Bruce's feet were badly affected and he was put on a sledge for the journey back to Base Camp, which he reached on 29 May.

While recovering at Base, Finch was able to ponder the results of the two high climbs of 22 and 27 May, the first without and the second with supplementary oxygen. Despite Bruce's minimal climbing experience, and the worse weather experienced by the second party, they had been able to achieve climbing rates of 900–1,000ft (275–300m) per hour using oxygen, compared with some 330ft (100m) per hour by the first party without oxygen. Clearly the benefit from oxygen amply compensated for the extra weights of the cylinders and equipment. For a summit attempt it seemed best to start using it between 21,000ft and 23,000ft (6,400–7,010m) so that a climber could reach the North Col at 23,000ft without becoming too fatigued. From a single higher camp at 26,500ft (8,080m), in good conditions, the summit might then be attained with a full oxygen supply in less than four hours. However, an extra cache of oxygen previously dumped at, say, 27,500ft (8,380m) would further increase the chance of a successful dash to the summit. Much would depend, as always, on the will-power of an assault team to pull out the last reserves of energy from their exhausted bodies.

A Disastrous Third Attempt

They also discussed together the possibility of a third attempt for which there might just be time before the monsoon broke, usually expected around 10 June, according to the Rongbuk Lama. But who would be available? Both Morshead and Norton were suffering from frostbitten feet, Bruce could not walk, Finch was exhausted but would hopefully recover after a few days' rest. Mallory had frostbitten finger tips and his heart had developed a flutter. Only Somervell seemed unscathed. After a week's rest, Longstaff agreed that Mallory and Finch might be fit enough to accompany Somervell on a third attempt, supported by Wakefield and Crawford, so General Bruce arranged to send the invalids back to Darjeeling in the care of Strutt and Longstaff.

The three climbers set off for Camp I on 3 June. Finch could barely keep going. It was clear he had not recuperated sufficiently, so next day he returned to Base in time to join the invalid party. Snow had begun to fall the previous evening and again the second night. Had the monsoon begun? Should they also return home? It seemed unworthy to do so if there was still a chance in an interval of fine weather. They decided to go on. At Camp III, there was up to 18ft (5.5m) of new snow; they had to re-erect the tents and dig out the stores. Next morning was fine and warm and the snow quickly began to consolidate. They were committed to an attempt with oxygen, Somervell being happy to take over Finch's role. The plan was to set their high camp at 26,000ft (7,920m), and use oxygen from there with a full set of four cylinders. Mallory and Somervell, with Wakefield and 24 porters, set off for the North Col on 7 June. They would have to be very wary of avalanches, particularly on the steeper slopes at the start and just below the Col. They had to make fresh tracks. At 1.30pm, they were on the gentler slopes of the corridor, with about 600ft (180m) to go, Somervell in the lead, with the porters strung out behind on three separate ropes. Suddenly, as Mallory records, they were 'startled by an ominous sound, like an explosion of untamped gunpowder'. Avalanche! In a moment, he was being buried under a wave of snow, trying to escape with a swimming motion but powerless to resist. He was able to break free, the rope tight at his waist to a porter who also emerged unharmed, as did Somervell and Crawford. One group of porters was carried down 150ft (45m), but the other two groups of four and five porters roped together were swept over a 50ft (15m) ice cliff and buried in avalanche snow in the crevasse at its foot. Frantically, they tried to dig them out. Two were extricated and survived. The other seven were killed. Thus ended this third attempt to climb Mount Everest.

Mallory took the blame on himself but observed that:

> The avalanche had started, not from the line of their steps, but about 100ft higher where perhaps the snow had drifted more deeply and remained powdery, ready to be triggered once the slope below had been disturbed ... One can never know enough about snow.

They were familiar with Alpine conditions, but had less experience of the additional effect of the monsoon in the Himalayas than, say, Longstaff, who wrote privately to a friend: 'To attempt such a passage in the Himalayas after new snow is idiotic. What the hell did they think they could do on Everest in such conditions, even if they did get up to the North Col?'

Somervell recorded his feelings:

> I remember well the thought gnawing at my brain. 'Only Sherpas and Bhotias killed – why, oh why could not one of us Britishers have shared in their fate?' I would gladly at that moment have been lying there dead in the snow, if only to give

those fine chaps who had survived the feeling that we shared their loss, as we had indeed shared the risk.

The expedition changed Somervell's life. On his way home, he visited a friend at the Neyyoor Mission Hospital in South India and was so impressed that he later joined the staff rather than taking up a much more prestigious post he had been offered at a London hospital.

The 1924 Expedition and the Mallory Mystery

'... for the spirit of adventure to keep alive the soul of man.'   George L. Mallory

On the 1922 Expedition's return home, the Mount Everest Committee was keen to maintain the momentum, at first proposing another attempt in 1923 but, after assessing the time it would take to assemble a strong team and improve equipment – particularly oxygen apparatus – it was postponed until spring 1924.

Mallory, without a job and with a wife and family to support, again undertook a series of lectures. It was while in the USA that he gave his famous reply to a reporter who asked him why he wanted to climb Mount Everest: 'Because it is there.' Was he just fobbing off an oft repeated question, or was there a deeper significance to his answer? Only recently I came across a more prosaic response attributed to him: 'For the stone from the top for geologists, the knowledge of the limits of endurance for the doctors, but above all for the spirit of adventure to keep alive the soul of man.' This US tour was not a financial success but when he got back, thanks probably to Everest publicity and some influential friends, he landed a job as Assistant Secretary and Lecturer at the Board of Extra Mural Studies in Cambridge.

Noel's film was not a commercial success either, although General

Bruce considered his efforts with the camera in most trying conditions to be unprecedented and a remarkable tour de force. This encouraged Noel to make a generous offer for the photographic and film rights in 1924 for the huge sum of £8,000, payable in advance. The Committee accepted with alacrity as it solved all their immediate financial problems in one go. Noel raised the money by forming a company, Explorer Films Ltd, with Younghusband as Chairman.

Bruce had taken over the chairmanship of the Mount Everest Committee from Younghusband and an Alpine Club selection committee set about choosing the team, including a deputy to Bruce. Bruce himself would probably not have passed a rigorous medical examination, but the committee unanimously agreed he should again be the leader. Perhaps they had no option! The nucleus of the climbing team was Somervell, Norton and Mallory, now joined by Noel Odell, a Cambridge geologist, and Bentley Beetham, a Lakeland schoolmaster and skilled photographer. Odell had spent the two previous summers on expeditions to Spitsbergen with Tom Longstaff, while Somervell and Bentley Beetham had just completed a superb Alpine season with 35 climbs in six weeks.

The last two places in the climbing team were filled by John de Vere Hazard and Andrew Comyn Irvine. Hazard, briefly mentioned in Norton's book, 'had previously served in India as a sapper, and had a great mountaineering record, and has been noted for feats of strength'. 'And finally,' writes Norton,

> our splendid 'experiment,' Irvine, bringing with him magnificent recommendations from Longstaff and Odell after Spitsbergen experiences, and, further, bringing his own great personality. He rapidly ceased to be an experiment, for we soon found that with a young body he possessed a mature judgement, combined with a very remarkable handiness and adaptability as a practical working engineer. All these valuable qualities, combined with infinite stamina and infinite unselfishness, made Irvine a very great asset to our party.

But in the meantime, where was Finch? Before each expedition financed by the Mount Everest Committee, the climbers were required to sign an agreement (I remember doing so solemnly in 1953 on a 6d stamp) whereby they were acting as agents and all their rights, including the copyright of the photographs taken by them, were handed over to the Committee. The income from subsequent lectures by team members was also to be handed over, after deducting a previously agreed fee. This proved rather irksome to some members who tended to forget that they had had a free trip to Everest, although they had received no salary or compensation for loss of income while preparing for or during the expedition. It was considered a sufficient honour just to be chosen. This was not enough for Finch who, on his personal initiative, had arranged a series of lectures on the Continent, taking advantage of his fluent German. This flagrant breach of the agreement, together with his outspokenness, created a permanent rift with the Committee, although he continued to help improve the oxygen equipment. It was a sad break because he was a fine climber and photographer and a clever scientist with practical ideas ahead of his time; for example, his innovative 'duvet jacket' and simple substitute for the uncomfortable oxygen masks. His splendid autobiography The Making of a Mountaineer, has two chapters on Everest in which he strongly defends the benefits of using oxygen, which the antagonists were only too ready to condemn on the grounds that it was unsporting and, therefore, un-British. Although he personally declared that Everest 'will never be climbed without oxygen', 25 years were to elapse after Hillary and Tenzing's ascent in 1953 before Messner and Habeler were to prove him wrong.

Norton Takes Over from General Bruce

The expedition left Darjeeling on 25 March, including Geoffrey Bruce again, E.O. Shebbeare of the Indian Forestry Department as Transport Officer instead of Captain Morris, who had been unable to get leave,

Hingston as doctor and naturalist and, of course, Noel as photographer with his own small retinue of assistants. Karma Paul came again as interpreter and Gyalgen as sirdar. Tragically, before they had got to Kampa Dzong, General Bruce went down with a severe attack of malaria and, although it yielded in four days, Hingston was adamant that he should return, and he had to be carried out of Tibet completely incapacitated. He handed over the leadership to Norton, in whom he expressed complete confidence. Norton, in turn, appointed Mallory as second-in-command and gave him free rein to develop the climbing plan.

Briefly, the plan was for three camps above the North Col, Nos. V, VI and VII at about 25,500ft, 26,500ft and 27,300ft, respectively (7,770/8,070/8,320m). When these had been stocked by the porters with necessary equipment and oxygen, two parties of two climbers would go for the top on the same day, one without oxygen from VII and one with oxygen from VI. Noel would be in support at one of the lower camps. Thus four climbers would remain in reserve, to repeat the plan if necessary. On 22 April, after dinner, Norton and Mallory named the assault teams: Geoffrey Bruce and Odell to establish Camp V; Somervell and Norton without oxygen from VII; Mallory and Irvine with oxygen from VI.

Odell had been placed in charge of the oxygen equipment, replacing Finch's role of 1922, but there seemed to have been very little rapport developed with the firm working on the equipment, Messrs Siebe, Gorman, over the previous two years. Some cylinders arrived empty and some only half full. Odell reported to the Committee: 'Every instrument leaked badly ... six sets had serious defects directly due to faulty design and workmanship, or bad material.' He praised Irvine's salvage work 'without whose mechanical faculty and manipulative skills, an efficient oxygen apparatus would hardly have been at the disposal of the expedition. Under difficult circumstances Mr Irvine had constructed an improved model of about 5lb less in weight than the original.'

Reading Julie Summers' recent book on Irvine, published in 2000, one gains the impression that during the march across Tibet, Irvine was working most nights alone in his tent until midnight with very limited tools to make the sets lighter and more reliable. He inverted the cylinders in their pack frame, thereby shortening the amount of connecting tubing, and relocated the reducing valves and flow meters so that they did not hamper the climber's freedom of movement quite so much while climbing. Despite his very limited mountaineering experience, this facility with the oxygen equipment (and the Primus stoves!) seems more than anything to have earned Irvine his place with Mallory on the planned assault with oxygen. Irvine's superb physical fitness from years of competitive rowing at Shrewsbury and Oxford, and the expedition the previous summer to Spitsbergen with Odell, coupled with his general athleticism, would hopefully compensate for his lack of experience when in Mallory's company. The impractical Mallory wrote to his wife: 'He will be an extraordinarily stout companion, very capable with the gas and with the cooking apparatus.'

Irvine wrote excitedly to his mother, Lillian: 'It will be a great triumph if my impromptu oxygen apparatus gets to the top. I hope it does ... If we reach the top, it will be probably May 17th.'

The Lama's Blessing and a Near Disaster

They arrived at Base Camp on 28 April. In order to save the Sahibs for work on the mountain itself, Camps I and II on the East Rongbuk Glacier were established and run by the Gurkha NCOs, Tejbir, Hurke and Shamsher, using locally recruited Tibetans. The 52 Sherpas were divided into two groups of 20, with 12 in reserve, to help establish and stock the higher camps. Norton was determined to get well ahead and not be caught out by an early monsoon as in 1922. Unfortunately, appalling weather between Camps II and III had forced the porters to make intermediate dumps and return to II, leaving those porters already at III in short supply. Already the immaculately planned transport system was crumbling. The tempest continued. At night, the temperature fell to –7°F. There was no hope of climbing the mountain until conditions improved. Norton ordered a general withdrawal to Base Camp, achieved by 12 May. There were several casualties, the most severe being Shamsher, who developed a clot on the brain, which we would nowadays refer to as cerebral oedema, the most acute form of high-altitude sickness, and the cobbler Mandhata, who had feet frostbitten to the ankles. Both died and were buried at Base Camp.

On 25 May, the whole expedition trooped down to the Rongbuk Monastery to obtain the Lama's formal blessing. He touched each one upon the head with his silver prayer wheel, and made a stirring speech which put fresh heart into the porters. The planned assault was deferred to 29 May. By 19 May, the first three camps were re-established and a route was forced through to the North Col. Remembering the disaster of 1922, a more direct route was taken up a 200ft (60m) ice chimney, protected with fixed rope, and Mallory and Odell found an easier way to the Col itself, returning well satisfied. According to plan, Hazard and 12 porters then occupied Camp IV. Bruce and Odell set out from III with 17 Sherpas, aiming to establish Camp V at 25,500ft (7,770m), but had to return as conditions became too difficult. Through the mist, they could see Hazard evacuating Camp IV but four porters refused to follow him down the first steep part in the avalanche-prone conditions and were marooned at IV. It is easy to criticise Hazard for not bringing all 12 down safely, but there were really too many for one Sahib to shepherd, even in reasonable weather conditions, and this was a weakness of the plan.

Next day, the three strongest climbers, Norton, Mallory and Somervell, climbed up to rescue the four. The rescue party were wallowing in deep snow, securing themselves with difficulty, ice axes plunged deep. Somervell, racked with fits of coughing, came to the end of his 200ft (60m) rope but was still 35ft (10m) short of the porters. So steep was the slope that Norton recalls Somervell standing almost upright in his steps, with his elbow resting on the snow, level with his shoulder. Two porters were persuaded to climb down separately and were passed along the taut rope to Mallory and Norton. The last two stupidly started together, their combined weight collapsing the snow and shooting them towards an ice cliff and impending doom. Miraculously, the snow balled up beneath them and brought them to a halt. The climbers unroped and by holding the ends of the rope at arm's length, Somervell, cool as a cucumber, and with his other arm outstretched, was just able to grab the terrified porters and haul them back to safety. By clutching the rope handrail, they were somehow able to get across to Mallory and Norton, their nerves totally shattered. 'Finally Somervell followed,' records Norton, 'after again tying the rope round his waist; and it was a fine object lesson in mountain craft to see him, balanced and erect, crossing the ruined track without a slip or mistake.'

Long after dark the party reached Camp III, and next day it was abandoned once again. The expedition members withdrew to Camp I for a council of war. Of the original 55 porters, only 15 were still fit to go to the North Col and above – henceforth nicknamed 'Tigers'. This limit to carrying capacity really precluded a serious attempt with oxygen, so the plan was revised for two parties to go up in sequence from Camp IV, stop at V, 25,500ft (7,770m) and VI, 27,200ft (8,290m), and then go for the summit. Mallory and Bruce would go first, then Somervell and Norton, with Odell and Irvine in support at the North Col, and Hazard at Camp III. Poor Bentley Beetham had had to return to base with an attack of sciatica.

Irvine's Rope Ladder

It was a bitter disappointment for Irvine no longer to be in a summit pair: 'Feel very fit tonight,' he wrote in his diary. 'I wish I was in the first party instead of a bloody reserve!' His fertile mind soon conceived another project: to construct a rope ladder for the ice chimney to assist porters carrying loads up to the North Col. Previously, he and Somervell had helped Hazard's party by hauling up the porters' loads on a rope, an exhausting process in which he narrowly escaped frostbitten hands. Helped by Odell and Shebbeare, Irvine used alpine ropes and a dozen large tent pegs for this 60ft (18m) masterpiece; every third rung was wood, with rope rungs spliced in between. Norton was impressed: 'like all the work of the well-known firm of "Odell and Irvine" this proved a complete success!' They had started a trend: in 1953, we were given a rope ladder by the Yorkshire Ramblers' Club!

The weather now began to improve. On 1 June, Mallory and Bruce with nine porters camped on the North Col and, the next day, pitched Camp V at 25,200ft (7,680m), slightly lower than intended because, although the sky was clear, the bitter north-west wind nearly blew the laden porters out of their steps. Three were kept for the carry to VI the next day, but the wind had sapped their morale so that even Bruce, with his eloquence, was unable to persuade them. They all had to go down. Halfway to the Col, they met Somervell and Norton ascending with six porters to occupy Camp V, retaining four 'Tigers'. Norton gives a detailed account of his dress designed to exclude the wind:

> Personally I wore thick woollen vest and drawers, a thick flannel shirt and two sweaters under a lightish knickerbocker suit of windproof gaberdine the knickers of which were lined with light flannel, a pair of soft elastic Kashmir puttees and a pair of boots of felt bound and soled with leather and lightly nailed with the usual Alpine nails. Over all I wore a very light pyjama suit of Messrs. Burberry's 'Shackleton' windproof gaberdine. On my hands I wore a pair of long fingerless woollen mitts inside a similar pair made of gaberdine; though when step-cutting necessitated a sensitive hold on the axe-shaft, I sometimes substituted a pair of silk mitts for the inner woollen pair. On my head I wore a fur-lined leather motor-cycling helmet, and my eyes and nose were protected by a pair of goggles of Crookes's glass, which were sewn into a leather mask that came well over the nose and covered any part of my face which was not naturally protected by my beard. A

huge woollen muffler completed my costume.

The porters were equally well equipped – each in a light green canvas windproof suit over a variety of woollen and leather garments.

Next morning, 4 June, Norton did his utmost to persuade three of the porters, Narbu Yishé, Lhakpa Chédé and Semchumbi, to climb higher than porters had ever climbed before. The fourth, Lobsang Tashi, a good-natured giant from eastern Tibet, was sick and could go no higher. At 1.20pm, Semchumbi reached his limits, Camp VI was set at 26,800ft (8,170m) and the porters returned. Norton had a better-stocked camp than in 1922, and surprisingly, as he wrote in his diary 'spent the best night since I left Camp I' – despite the cork coming out of a Thermos of tea, which he had taken into his sleeping bag. They had to melt more snow for breakfast tea but even so were off by 6.40am.

Norton and Somervell's Record Climb

The day was fine and nearly windless, but bitterly cold. Norton and Somervell could choose to climb the North-East Ridge or across the slabs of the North Face. The former had two steep prows, now called the First and Second Steps, favoured by Mallory but probably difficult to overcome, so they chose the latter, following the band of yellow limestone, underlying steeper crags which one cannot bypass until reaching a great couloir giving access to the final 700ft (213m) summit pyramid. Norton stopped to check his pulse – 64 – extremely low, although 20 above his normal very low level. Since leaving the snow, he had removed his goggles as the rim slightly impeded his vision. Now he began to see double, which Somervell assured him was due to a lack of oxygen rather than incipient snow-blindness, which was to afflict him severely later on. In the cold dry air, breathing many times for each step, Somervell's sore throat grew worse, giving rise to fits of coughing. At midday, he just had to stop and urged Norton to go on alone to the top.

As he did so, towards the shelter of the big couloir, the ledges narrowed and powdery snow concealed the precarious footholds. In the couloir, the snow lay deeper but still powdery, a dangerous place for a single unroped climber as one slip could prove fatal.

At 1pm, at a height later fixed as 28,126ft (8,753m), he was near the end of his powers. He calculated he had no chance of climbing the remaining 800ft or 900ft (240–270m) and returning safely. He turned back to rejoin Somervell, having gone on some 300yd (90m) but probably gaining less than 100ft (30m) in height.

On the descent, Somervell's axe slipped from his numbed fingers and cart-wheeled down the slope. Once he hung back when a fit of coughing nearly choked him until, in desperation, he vomited a slough of mucous membrane lining the larynx, caused by frostbite. Although in great pain, he could now breathe freely and quickly rejoined Norton. They continued by torchlight until Mallory and Odell guided them into the North Col camp where Irvine had tea and soup ready for them. An hour later, Norton was smitten with a severe attack of snow-blindness that lasted 60 hours. I, personally, have never suffered it, fortunately, but remember John Jackson on Kangchenjunga telling me it was like having powdered glass beneath your eyelids.

Norton had set a height record that lasted for nearly 30 years. He did not feel that he had necessarily reached man's upper limit, only his own. He declared: 'I still believe there is nothing in the atmospheric conditions even between 28,000ft and 29,000ft to prevent a fresh and fit party from reaching the top without oxygen!'

One More Try

While Norton and Mallory lay in their tent at Camp IV, Mallory explained that although the current attempt had failed, he was determined to make one more try, this time with oxygen. He had been down to Camp III with Bruce who had been able to reinvigorate the porters, helped by continued fine weather, to enable enough cylinders to be carried up for the attempt to be staged. Norton agreed, but was concerned that Mallory wished Irvine to accompany him rather than Odell who was the more experienced climber. Although both were familiar with the oxygen equipment, Mallory felt that Irvine had the better practical knack to cope with any unexpected failure. In his present exhausted state, Norton was hardly in a position to argue when Mallory had already completed his plans. Hingston, the doctor, although not a climber, had pluckily come up to Camp IV to examine Norton's eyes and now with the aid of two porters helped to escort him down, Hazard giving him a top rope down the steepest parts including the ice chimney. In two more days, Norton had recovered and he decided to remain at Camp III with Bruce, Noel and Hingston until the fate of Mallory and Irvine's attempt had been decided.

Odell, in charge of Camp IV at the North Col, now takes up the story. On the evening of 4 June, Mallory and Irvine had come up from III making a final test of the oxygen sets they would use higher up. It was while sledging across Spitsbergen the previous year that Odell had got to know Irvine intimately and had recommended him for Everest. Clearly Irvine had hoped for a real chance of 'a shot at the summit', although he had told Odell that despite his devotion to improving the oxygen equipment, he would have preferred to tackle it without. However, when the call came from Mallory, he was only too ready to seize the chance. His sore throat and painful sun-scorched face were forgotten in his enthusiasm.

Odell photographed Mallory and Irvine as they set out from IV at 8.40am on 6 June, having hardly done justice to the choice meal of sardines, biscuits and tea prepared for them by Hazard and Odell. Their personal loads, with two oxygen cylinders, weighed about 25lb (11kg), and they had eight porters with similar weight loads, including more oxygen. Four porters were sent back after leaving their loads at Camp V, bringing

Odell a note from Mallory: 'There is no wind here, and things look hopeful.'

On 7 June, Mallory's party went on up to Camp VI, and Odell, taking one Sherpa, Nema, followed up in support to V. Soon after he arrived there, a shower of stones heralded the return of Mallory and Irvine's four porters. They brought a hastily scribbled message:

Dear Odell,

We're awfully sorry to have left things in such a mess – our Unna cooker rolled down the slope at the last moment. Be sure of getting back to IV tomorrow in time to evacuate before dark as I hope to. In the tent I must have left a compass – for the Lord's sake rescue it; we are without. To here on 90 atmospheres for the two days – so we'll probably go on two cylinders – but it's a bloody load for climbing. Perfect weather for the job.

Yours ever,

G. Mallory

Odell's Lone Vigil

Nema was not feeling well, so Odell sent him back down with the other porters. This left Odell free to study the rocks, to look for fossils and to enjoy the fantastic scene around him, enhanced by the solitude – to the west, the giant peaks of Cho Oyu and Gyachung Kang bathed in pinks and yellows and to the east, 76 miles (122km) away, the snowy top of Kangchenjunga. After a meal of cereal and a little jam with macaroni, he stretched out in two sleeping bags diagonally across the tiny tent and fell asleep.

Odell was off next morning at 8am carrying a few provisions in case of shortage at VI and climbed up to the crest of the main North Ridge. It was fine, not unduly cold, and banks of mist drifted across from the west. With only a light wind, he felt Mallory and Irvine should be making good progress up the final summit pyramid. The general slope here was 40° to

45°, but as the slabs dipped outwards from the mountain at about 30°, when they were sprinkled with rock debris from above or freshly fallen snow, they could be awkward rather than technically difficult.

At 26,000ft (7,925m) he climbed a little crag, just to test himself, and as he reached the top there was a sudden clearing of the mist and he could see the ridge and final peak above. In the expedition book he wrote:

> I noticed far away on a snow slope leading up to what seemed to me to be the last step but one from the base of the final pyramid, a tiny object moving and approaching the rock step. A second object followed, and then the first climbed to the top of the step. As I stood intently watching this dramatic appearance, the scene became enveloped in cloud once more, and I could not actually be certain that I saw the second figure join the first. It was of course none other than Mallory and Irvine, and I was surprised above all to see them so late as this, namely 12.50, at a point which, if the 'second rock step', they should have reached according to Mallory's schedule by 8am at latest, and if the 'first rock step' proportionately earlier. The 'second rock step' is seen prominently in photographs of the North Face from the Base Camp, where it appears a short distance from the base of the final pyramid down the snowy first part of the crest of the North-east Arete. The lower 'first rock step' is about an equivalent distance again to the left. Owing to the small portion of the summit ridge uncovered I could not be precisely certain at which of these two 'steps' they were, as in profile and from below they are very similar, but at the time I took it for the upper second step.

Odell continued up to Camp VI at 2pm when snow began to fall and the wind freshened. They had left no note amongst the debris of sleeping bags, scraps of food and spare clothes so he could not tell what time they had actually started out. Camp VI was slightly hidden from above, so in case they might have difficulty in locating it, he scrambled up some 200ft (60m) and whistled and yodelled. It clouded over and he could only see a few yards ahead so within an hour he turned back. The squall blew over and it cleared. The whole North Face and the freshly fallen snow was bathed in sunshine, but there were no signs of the party. Recalling that Mallory had asked him to return to the North Col, and that the small tent at VI was only just big enough for two, around 4.30pm he left the provisions he had brought, together with Mallory's compass, closed the tent and descended. Passing V at 6.25, and then taking the snowy crest of the North Ridge, he was able to glissade a few hundred feet and so quickly reached IV at 6.45pm. The distance between IV and V, which took three to four hours uphill, could be descended in half an hour!

Hazard plied him with a wonderful brew of Maggi soup. That evening and next morning they scanned the slopes above, and the tiny tents, through binoculars but could see no movement. At noon, Odell decided to go up in search, taking two of the three porters who were then at IV. They spent the night in the two small tents at V. It was an intensely cold and windy night and they were unable to sleep. In the morning, the porters felt unable to climb further, so after seeing them on their way down, Odell continued up to VI. He had brought up an oxygen set which he now used but seemed to derive very little benefit from it; perhaps he was using too low a flow rate or else he had become so well acclimatised that he did not need it.

On reaching VI, he found everything just as he had left it. He dumped the oxygen set and went on up in search of his friends. After going for nearly two hours he realised how small were his chances of finding them on that vast expanse of crags and broken slabs. A more extensive search would need to be organised. Returning to VI, during a lull, he dragged two sleeping bags out onto a patch of snow visible from below, arranging them in the form of a T, as a pre-arranged signal to Hazard that there was no trace of the missing climbers.

He wondered whether to stay another night at VI and prolong his search next day. If he did, what hope was there of finding them still alive? Looking down to the North Col, he remembered his other companions anxiously awaiting his return to hear any news. He decided to take Mallory's compass and the oxygen set of Irvine's design, the only things worth retrieving. Alone and in meditation, he slowly commenced the long descent. At times, he sheltered from the biting gale in the lee of rocks, wriggling his toes to reassure himself that he was not getting frostbite. Hazard welcomed him with a note from Norton that confirmed he should return and not prolong the search. Together they descended and rejoined the main party at Base Camp, where the first joys of spring – flowers and insects – were transforming the erstwhile Arctic environment.

The Loss of Mallory and Irvine

What had happened to Mallory and Irvine? The 'first step' was at about 28,000ft (8,530m) and the 'second step' determined by theodolite at 28,230ft (8,605m). If indeed Odell did see them at the second step, they had about 800ft (245m) vertically still to climb, across some 1,600ft (490m) of ground. If it was not particularly difficult, and the weather and wind allowed, they should have reached the top by 3.30pm. This was five to six hours later than their originally planned schedule to reach the foot of the final pyramid (about 28,300ft) by 8am. Allowing five or six hours for return, they would have reached VI again well after dark – provided they had not missed their way, or met with an accident. In either case, to spend a night in the open at that altitude, and with their relatively modest clothing, they would have been very lucky to survive. Odell's conclusion was that there was a strong probability that Mallory and Irvine had reached the top, but that they had met their death by being benighted.

Odell's own achievement was outstanding. He was considered to be a slow acclimatiser but, in the long run, the most enduring. In the 12 days from 31 May to 11 June, he went three times up and down from III to IV, once from IV to V, and twice from IV to VI, the last two journeys over four consecutive days. During those 12 days, with one exception, he slept at 23,000ft (7,010m) or higher. He suffered no long-term ill effects.

Odell lived to the age of 96; his genial nature and patriarchal figure earning him the nickname 'Noah'. Wearing a broad-brimmed hat and flowing cloak, he became a familiar figure at The Alpine Club and the Royal Geographical Society (RGS), retaining in old age his earnest enthusiasm and the tall, spare figure and purposeful gait that had carried him to record heights. He died in Cambridge on Saturday 21 February 1987, in his chair at breakfast. The previous Wednesday, I had sat beside him in the front row at the RGS for a special lecture evening commemorating the life and times of another mountaineer who had distinguished himself on Everest – Don Whillans. Norton wrote:

Mallory was no common personality. Physically he always seemed to me the beau ideal of the mountaineer; he was very good looking, and I have always thought that his boyish face – for he looked absurdly young for his 37 years – was the outward and visible sign of a wonderful constitution. His graceful figure was the last word in wiry activity and he walked with a tireless swing which made him a man with whom few could live uphill; he was almost better downhill, for his years of mountain training had added balance and studied poise to his natural turn of speed.

But it was the spirit of the man that made him the great mountaineer he was: a fire burnt in him and caused his willing spirit to rise superior to the weakness of the flesh; he lived on his nerves, and throughout two campaigns on Mount Everest (I never climbed with him elsewhere) it was almost impossible to make out whether he was a tired man or not, for he responded instantly to every call that was made on him, and while the call lasted his would remain the dominant spirit in any enterprise. The conquest of the mountain became an obsession with him, and for weeks and months he devoted his whole time and energy to it, incessantly working at plans and details of organization ... His death robs us of a right loyal friend, a knight 'sans peur et sans reproche' amongst mountaineers and the greatest antagonist that Everest has had – or is likely to have.

Young Irvine was almost a boy in years – he was 22; but mentally and physically he was a man full grown and able to hold his own with all modesty on terms at least of equality with the other members of our party, who averaged

12 years older than he. Physically indeed he was not only a man full grown, he was a splendid specimen, as befitted an Oxford rowing blue, with the powerful shoulders and comparatively slim legs characteristic of the best oars.

His experience as a mountaineer was limited to the rocks of the British Isles and a climb in which he distinguished himself in Spitzbergen; but the previous summer he had been a member of the Oxford Expedition to those islands, and it was largely the outstanding reputation he had there gained for endurance, initiative, and all those moral qualities which go to make the right man for such an enterprise that had led to his being selected for the Mount Everest party.

He had further added to his reputation by the extraordinary aptitude he had shown for skiing as a novice in Switzerland the preceding winter. One more invaluable characteristic was his turn for things mechanical, for in this respect he was nothing short of a genius, and he became our standby in dealing with the troubles and difficulties we encountered over this year's oxygen apparatus, and, for the matter of that, in every department – from a lampshade to a rope ladder.

Sandy Irvine's cheerful camaraderie, his unselfishness and high courage made him loved, not only by all of us, but also by the porters, not a word of whose language could he speak. He shares with Odell the credit of having shown us all how to 'play for the side', stifling all selfish considerations, for nothing in the record of 1924 was finer than the work these two put in as 'supporters' at Camp IV.

By midday on 15 June, the last yak had left Base Camp. The monsoon broke on Everest the following day, presaging a return to bleaker conditions with constant snowstorms. At Rongbuk, there was a new feature on the landscape. A huge cairn built under the direction of Somervell and Beetham stood conspicuous on the highest stony hillock over the camp, commemorating the names of those who had been lured to their death on the great mountain.

The Mallory and Irvine Mystery

That was not the end of the Mallory and Irvine story. In the face of repeated questioning, it is perhaps not surprising that Odell changed his mind slightly in the various accounts of his final sighting. Initially, in his tiny diary, measuring a mere 3 × 2in, which I have seen, written in minute lettering with a special mapping pen, he recorded that he saw the two men 'on ridge nearing base of final pyramid'. In the expedition book, he places them at the last step but one from the final pyramid – corresponding to what is now called the Second Step. We now know that this is a wall about 100ft (30m) high with a short but technically difficult 15ft (4.5m) rock pitch at the top, and one conjectures whether Mallory would be able to climb it at that altitude in the way that Odell describes. When the Chinese first climbed the Step in 1960, it took them some four hours. Then in 1975, British climbers placed an aluminium ladder to overcome the top pitch, which most people now use, although in 1999 a brilliant American climber, Conrad Anker, managed to climb it free. Possibly

the hump which Odell saw Mallory and Irvine climb was a third step, above the second one, which might help to account for their being so late. In 1999, Andy Politz went to the point where Odell had stood and took a photograph of the ridge above, where the three steps are clearly visible. Only the third step could be said to be 'at the base of the final pyramid'.

Earlier, in 1933 on another expedition, Percy Wyn Harris discovered an ice axe which must have belonged either to Mallory or Irvine. It was at about 27,700ft (8,440m) lying on a slab about 60ft (18m) from the crest of the ridge and 250 (227m) yards north-east of the First Step. This was lower than the point where Odell saw the two men. They might have dropped the axe on the way up and decided to press on without it, or it might have marked the scene of an accident on the descent. The axe was noted to have three small nicks cut into the wooden shaft, an identification which Irvine also used on his officer cadet's swagger stick at Shrewsbury. It was, therefore, assumed to be Irvine's axe, although Hattersley Smith, in a letter to the *Daily Telegraph*, said that Wyn Harris had told his servant, Kusang Pugla, to cut the three nicks so that the axe would not then be confused with any others being used at the time. Or did Kusang just scratch a small cross on the shaft to identify it? The axe was later donated to The Alpine Club, but is, at present, on display in the permanent National Mountaineering Exhibition at Rheged near Penrith, so you can go and see it for yourself!

Another event added to the mystery. The Chinese climber Wang Hongbao was a member of a search party looking for a fellow climber who had disappeared on 4 May 1975. Wang was at their Chinese Camp VI and, returning from a short stroll, told another climber, Zhang Junyan, that he had come across the body of a foreign mountaineer dressed in old-fashioned clothing. Four years later, Zhang described this to a Japanese climber, Hasegawa Yoshinin, as an 'English dead'. The body's cheek had been pecked at by birds. The day after his discovery, Wang himself was killed in an avalanche, but the story was checked with Hasegawa by an American, Tom Holzel, who, helped by the British mountaineering historian Audrey Salkeld, had become obsessed by the mystery and organised an expedition in 1986 to try to find Mallory and Irvine.

Holzel was not successful, but in 1999 a dedicated Anglo-American 'Mallory and Irvine Research Expedition' tried again. This was partly in-spired by a BBC producer, Graham Hoyland, a great-nephew of Howard Somervell. Apparently, Somervell had lent his Kodak Vest pocket camera to Mallory on that fateful day. It is possible that any photographs taken would still be preserved in the cold conditions and, with special care, could be developed. A shot of Mallory on the summit would be the proof that they had climbed it!

A German student, Jochen Hemmleb, equally obsessed with Everest, was the 1999 expedition's historian. The expedition book, *Ghosts of*

Everest, describes how he used old photographs to predict the location of the 1975 Chinese Camp VI. 'Forget the ice axe,' he said, 'find the camp and you'll find Irvine.' On 1 May, the search party spread out over the 30–40° slope. That year, there was exceptionally little snow cover so there was a better chance than usual of uncovering something. In a shallow depression – a natural fall zone – they stumbled into 'a virtual graveyard of mangled, frozen bodies'; but all wearing recent clothing. Conrad Anker, going on intuition, had been looking further down at the lower edge of the terrace where it dropped away 6,000ft (1,800m) to the Rongbuk Glacier. Coming up again to about 26,770ft (8,160m), he saw 'a patch of white that was whiter than the rock around it and whiter than the snow'. It was a body lying prone with a broken leg, arms outstretched, fists clenched, wearing fragments of old clothing, the bare skin bleached white like porcelain. He wore hob-nailed boots, and had a rope tied around the waist. A piece of shirt collar revealed a name tape: G. Mallory.

They recovered some artefacts and later covered the body reverently with stones to let it rest in peace. Unfortunately, and possibly un-intentionally, photographs of the scene received instant worldwide distribution. It was a distressing time for the Mallory family. Snow goggles were found in Mallory's pocket, suggesting that they were descending in the dark when an accident occurred. Notes on the back of an envelope recorded pressures in numbered oxygen cylinders. They might have started with three cylinders each, instead of two, giving them a longer duration on oxygen than had previously been thought. Even so, I rather doubt whether they ever reached the summit. Of the camera, there was no sign. Possibly, some day, Irvine's body will also be found and the issue resolved beyond doubt. Personally, I have a less obsessive or enquiring mind and am reconciled to let it remain forever a mystery.

04

'We'll Do It Next Time!' – The 1930s

'It must be climbed one day and I hope I will be one of the men to do it.'

Major F. M. Bailey

Eight years were to pass before the Dalai Lama allowed another expedition to Everest. At that time, Sir Charles Bell had been the Political Officer in Sikkim whose close friendship with the Dalai Lama had enabled the first expedition to be granted permission in 1921. However, his successor until 1928, Major F.M. Bailey, although a great explorer himself, seemed less inclined to help and even tried to obstruct subsequent expeditions in the late 1920s. In 1913, he had explored the Tsangpo in Tibet with Morshead, proving that it and the Brahmaputra were one and the same river, and also discovered and brought back the wonderful blue poppy, *Meconopsis baileyi*. But after the 1924 Expedition, he told Noel's wife in India that he did not like the Everest expeditions because of the trouble and work they gave him. True, one or two incidents had occurred but were blown out of proportion: Heron's geologising; Morshead's and later Hazard's extended travels; and part of the team's rest and recuperation excursion in 1924 down the Rongshar Gorge briefly into Nepal. Noel capped these minor transgressions by bringing several lamas from the monastery at Gyantse to England to help

↑ Mount Everest – Record of First Ascents 1953–1996

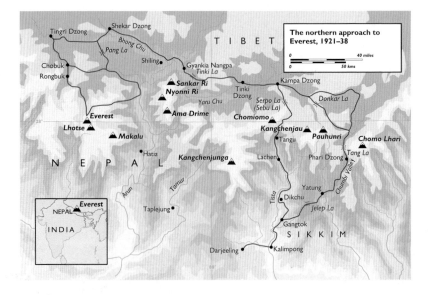

↑ From Darjeeling to Everest through Sikkim and Tibet

↓ The North Face, showing camps and points reached

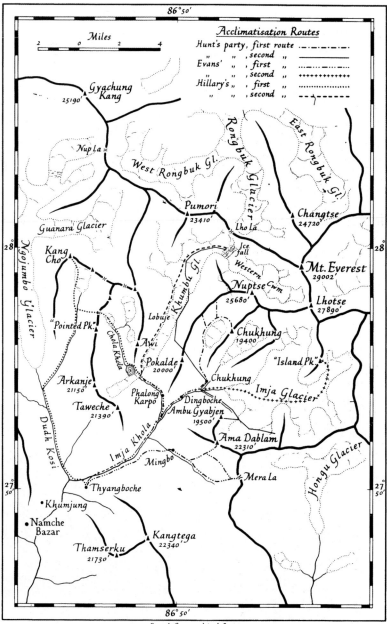

↑ Everest from Nepal with 1953 acclimatisation routes

↑ Lamas of Kharta Monastery, with long horns

↓ The Head Lama at Rongbuk Monastery

↓ Sir George Everest (1790–1866), Surveyor General of India

Somervell's watercolour of Everest from Shiling, 80 miles away

The 1921 team: standing, Wollaston, Howard-Bury, Heron, Raeburn; seated: Mallory, Wheeler, Bullock, Morshead

↑ Everest from Base Camp at the snout of the Rongbuk Glacier

↓ Mallory's view in 1921 of the Khumbu Icefall and the Western Cwm, photographed recently

↑ Everest from the Camp on the Lhakpa La

↓ Alfresco breakfast in 1922: Wakefield, Morris, General Bruce, Norton, Gurkha, Geoffrey Bruce

↑ Finch testing oxygen equipment

↓ Norton's watercolour of a Buddhist monk

↑ Everest sunrise, 18 September 2003, showing the pinnacles near the top of the north-east ridge

← Camped in the forest of the Arun Gorge

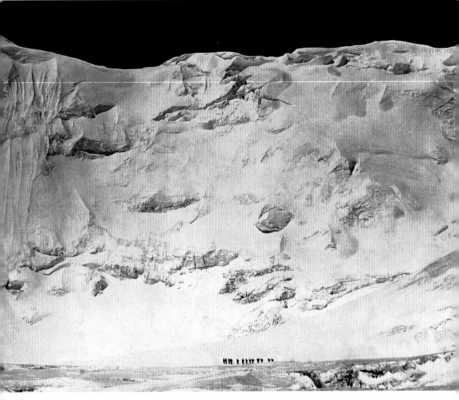

↑ The ice wall below the North Col – prone to avalanche after fresh snow

← Camped on the plain below Shekar Dzong

↓ Somervell's watercolour of seracs on the East Rongbuk Glacier

↑ Mallory and Norton reached 26,985ft (8,225m) in 1922

↑ Edward Felix Norton

↑ George Leigh Mallory

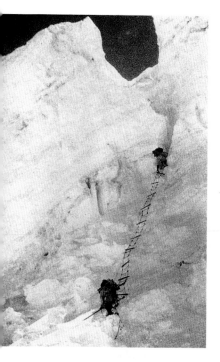

↑ Irvine's rope ladder below the North Col

↓ Leaving Camp IV, 6 June 1924, the last photograph of Mallory and Irvine

↑ Norton near the highest point reached in 1924, 28,126ft (8,572m)

JUNE 1924

SUN. 8 *Whit Sunday* *W/p 6. Off 8*
Went up & over N. ridge on to N. face
frequent mists. At 12.50 saw M. & I on ridge
nearing base of final pyramid. Had a little
rock climbing at 26,000 at 2 on reaching tent
at 27,000 waited 1 hr. they went out & stopped
& started to join M. & I. direction. Blizzard cleared
so decided to go back, reached IV. c. 6.45, no

MON. 9 *Whit Monday* signs, lights, on mt.
Made arrangements for coolie with Hazard, &
also no M. on I. started off 12 with 2 coolies
for V, arr. 3.30, v. cold wind on ridge,
& gusty at camp: prep. over. app. for going
on to VI. tomorrow. Nothing further of M. & I.

TUES. 10 *Whit Tuesday* D V. cold night
Tent coolies down to IV. Used oxygen
which allayed tire on legs somewhat: very
bitter N. wind of great force all day. climbed
up slopes to W. of VI, & finally reached tent, but
no signs of M. & I. around. Signalled by
sleeping bags on snow patch to Hazard at 1 th

WED. 11 *S. Barnabas. Ember Day*
Packed up camp IV. leaving tents
standing, & with heavy loads Hazard Nima
& I got down so slopes by 22 avalanche
rt. — 1 hr., & on to III., where after tiffin,

→ A page from Odell's tiny diary,
8–11 June 1924

↓ Noel Odell, aged 87, at Pen-y-
Gwryd, 1978

↑← Mallory's goggles, altimeter,
watch, neckerchief and hob-nailed
boot, retrieved 1 May 1999

→ Dawson Stelfox below the tricky 2nd Step, 27 May 1993

↓ Andrei Louchnikov on the Chinese ladder at the 2nd Step, 26 May 1999

↑ Hugh Ruttledge, leader in 1933 and 1936

↓ The brave 'Tigers' who set up Camp VI in 1933

↑ Frank Smythe in deep snow at 27,300ft (8,320m), the highest point in 1938

↑ Angtharkay, Shipton's favourite sirdar

popularise his film of the expedition – Bailey took exception to these 'dancing lamas'. He was perhaps envious that, as a younger man, he had not had the chance to go to Everest himself. Amongst his papers after he died in 1967 was found the comment: 'It must be climbed one day and I hope I will be one of the men to do it.'

In 1931, the Mount Everest Committee was reconstituted under the newly elected President of the Royal Geographical Society, Admiral Sir William Goodenough (a first cousin of my wife's grandfather!) who had been Commodore of the Second Light Cruiser Squadron at the Battle of Jutland, and he immediately made a tentative approach via the Secretary of State for India, Wedgwood Benn. The new Political Officer in Sikkim was Colonel Weir (grandfather of the actress Joanna Lumley). The response was not encouraging (despite these modern-day associations), and it was another year before permission was reluctantly granted by the Dalai Lama for 1933, provided all the expedition members were British.

The 1933 Expedition

RUTTLEDGE HEADS THE TEAM FOR 1933

Norton was not available as leader, so the Committee chose 'a safe pair of hands' in Hugh Ruttledge, 48, an ex-Commissioner of the Indian Civil Service who, although not an outstanding mountaineer, had made several exploratory Himalayan trips while serving in Almora, so he had a good knowledge of the local people and had climbed with the Gurkhas and Sherpas. He was not expected to go above the North Col. From previous expeditions, Odell and Crawford were included, with Shebbeare as Transport Officer, but the core of the 14 member team were younger climbers, bringing the average age down to 34, often considered ideal for Himalayan climbing.

Frank Smythe, 32, had perhaps the greatest reputation because of his two superb new routes with Graham Brown on the Brenva Face of Mont Blanc in 1927 and 1928, after which he had gone to Kangchenjunga with Dyhrenfurth in 1930, climbing the Jongsong Peak, 24,344ft (7,420m). In 1931, he led his own expedition to climb Kamet, at 25,447ft (7,757m), the first peak over 25,000ft to be climbed. Smythe had a reputation for irritability, but his friends said his temper improved with altitude! Others selected from the Kamet team were Eric Shipton, E. St J. Birnie (a Cavalry Officer) and Dr Raymond Greene (brother of the writer Graham Greene) as Chief Medical Officer.

Shipton, 25, had cut his teeth on Ruwenzori, Kilimanjaro and the first traverse of Mount Kenya while a planter in that country. He was destined to become one of the greatest mountain explorers of the century, his name forever associated with Everest. The telegram from Admiral Goodenough inviting him read: 'MOUNT EVEREST COMMITTEE INVITE YOU JOIN THE EXPEDITION SUBJECT MEDICAL APPROVAL PLEASE REPLY GOODENOUGH.' As Shipton was probably halfway up a mountain at the time, a friend drafted a reply on his behalf: 'GOODENOUGH – SHIPTON' but luckily Eric was able to stop it in time!

Two others with Himalayan experience were George Wood-Johnson, a tea planter from Darjeeling who was with Dyhrenfurth in 1930, and Hugh Boustead, who commanded the Sudan Camel Corps and later wrote a superb autobiography, Wind of Morning. The others had not previously been to the Himalayas but were drawn from Britain's best alpinists: Percy Wyn Harris, who had traversed Mount Kenya with Shipton; Jack Longland, top rock climber, and a pole-vault blue who reputedly was the first to ascend the vertiginous tower of St John's College Chapel, Cambridge; Tom Brocklebank, the youngest at 24 and a rowing blue; and Dr W. McLean to act as Greene's assistant. In November, Odell had to withdraw, and was replaced by Lawrence Wager, another distinguished geologist who had explored in Greenland with Gino Watkins, and later became Professor of Geology at Oxford. Altogether it was the strongest team yet to attempt Everest. As one might expect from those days, the Services and universities were well represented; the hardy gritstone climbers from the north of England were not yet well enough known to be considered, even if they could have afforded to take the time off.

The expedition's finances were secured on a more competitive basis than previously; the *Daily Telegraph* paid £3,500 to outbid *The Times*, who were furious, and Hodder & Stoughton replaced Edward Arnold, paying £3,000 for the book rights. Hodder continued to be a favourite publisher among mountaineers for many years following.

Some lessons had been learned from the expeditions of the 1920s: the need to place the last camp higher than 27,000ft (8,230m), and the importance of timing the summit attempts during the expected fortnight of calmer weather just before the monsoon. So as to receive early warning of the approach of the monsoon, radio equipment was taken for the first time, operated by two officers from the Royal Corps of Signals, Thompson and Smijth-Windham.

Grenfell cloth was used for windproof clothing and the highest tents. High-altitude boots were designed specially by Robert Lawrie to minimise frostbite. Oxygen apparatus was taken, but not for essential use if climbers could become sufficiently acclimatised to scale the mountain without it.

The expedition arrived at Rongbuk Monastery on 16 April – 12 days earlier than in 1924 – and received the customary blessing from the Head Lama. With time in hand, they were able to ride out periods of bad weather. Camp III was established below the North Col on 2 May, and Smythe and Shipton started to find a safe route to the Col. Considerable changes had occurred since 1924, the most difficult feature now being a near vertical ice cliff about halfway up, 40ft (12m) high at its lowest point. Ten days of storm intervened before Smythe was able to tackle the ice wall on 12 May. The ice was tough and rubbery, requiring handholds as well as footholds and a ringed spike or piton for security to safeguard progress. Gasping for breath, and beating his hands together to restore circulation, he later recalled: 'I was feeling pretty done and my heart was pumping as though it would burst, yet I remember a thrill of exhilaration. This was altogether different from the monotonous work we had so far endured; it was mountaineering.'

Next day, they fixed a 60ft (18m) rope ladder on the wall – a gift from the Yorkshire Ramblers' Club – and the following day five Sahibs escorted a dozen laden porters to Camp IV. This was probably on the same ledge used in 1922 and 1924, but because of the movement of the ice it was now some 200ft (60m) below the Col itself.

An Early Monsoon?

Sickness and bad weather continued to plague the party. The monsoon had arrived in Ceylon, earlier than usual, and in two weeks it would reach Everest. In these situations, frustration can easily build up and sparks fly. On 20 May, there was an abortive attempt to set up Camp V around 25,500ft (7,770m) with 11 porters, but because of the cold wind Birnie had allowed them to stop a thousand feet short. Wyn Harris was furious, and next day Ruttledge went up to Camp IV himself to sort out the argument, and put Wyn Harris in charge. Two days had been lost. The next day was calm and clear and Camp V was set up successfully at 25,700ft (7,830m), but they had to withdraw after a furious storm on 24 May. The monsoon clouds were building up ominously to the south-east ready to take over when the west wind failed.

On 28 May, a team with eight of the finest Sherpas managed to establish Camp VI, a Burns Grenfell cloth tent weighing 10lb (4.5kg), pitched at 27,400ft (8,350m), halfway up the Yellow Band, about 400yd (365m) west of the First Step and 600ft (180m) higher than in 1924. The summit was just 1,600ft (490m) above. Wyn Harris and Wager moved in while Longland escorted the porters down. Rather than committing them to the featureless shelving slabs of the North Face, where they could easily slip, he led them across to the better-defined North Ridge. A sudden storm enveloped them and within moments they were fighting for their lives. In Longland's words: 'visibility suddenly narrowed to a snowswept circle of some 20 yards, and ... I was taking a party of porters down a ridge which I had never been on before, but which I knew to be ill-defined and easy to lose, particularly in such conditions.'

They came across the green tent where Mallory and Irvine had spent their last night in 1924. Longland had a dreadful thought that he had gone too far onto a minor ridge leading onto the ice slopes above the East Rongbuk Glacier but he kept his head until at last the green tent of Camp V appeared through the swirling mist, not a hundred feet below, where Smythe and Shipton were anxiously awaiting them. Smythe describes the moment:

> The afternoon lengthened and a premature gloom gathered as the blizzard thickened. Suddenly we heard something above the roar of the wind. A dim figure showed through the murk, then another and another. There was a relieved shout and one by one the porters came scrambling down the rocks to the camp. Among them was Jack. He was unrecognizable; his eyebrows, his eyelashes, his moustache, were rimed and caked with snow and ice; icicles inches long hung from his nostrils.

After a short break, they continued down, reaching Camp IV at dusk, utterly exhausted, as fine a performance on Everest as any. The names of these gallant Sherpas were Ang Tarke, Da Tsering, Nima Dorje, Ang Tsering, Kipa Lama, Pasang, Tsering Tarke and Rinzing, henceforth known as 'Tigers'.

Two Summit Attempts

The team was now well disposed for an attack on the summit, with the top three camps fully stocked and manned. All they needed was good weather. Wyn Harris and Wager left Camp VI at 5.40am, an hour before the sun reached them. They planned to try the North-East Ridge rather than following Norton's route. They were within 60ft (18m) of the crest and 230yds (209m) from the First Step when Wyn Harris spotted an ice axe lying on a slab, held only by friction. It must have belonged to either Mallory or Irvine! Leaving it to be retrieved on their return, they continued to the First Step, which they reached at 7am. They could have climbed around it, but the narrow and jagged ridge above leading to the Second Step appeared considerably more difficult than the alternative of following along the outcrop of the Yellow Band to their right and then climbing directly to the Second Step when they came under it, but this also appeared unclimbable. Gradually they became committed to following Norton's route. They entered the great couloir which was deep in unstable powder. Now roped up, they crossed it and traversed up steeper snow-covered rocks to some 50ft (15m) above the Yellow Band. They were in a sensational position, with no belays. It was 12.30pm; the summit 1,000ft (300m) above, or at least four hours' climbing, giving no time to return to Camp V, as Smythe and Shipton would now be occupying Camp VI. They decided to turn back, having equalled the height reached by Norton in 1924. Wyn Harris retrieved the ice axe, leaving his own in its place. Too exhausted to re-examine the First Step, Wager climbed to the edge of the ridge instead to look down the sheer ice slopes of the East Face, and up at this flank of the Second Step which was plastered with 60° ice. They got back to Camp VI at 4pm, continued on down and were welcomed by Birnie in support at Camp V.

Next day, Wyn Harris had a near escape when he glissaded out of control towards a precipice but was able to arrest himself with his ice axe just in time. Meanwhile, Smythe and Shipton were stormbound at Camp VI and had to spend a second night there. It was too cold to start before 7.30am. Shipton did not feel well and when they had almost reached the First Step he could go no further, but he encouraged Smythe to continue alone while he returned to Camp VI. Smythe again followed Norton's route, remarking that the Second Step resembled 'The sharp bow of a battle cruiser'. Loose snow had accumulated more deeply on the rocks beyond the great gully, making the climbing more difficult and dangerous. All alone, he realised the game was up, and turned back from much the same point as his predecessors, around 28,200ft (8,595m).

On his descent to Camp VI, Smythe experienced two curious incidents. He felt strongly that he was roped to a second man, even to the extent of offering him some Kendal mint cake when he stopped for a bite. Then later, glancing towards the North Ridge, he saw two dark objects hovering in the sky, pulsating but more slowly than his heart beat. Then an obscuring mist drifted across and they vanished. Were they UFOs, or just the mental state of an exhausted man under stress that produced what Raymond Greene called 'Frank's pulsating teapots'? Although Smythe slept well that night at Camp VI, both he and Shipton were caught in a storm on the descent with a similar experience to Longland. They were lucky to survive. McLean examined them afterwards and Smythe was one of the few to go high on Everest without suffering a dilated heart. Ironically, as a boy he was said to have a weak heart and, at 27, was discharged from the Royal Air Force as medically unfit!

Defeat and Indecision

On 3 June, the general retreat from Camp IV was described by Smythe as 'a descent of broken men'. Rest was essential and Ruttledge ordered the retreat to Base. A week later they moved back to Camp III but snow continued to fall. The monsoon had broken so gradually one could not say which day it arrived. An unusually early monsoon had coincided with unusually frequent western storms so the expected lull had never occurred. The mountain never came into reasonable condition and was unclimbable. The expedition was over.

What happened about the use of oxygen? Both Wyn Harris and Smythe conceded it would have been useful for crossing the couloir and the rocks beyond, where fixed ropes would also have increased security.

However, there was still a belief that oxygen was of little benefit to a fully acclimatised person, and that the final summit pyramid could be climbed without it. The outspoken George Finch was infuriated by this attitude, writing in *The Listener*:

> This wretched state of indecision about oxygen must be ended, and in good time, too, if the next expedition is to succeed. Either oxygen should be taken and used full blast in the attack above 25,000 or even above 23,000ft, or it should be utterly tabooed on moral or material grounds, or indeed for any other reason that the wit of man can conceive. And if the prospective Everest Committee cannot bring itself to decide one way or the other then sack the lot!

1935 – A Monsoon Reconnaissance

On his return to England, Ruttledge had the daunting task of reporting back to the Mount Everest Committee. They covered their disappointment by applying for yet another attempt and asking him to lead it. But he was not everybody's choice. He had been quite surprised himself to be appointed leader in 1933 for he was a kindly, modest man and, at 48 years of age with a slight limp, caused by a pig-sticking accident, he was never expected to go high on the mountain. There was a growing feeling that Everest was now becoming a technical climbing problem and the next leader should be capable of being well up front.

Jack Longland, ever one to express a candid opinion, wrote many years later: 'It is difficult to overemphasize the frustration felt by young climbers in the mid-nineteen thirties, believing, as they did, that the conduct both of The Alpine Club and of Everest affairs was largely in the hands of people who had not been near a serious climb for years.'

Ruttledge, sensing the mood, offered his resignation to save both the Committee and himself from embarrassment. Then, unexpectedly, the Tibetans gave permission for another expedition between June 1935 and June 1936. There was not time to organise a full-scale one in spring

1935, but the Committee, now chaired by Major General Percy Cox of the Royal Geographical Society, agreed on a monsoon reconnaissance to gather information, followed by another full attempt in spring 1936. Ruttledge was asked to be leader in 1936, which he surprisingly accepted. Factions immediately developed, both in the Committee and The Alpine Club, with an anti-Ruttledge group becoming pro-Crawford, but after considerable machinations the Committee decided, by the Chairman's casting vote, to confirm Ruttledge.

Meanwhile, Shipton was asked to lead the reconnaissance. After going high in 1933, he had further enhanced his reputation by discovering, after many other distinguished mountaineers had failed, a route up the Rishi Gorge into the inner sanctuary of Nanda Devi in Garhwal. He was accompanied only by H.W. Tilman, with whom he had traversed Mount Kenya, and three Sherpas, including Angtharkay. It was a brilliant reversion to the principle of lightweight exploration pioneered by Graham, Mummery, Longstaff and others, in contrast to the more recent massive assaults on the giants, Everest, Kangchenjunga and Nanga Parbat. The Committee still had £1,400 in its coffers, so Shipton offered to lead a team of six climbers for £200 each.

The main objectives of the reconnaissance were to investigate snow conditions during the monsoon, and a possible alternative route up the West Ridge, and to try out new men for 1936 – particularly in their ability to acclimatise. Astonishingly, there was a clause in Shipton's contract forbidding them to make an assault. As he later wrote:

> But I had a private motive: my dislike of massive mountaineering expeditions had become something of an obsession, and I was anxious for the opportunity to demonstrate that, for one-tenth of the former cost and with a fraction of the bother and disruption of the local countryside, a party could be placed on the North Col, adequately equipped to make a strong attempt on the summit.

Shipton's team consisted of: H.W. Tilman; Dr Charles Warren, who had been with Marco Pallis in Garhwal in 1933; Edwin Kempson, a schoolmaster at Marlborough with 12 years' Alpine experience; Edmund Wigram, a medical student; L.V. Bryant, a tough young New Zealander; and Michael Spender, with a double first from Oxford, whose task was to extend the photo-theodolite surveys of the 1920s. In Darjeeling they engaged 15 Sherpas, including Angtharkay and several other Tigers. One of the humblest was Tenzing Bhotia, later known as Tenzing Norgay, who was to become the first, with Edmund Hillary, to climb Everest. By coincidence, it was Bryant's inclusion in the team which led Shipton to think highly of New Zealand climbers and to invite two, one of them being Hillary, to join him on the Everest reconnaissance of 1951, years later in Nepal.

The expedition left Darjeeling at the end of May, dallying two weeks to explore an unknown range of 20,000–22,000ft (6,100–6,710m) peaks to the east of the Arun Gorge. From there, they could see Everest was relatively clear of snow and in perfect condition. If they had gone there directly, one wonders how high they might have climbed. Ironically, the monsoon did not break until 26 June.

They arrived at Rongbuk on the 4 July and went straight up to Camp II on the East Rongbuk Glacier with 40 Tibetans carrying five weeks' food. The weather was still perfect and they occupied Camp IV on 8 July.

A few yards beyond, beside an old food dump, they came upon the pathetic remains of a lone Englishman, Maurice Wilson, who had died in his tent. Charles Warren retrieved his diary, from which they were able to unravel a strange story. Wilson was an ascetic who believed that by abstinence he could purify himself and be born again. To draw attention and convert the world to his ideas, his first act would be to climb Everest. Possibly influenced by the daring first flight over Everest in 1933, although he could neither fly nor climb, he thought of crash-landing a light aircraft on the mountain, going to the top and then descending to Rongbuk.

He therefore learned to fly, bought a small plane, which he named Ever Wrest, and flew it to India where it was seized by the authorities. Undeterred, he went to Darjeeling, hired three Sherpas and travelled surreptitiously to Rongbuk, where he made a very favourable impression on the Head Lama. He then set off alone for Everest and, incredibly, got within a couple of miles of Camp III before retreating, stumbling more dead than alive, back to the monastery after nine days. He stubbornly tried again; this time two Sherpas helped him to get to Camp III but then deserted when they were unable to persuade him to return. He discovered the food dump and his asceticism did not prevent him polishing off a 1lb box of King George chocolates. In trying to reach the North Col, he got as far as the 40ft (12m) ice wall but not surprisingly this utterly defeated him and he finally appears to have died in his sleep, of exhaustion and exposure. A sad story. They buried his body in a crevasse.

Shipton's party now turned to investigate the slopes leading up to the North Col. The dreadful avalanche of 7 June 1922 which had killed seven Sherpas was probably a form called 'wind slab', caused by the strong west wind blowing fresh snow over the Col onto the east side where it packed down to form the wind-slab, but with an underlying unstable surface. It was now July, the west wind had moderated, and after careful inspection they considered the slope to be safe. Shipton, Kempson and Warren, therefore, set up camp on the North Col with nine Sherpas and food for 15 days on 12 July – only six days out from Rongbuk. Shipton planned to set a camp at 26,000ft (7,925m) and then examine the slabs above 27,000ft (8,230m). If the snow there had consolidated instead of remaining powdery, at this season it would become a feasible route. Sadly, the weather broke and it was deemed prudent to retreat. They decided to climb some smaller peaks until the weather improved, when they could return. They started the descent. Two hundred feet (60m) below the crest, they discovered an enormous avalanche had peeled off to a depth of 6ft (1.8m), utterly obliterating the tracks of their ascent. They had heard nothing. Should they go on or back? The avalanche track itself was most likely to be safe so they pressed on down to Camp III. It was a salutary lesson on how difficult it was to judge monsoon snow conditions at high altitude. They decided to abandon their camp on the Col and not return.

Twenty-six Peaks – An Orgy of Climbing!

The party were now free to climb where they wished. While Spender continued his survey, the others split into groups and enjoyed a veritable orgy of climbing. In two months they climbed 26 peaks, nearly all first ascents. Several times they exceeded 23,000ft (7,010m) and confirmed that during the monsoon season, snow above that altitude never consolidates, nor does the wind blow the rocks clear. It appeared that Everest was virtually unclimbable by the northern route during that time. They climbed a peak beside the Lho La, the col at the base of Everest's West Ridge, and had a clear view of the Ridge, which they considered impracticable. From another col north-east of Pumori, they could see the great Khumbu Icefall issuing from the Western Cwm but, like Mallory and Bullock in 1921, they could not see into the Cwm itself nor the South Col. So, in its whirlwind tour, the Shipton reconnaissance accomplished its main objectives but brought back very little new information as far as Everest was concerned.

With regard to the new men, Tilman and Bryant had difficulty acclimatising to 23,000ft, so they were turned down for the expedition of 1936. How unpredictable is the matter of acclimatisation? In the same year, Tilman and Odell (another Everest reject) made the first ascent of Nanda Devi, 25,645ft (7,817m), the highest mountain to be climbed by that date!

At least Shipton had cost the Mount Everest Committee very little money. While on the march, being a small party, they lived largely off the country instead of relying on 'Fortnum & Mason'. Mutton was pressure-cooked, and local potatoes and onions were supplemented with dried vegetables from England. Shipton added:

> Eggs were always plentiful in the villages, and though many of them were rather
> stale we consumed enormous quantities. Our record was 140 in a single
> day between four of us, and many times our combined party of seven put away
> more than a hundred. Tilman could bake an excellent loaf with the local flour
> and the dried yeast which we had brought as a supply of Vitamin B. Excellent
> butter made from yak's milk was always available. So food presented no problem
> while we were in inhabited parts of Tibet; appetites were healthy and no one was
> inclined to be fussy about lack of variety.

They returned to Darjeeling by an obscure pass from Tibet into the
Lhonak Valley of north Sikkim called the Chorten Nyima La, 19,090ft
(5,819m), the same one used by Captain J.B. Noel in 1913. This particularly
intrigued me because in spring 2002 I obtained special permission to
take a party into the Lhonak Valley where we hoped to climb up to this
pass and to the higher Jongsong La, 20,160ft (6,145m), just to the north
of Kangchenjunga. We were the first Westerners to enter the valley since
the 1930s and made the mistake of paying a courtesy call on the local
army unit, the only people we encountered. Unfortunately, owing to a
lapse in communication, they had not been informed by their higher
command that we were coming, so we were not allowed to proceed
further, despite our valid permit.

Tenzing Norgay's First Expedition

What did Tenzing think of his first Everest expedition? He was lucky
to be chosen as he had no previous experience. Shipton had picked
out only those with whom he had climbed before or who had been
specially recommended. Then it was announced they needed just two
more men. Tenzing slipped into the line of 20 candidates wearing a new
khaki bush jacket, which he hoped made him look very professional. He

was chosen! Eighteen years later when he met Eric Shipton at a 1953 reception in London, Tenzing reminded him that it was he who had given him his first chance.

Tenzing clearly did very well in 1935, working hard and carrying a load to the North Col at 23,000ft (7,010m):

> It was there on the Col, before we turned back, that I first realized that I was in some way different from the other Sherpas. For the rest of them were glad to go down. They did their work as a job, for the wages, and wanted to go no farther than they had to. But I was very disappointed. I wanted to go still higher on the mountain.

Tenzing's father, who was then living in Thame in Nepal, decided to cross the Nangpa La to visit his son at Rongbuk. Tenzing relates his father's story:

> One night he stayed alone at Camp I, on the glacier, while the rest of us were either at the base camp below or at the other camps higher up and, in the morning, when it was just starting to be light, he heard a whistling sound outside the tent. He raised the flap and looked out, and there was a creature a little way off, coming down the glacier from south to north. Again, of course, my father was frightened. He did not want to look at the yeti, but also he did not want just to hide in the tent, for fear it would then come closer, or even enter. So he stayed where he was until it had gone on down the glacier and was out of sight, and then he came as fast as he could up to Camp II, where I was at the time. When he arrived he embraced me and said, 'I come all this way to see my son. And instead what I see is a yeti.'

I relate this story because two years ago a local friend brought me a postcard-size photograph of yeti footprints which on the reverse was pencilled 'Photo taken by Eric Shipton about 1935'. It had come from her stepfather, Michael Roberts, who had married her mother in 1975, but died in 1977 in his 80s. He had commanded the 10th Gurkhas, retiring as a Brigadier. He had travelled widely in Nepal, getting to know Shipton quite well. Although there is no record of the above incident in any of the expedition reports, one may conjecture that Tenzing's father relayed his frightening experience to Shipton, who then went out in search of the tracks and took the photograph. I have not come across any other report of this incident.

Ruttledge Again for 1936

Ruttledge's team for the 1936 expedition was of eight climbers: Smythe, Shipton, Wyn Harris, Kempson, Warren, Wigram and two newcomers, P.R. Oliver and J.M.L. Gavin, who had both climbed with Smythe in the Alps. Oliver, an army officer, serving on the North-West Frontier, had made the second ascent of Trisul. He was also an accomplished artist, his pencil sketches of the team being included in the expedition book. There were three non-climbing members of the team: John Morris from 1922, again in charge of transport; W.R. Smijth-Windham from 1933 for wireless (he had set up a telephone link to the North Col); and G. Noel Humphreys as doctor, a polymath surveyor, botanist, aviator, mountaineer and explorer of the Ruwenzori, who at 48 had qualified as a doctor to facilitate his interest in exploration.

The expedition arrived at Rongbuk on 25 April. The mountain was in perfect condition but on 30 April came the first sudden snowfall, repeated on 10 and 11 May. It was never to be in condition again that season. They took a right-hand route up to the North Col on 12 May. To save his strength for the upper mountain, Smythe handed over some of the step cutting to the Sherpa Rinzing, who handled it like 'a first-class Alpine guide' said Oliver. In 15 years, the best of the Sherpas had evolved from mere 'coolies' to very competent climbers. Next day, Wyn Harris and Kempson took up the 46 porters, followed on 15 May by Smythe and Shipton with 50 porters, 36 of whom remained on the Col ready to carry loads to higher camps. Morale was high, among both Sahibs and

Sherpas, and this year they planned to set a higher Camp VII at around 27,800ft (8,470m). For the first time, they took lightweight radios – with valves, of course, as transistors had not yet been invented – to link the higher camps to Base, but deep snow lay everywhere, and certainly the upper slabs and Norton's couloir would be impossible at present. It was also far too warm. When more snow fell on the 18 May, there was an increasing risk of the 38 men on the North Col being cut off.

General retreat

Ruttledge ordered a general retreat to Camp I. Simultaneously, the monsoon was reported to be forming off Ceylon. Instead of taking the usual two weeks to reach the Everest area, in four days, by 22 May, it had struck the Darjeeling hills, and it arrived on Everest on 25 May. This was unprecedented. Although further trips back to Camp III were made, it was folly to risk taking porters up to the North Col. As a final test, Ruttledge reluctantly agreed that Shipton and Wyn Harris should have a go, although conditions were ideal for the formation of 'wind-slab'. Halfway up to the Col, Shipton started the traverse left, with Wyn Harris well belayed on the lower lip of a crevasse. After going 40ft (12m), suddenly the whole slope gave way carrying Shipton, as if on a down escalator, towards the brink of an ice cliff 200ft (60m) below. Wyn was just able to hold him. The rope went taut and the surface broke into blocks, piling on top of Shipton. Then miraculously the slide stopped. They descended safe but shaken. Never again would they try these North Col slopes during the monsoon. The expedition was abandoned. A final reconnaissance was made of the western approach to the North Col from the Rongbuk Glacier, as this could be a useful escape route for a party marooned on the Col by such conditions. It was bad luck for Ruttledge, and not his fault that his two expeditions – composed of the strongest teams – should suffer the two earliest monsoons, while it was the two reconnaissance parties of 1921 and 1935 who enjoyed the latest.

These were the dates for the onset of the monsoon:

1921	7 July
1922	early June
1924	16 June
1933	30 May
1935	26 June
1936	25 May

Leaving Rongbuk Monastery for the last time, on 17 June, Ruttledge presented his friend, the Head Lama with a small (but empty!) wooden rum cask, supplied by the Royal Navy through the good offices of Admiral Sir William Goodenough. Fitted with a spindle and filled with written prayers, it revolved for many years as a Buddhist prayer wheel proclaiming: 'Om mani padme hum – Hail to the Jewel in the Lotus.'

1938 – Tilman on a Tight Budget

The 1936 Expedition had been another costly failure. Unless an assault party was favoured with fine weather and compacted snow conditions above 27,000ft (8,230m), repeated failures seemed inevitable on this northern route. Was the answer to launch a series of small economical expeditions annually until one was lucky enough to be granted the expected lull before the monsoon and favourable snow conditions?

Tilman had shown what could be achieved on Nanda Devi in 1936 with quite modest resources. Granted, Everest was more than 3,000ft (900m) higher, so a broader-based pyramid of support would be required, but this could still be organised quite economically. Besides, the public interest and the ability to raise funds was also diminishing. So when permission was again granted for 1938, the Mount Everest Committee virtually had no choice. There was only £355 left in the Committee's expedition account. Fortunately, Tom Longstaff offered to underwrite the costs up to £3,000, and The Times, who had been rejected since 1924, also came to the rescue.

Tilman was appointed leader, and managed to pare down a budget drawn up by Shipton for a small Everest expedition from £2,500 to £2,360 – less than a quarter of that for the 1936 expedition. Tilman was well known for his dicta that 'anything beyond what is needed for efficiency and safety is worse than useless' and that 'any expedition that cannot be planned on the back of a used envelope is over-organized'.

Tilman chose a highly competent 'socially harmonious' seven-man team, all of whom had been on expeditions together: Smythe; Shipton; Warren; Oliver; Odell, who was 47 years old, but still extremely fit; and the only newcomer to Everest, Peter Lloyd, who had also been on Nanda Devi in 1936. Peter, who had become a personal friend of mine, died on 11 April 2003, aged 95 – the last surviving team member of the pre-World War II Everest expeditions. Initially graduating in Chemistry, Peter worked on combustion and gas-turbine development, ran the rocket range at Woomera, Australia, and was deeply involved in the development of the Harrier vertical take-off fighter. He retired to Toowoomba, Queensland, and only three years ago he was trading in his old car for a new Volvo! Jack Longland was also invited to be part of the team, but his employers refused him leave of absence. 'I could not afford to lose my job,' he wrote in 1977 to Walt Unsworth. 'Perhaps regular jobs were taken rather more seriously than they seem to be in the expedition world of today.'

The expedition's equipment was pretty basic: no radio equipment this time, but they did take oxygen, even though Tilman was not very convinced of its value. He took it possibly on the grounds that if they got close to the summit in good weather and they were still defeated for want of oxygen, then they would look 'uncommonly foolish'. They took just four sets: two open-circuit, whereby the oxygen is supplied to the mouth through a tube and then exhaled and lost to the atmosphere; and two closed-circuit, an experimental system where the exhaled air is recirculated after extracting the carbon dioxide with a chemical such as soda-lime. The open-circuit equipment weighed 25lb (11kg) and was similar to that used successfully by Finch in 1922. Two cylinders holding 500 litres each would last eight hours at the normal consumption rate of 2 litres per minute. Warren had been trying out the closed type in the Alps and was very enthusiastic about it. Although it was 10lb (4.5kg) heavier, mainly because of the soda-lime, in theory it gave the user a great boost because he was breathing pure oxygen. A single 750 litre cylinder would last 5½ hours. Warren took charge of the oxygen apparatus, assisted by Lloyd.

As usual, food was a bone of contention. Tilman and Shipton were renowned for managing on a very restricted diet, as explained by Tilman:

> As we once lived perforce for a few days on tree mushrooms and bamboo shoots there is a general impression that this is our normal diet, eked out with liberal doses of fresh air, on which, thanks to a yogi-like training, we thrive and expect everyone else to do likewise. Nothing could be farther from the truth. Like Dr Johnson, we mind our bellies very strenuously: 'for I look upon it', he said, 'that he who will not mind his belly will scarcely mind anything else.' The more restricted a ration is, the more need is there for careful thought in its selection. For normal men a ration of 2lb a day is ample (I have kept Sherpas happy for two or three weeks on 1½lb) and the whole art lies in getting the most value for weight.

Warren recalls the delight of the other expedition members when they discovered and fell upon cases of 'Fortnum & Mason' food left at Rongbuk by the 1936 Expedition.

The expedition reached Rongbuk on 6 April, ten days earlier than any previous expedition, determined not to miss any opportunity should the monsoon come early. The mountain was black, blown clear of snow by the winter winds. Thirty-one porters set up the glacier camps and Camp III was fully set up by 26 April. Tilman had recruited some of the best Sherpas: Pasang, Kusang, Rinzing, Tenzing, led by Angtharkay as sirdar. Being early, it was still extremely cold up high and most of the party had caught coughs, colds and 'flu, so they decided to cross the Lhakpa La for a week's recuperation in the more hospitable Kharta Valley, at around 11,000ft (3,355m). When they got back to Rongbuk, they were astonished to see Everest now clad in white. It had started to snow daily from 5 May. Surely the monsoon could not have broken that early? They returned to Camp III on 18 May and next day had a surprisingly easy breakthrough almost to the North Col on good snow, with Oliver leading most of the way. That night snow fell heavily and raised the spectre of avalanches on the North Col slopes, but by 24 May conditions had improved and 26 porters were escorted to dump their loads at the site of the 1936 Camp IV. Fifteen more loads were carried next day, but the climbers were not optimistic. The snow was soft and deep and the air too warm. They were experiencing monsoon conditions.

The North Col from the West

Tilman decided to split the party: Odell, Oliver, Warren and Tilman to occupy Camp IV, and Smythe and Shipton to go via Rongbuk to climb the North Col from the west side, as had been reconnoitred in 1936, to provide a safer escape from the Col if required.

On 30 May, the Camp IV team pushed on up the North Ridge through deep snow to some 24,500ft (7,470m), with young Tenzing making some of the trail. However, with all the fresh snow, there was little point in setting up Camp V. They decided to retreat to Camp III and withdraw from the East Rongbuk Glacier concentrating all their efforts on the west side. They set up a west-side camp at about 21,500ft (6,550m), corresponding to Camp III on the other side. Starting at 7am, they soon came across the debris of a huge avalanche, so this side was also potentially dangerous. It had exposed a slope of hard ice requiring arduous step cutting for 500ft (150m) before they could regain the snow, but this was now softening in the sunshine, so it was with great relief that they reached the Col at 11am, the first ascent from the west.

Next day, 6 June, they began the ascent of the North Ridge again. Smythe and Shipton went back to Camp V. Tenzing and Pasang enhanced their reputations by making a second carry of loads which had been abandoned by two exhausted porters. Camp VI was set at 27,200ft (8,290m) on 8 June, just below the Yellow Band, where Smythe and Shipton spent the night. Next day was almost a repetition of 1936. The snow was deep and unconsolidated; Norton's traverse line and the gully beyond it were impossible. Towards the crest of the ridge there was waist-deep snow waiting to avalanche where it steepened. They retreated, meeting Tilman and Lloyd on their way up to Camp V, but they too soon returned. They began to evacuate all the camps. The expedition was over. At least Lloyd had gained some useful experience with the oxygen. The closed system never worked properly, but he had used the open system continuously above Camp IV. He found it reduced fatigue considerably, and above 26,000ft (7,925m) definitely increased his climbing rate.

Once again, they were able to demonstrate, like Norton in 1924, Smythe in 1933 and Ruttledge in 1936, that during the monsoon, with fresh unconsolidated snow, the mountain was virtually unclimbable by this northern route, although Tilman had demonstrated it rather more cheaply than the others. Therefore, there would be a case for launching a consecutive series of three, four or five 'Tilman-sized' expeditions until at last one of them hit the right weather conditions and was crowned with success. This must have been the Committee's view when they met on 14 June 1939 and decided to ask for permission for Everest in 1940, 1941 and 1942, but three months later Poland was invaded and Adolf Hitler began his ill-fated attempt to gain mastery over Europe. Perhaps he had heeded the words of Julius Kugy quoted by Tilman: 'I cannot imagine any place less suitable to choose than high mountains wherein to display the mastery of mankind.'

05

Everest from Nepal –
The Early 1950s

'Sola Khumbu ... an ultimate goal in Himalayan exploration.' Eric Shipton

After World War II, further requests to enter Tibet to climb Mount Everest from the north met with no response. Then in 1950, the Dalai Lama fled to India and Chinese Communists seized control of Tibet. By coincidence, the Government of Nepal, which controlled the southern approach to Everest, began to relax their policy of total exclusion and from 1947 onwards several mountaineering and scientific expeditions were permitted to visit various parts of the Nepal Himalayas which included eight of the world's 14 peaks over 8,000m (26,240ft) in height.

The French were the first to climb one of these giants – Annapurna, 26,545ft (8,091m), in 1950. That same year, Dr Charles Houston, who had been with Tilman on Nanda Devi in 1936, was granted access to the Sola Khumbu region where the Sherpas live and where Everest lies. Tilman joined him and pushed on beyond the Sherpa capital of Namche Bazar up the valley towards the foot of Everest. He reached the Khumbu Glacier but only had a superficial look at the great Icefall disgorging from the Western Cwm and was unable to see the approach to the South Col, which was obscured by the bastion of Nuptse, so he could barely add to Mallory's conclusion in 1922: 'The single glimpse obtained last year of the western glacier and the slopes above it revealed one of the most awful and utterly forbidding scenes ever observed by man.'

A more detailed look was required and the person to initiate this was Michael Ward, a doctor doing National Service but studying to become a surgeon, whose limited Alpine climbing experience did not deter him from challenging the greater scale of the Himalayas. He assembled all the relevant photographs he could obtain, including some taken by pilots illicitly flying near the mountain during the war, and studied a possible approach from the south. There was no reason to believe the Icefall was unclimbable. The South-East Ridge of Everest dropping over 3,000ft (900m) to the South Col was broad, snow covered and seemingly not difficult. The lack of information about the western approach to the Col seemed to cry out for a reconnaissance expedition to ascertain whether there was a practicable route through the Icefall to the Western Cwm, and from there to the South Col. Ward enlisted the support of Campbell Secord and the noted Scottish climber W.H. Murray, and a proposal for an autumn reconnaissance was put to the Joint Himalayan Committee in June 1951. This was the successor to the former Mount Everest Committee, similarly constituted from members of The Alpine Club and the Royal Geographical Society. They were hardly enthusiastic, but agreed to seek permission from the Government of Nepal which, rather to their surprise, was granted. The team was to be Ward, Secord and Bourdillon with Murray as leader – a purely private party.

Then in July, Eric Shipton unexpectedly turned up from China and was persuaded with his much greater experience to lead the party instead. He stipulated the Committee should take on the financing and this was largely covered by an exclusive contract with *The Times*. There was barely a month to get everything ready for shipment to India. Sadly, Secord had to drop out, but rashly allowed the stores and equipment to be accumulated at his house in Carlton Mews. Shipton recalled that: 'Mrs Secord had to bear the brunt of endless telephone calls from the press, equipment firms, applicants for a place in the party, inventors of helicopters and portable radio sets, food cranks, moneylenders and members of the expedition.' The day before everything was due at the docks still nothing was packed, so in desperation he sent an SOS to the Women's Voluntary Service. They responded magnificently and had everything boxed and listed before evening!

The 1951 Reconnaissance

Murray and Ward sailed with the baggage on 2 August, while Bourdillon and Shipton flew to Delhi, arriving on 19 August. Two days before leaving, Shipton had received a cable from the President of the New Zealand Alpine Club asking whether two members of their first Himalayan expedition, currently climbing in Garhwal, might accompany the party. Shipton had already turned down several applications and was about to reject this one when he nostalgically recalled his warm impressions of the New Zealander, Dan Bryant, who was on the 1935 Everest Reconnaissance. He took a snap decision, which was to have far-reaching consequences, and wired: 'Invite any two of you to join my party.' There were four: Hillary, Lowe, Riddiford and Cotter, who, up to this point, had climbed as a good co-operative team, although Earle Riddiford had done much of the initial planning and had read out the telegram. 'We were all shaken,' recalls George Lowe, 'by Earle's first words: "Well, I shall be going," he said coolly, "and I will decide by the morning who will go with me!"' Earle did not agree with George's version of events. In truth, the real tussle lay between Earle and George; Ed Cotter could not afford the extended trip, neither could George really but this did not diminish his belief that he qualified on grounds of fitness alone. Ed Hillary was a natural choice; he could afford it and was now powerfully fit. Riddiford, as a barrister, could also afford it but was not as fit as George in the latter's opinion. In the end, it was settled that Riddiford and Hillary would go. Cotter and Lowe were filled with envy and disappointment but, thanks to Hillary, George Lowe's chance was to come the following year.

There were several routes into the Khumbu: from Darjeeling, Kathmandu or from an Indian railhead at either Jainagar or Jogbani. As they would be travelling during the monsoon, they settled on the shortest, from Jogbani, which Houston and Tilman had used the previous year. It had taken them two weeks in the dry post-monsoon; now the 1951 party would take twice as long, following muddy paths in continuous rain through leech-infested forests. Shipton recalled one section:

> For three days we made our way slowly along it in a northerly direction, unable to see anything of our surroundings because of alternating spells of heavy rain and equally drenching Scottish mist. After a while we lost all sense of direction and distance; it was a curious sensation, blindly following this narrow crest, the ground on either hand falling steeply into the silent, forested depths below, while rocky peaks loomed, one after another, ahead. The undergrowth was infested with leeches; on a single twig a score of the creatures could be seen, stiff and erect, like a cluster of little black sticks, ready to attach themselves to our legs and arms and clothing as we brushed past.

Hillary and Riddiford caught up with the main party at the village of Dingla. Travelling fast, they were ragged and unkempt, a couple of forthright Antipodeans. Hillary, living in awe of Shipton's reputation, and not knowing the other members, felt they might have to smarten up and watch their language:

> Feeling not a little like a couple of errant schoolboys going to visit the headmaster, we followed our Sherpa into a dark doorway and up some stairs into the upper room of a large building. As we came into the room, four figures rose to meet us. My first feeling was one of relief. I have rarely seen a more disreputable bunch, and my visions of changing for dinner faded away for ever.

On 19 September, they crossed a pass into the valley of the Dudh Kosi. The monsoon rains were left behind and the sky was a cloudless blue. Shipton was realising an ambition he had held for 20 years, since he had first known the Sherpas:

> I had longed, above all else, to visit their land of Sola Khumbu, through which the expedition would travel. I had heard so much about it from the Sherpas; indeed during our journeys together in other parts of the Himalaya and Central Asia, whenever we came upon a particularly attractive spot, they invariably said, 'This is just like Sola Khumbu,' and the comparison always led to a long, nostalgic discourse about their homeland. It required only an intelligent glance at the map and a little imagination to realize that their praise was not exaggerated; moreover, we had looked down into the upper valleys of Khumbu from the peaks west of Everest. Almost unknown to Western travellers, it had become, to me at least, a kind of Mecca, an ultimate goal in Himalayan exploration. So it was that I finally decided to accept the invitation to lead the expedition.

What a contrast between the lushness of Sola Khumbu and the endless march in the 1930s across the windswept Tibetan plateau to reach the bleak Rongbuk Valley on the north side of Everest!

The First Clash with the Khumbu Icefall

The party left Namche Bazar on 25 September with food for 17 days. They hoped to find a way through the Icefall, reach the Western Cwm and see if there was a feasible route up to the South Col. If so, they could have more supplies sent up and see how far they could get. They camped at places which have now become familiar to thousands of trekkers: the Buddhist Monastery at Thyangboche, yak pastures at Pheriche and Lobuje; then along the west side of the desolate moraine-covered Khumbu Glacier to the small lake at Gorak Shep.

On 30 September, while Riddiford, Ward and Bourdillon with two Sherpas took a first look at the Icefall, Shipton and Hillary climbed some way up the peak of Pumori to get a view into the Western Cwm. At about 20,000ft (6,100m), Shipton took a photograph, later published in *The Times*, that so impressed me I ordered a personal copy which still hangs in my study today. Hillary assumes a prophetic stance in the bottom right-hand corner (p. 18 of plates). Shipton described what they saw:

We found to our surprise that from the point reached we could see right up to the head of the Western Cwm, the whole of the west face of Lhotse, and the South Col. We estimated that the floor of the Cwm at its head was nearly 23,000ft high, about 2,000ft higher than had been expected. There appeared to be a perfectly straight-forward route from there up the face of Lhotse to some 25,000ft whence, it seemed, a traverse could be made to the South Col.

Our study of the Icefall was less encouraging than our view of the Cwm. From the top of the lower half there was an easy route running through to the left; but this was obviously swept by ice avalanches from the West Ridge of Everest, while to the right nothing could be seen but a wild tangle of seracs and ice cliffs. However, we made a further reconnaissance the following day from a ridge near the Lho La, which revealed the upper icefall in a more hopeful light.

Meanwhile, in the Icefall, Riddiford and Pasang had had a good day: keeping to the left, they had climbed most of the lower section but had not been in a position to judge the avalanche danger higher up. Ward and Bourdillon, further right, had been stymied by ice cliffs, but both parties were optimistic that the Icefall could be climbed.

However, it was potentially a very dangerous place; the whole unstable mass moves inexorably downwards at some 100ft to 300ft (30–90m) annually, so that at any moment leaning pinnacles or walls of ice the size of a row of cottages could crash down without warning and obliterate anyone beneath. On either side, the Icefall was squeezed between the lower cliffs of Everest and Nuptse from which huge ice avalanches could fall unpredictably. It was the sort of place where a bold man given the chance of climbing Everest would be prepared to go once or twice, but not if it meant risking the lives of porters repeatedly ferrying loads up into the Western Cwm. It posed a dilemma for Shipton, at which he baulked:

> To abandon this wonderful new route to the summit of Everest that had appeared like a vision, this chance that we had scarcely dared to hope for, not because the way to it was beyond our powers, but because on a small section of the approach the party, and particularly the Sherpas, must repeatedly be exposed to the risk, however slight at each individual exposure, of extermination.

Hillary did not share Shipton's qualms:

> In my heart, I knew the only way to attempt this mountain was to modify the old standards of safety and justifiable risk and to meet the dangers as they came; to drive through regardless. Care and caution would never make a route through the Icefall. If we didn't attack it that May, someone else would. The competitive standards of Alpine mountaineering were coming to the Himalayas, and we might as well compete or pull out.

On 4 October, Shipton, Hillary, Riddiford, Bourdillon and three Sherpas tried again, in a concerted effort, following Riddiford's earlier reconnaissance. Shipton again:

> The upper half was a far tougher proposition. Threading our way through a maze of seracs, ice walls and crevasses which split the surface in every direction, we could never see more than about 200ft ahead. The snow was often hip deep, so that even with so many to share the labour, progress from point to point was very slow, and a false line costs a great deal of time.
>
> However, by the middle of the afternoon we seemed to be approaching the top of the Icefall. We had decided to turn back not later than 4 o'clock in order to reach

camp before dark. Even that was running it a bit fine, since it did not allow for accidents, such as the breaking of a snow bridge. We reached the last of the seracs at an altitude, according to our aneroid, of 20,600ft. We looked across a deep trough to a level crest of ice marking the point where the glacier of the Cwm takes its first plunge into the Icefall like the smooth wave above a waterfall. Crossing the trough was difficult, as it was riven with crevasses, but by 3.50 we had reached the steep slope below the crest. This had to be climbed diagonally to avoid an ice cliff directly above. The snow was obviously unstable, but the slope was not high enough to constitute a serious danger. The leading rope was half-way across, and not more than 30ft from the crest, when, as we had half expected, the slope avalanched. Pasang and I, at either end of the break, managed to scramble off the moving sheet of snow, and Riddiford was left suspended between the two of us while the sheet broke into great blocks and slid silently into the trough.

Luckily, nobody was hurt. They turned back and reached camp before dark. Shipton agreed that access to the Western Cwm was feasible, but there was too much soft snow to make further progress. If they left it for a couple of weeks to melt and consolidate, they could use the time profitably to acclimatise further and seize the opportunity to explore the totally unknown mountain country surrounding them, something much closer to Shipton's heart. So they split into two teams, exploring to east and west.

When they reunited on 26 October, and climbed up the Pumori Ridge for another look, it was all much the same and the Icefall was as unstable as ever. Nevertheless, they decided to make one last assault with the whole team, and on 28 October, they successfully reached the lip of the Western Cwm, but two enormous crevasses still barred their way. Shipton decided to retreat to Base Camp – a decision not welcomed by everybody – but he had been to the Cwm, without mishap, and that was enough for him. He did not wish to tempt Providence further. In his despatch to The Times he wrote:

Icefalls throughout the world are subject to great seasonal variations, and autumn is usually the season when they are at their most difficult. This dragon guarding the Western Cwm is now in a restless mood; it is not unreasonable to expect that in the spring he may be found sleeping.

Beyond the Menlung La

As they had returned early there was time for a further round of exploration, so again they split into groups. Murray and Bourdillon went to the Nangpa La, the 19,000ft (5,790m) pass by which the old trade route crosses from Sola Khumbu to Tibet, and the route of pilgrimage to the Rongbuk Monastery. They also looked for possible routes up the north-west side of Cho Oyu, 26,906ft (8,201m) – the eighth highest 8,000m peak. Shipton and Ward went to the group of mountains further west, crossing a Col they called the Menlung La, and found themselves in a vast amphitheatre, not unlike the Nanda Devi Sanctuary, in the centre of which stood an isolated peak of pale granite which they called Menlungtse. The basin drained to the north-west and then plunged into a series of canyons flowing into the Rongshar Chu which, similar to the Arun River to the east of Everest, cut through the great Himalayan range. It was on one of the Menlung basin glaciers at about 19,000ft (5,790m) that they came across one of the best sets of recorded 'yeti' footprints. They were very fresh but when Murray and Bourdillon followed a few days after, they had been almost obliterated by melting. Sen Tensing was in no doubt that 'yetis' had made the tracks, claiming that he and other Sherpas had seen one two years previously at a distance of about 25yds, at Thyangboche. He described it as half man and half beast, standing about 5ft 6in tall, with a tall pointed head, its body covered with reddish-brown hair, but with a hairless face.

What was not mentioned was that the party had inadvertently strayed into Tibet and had a narrow escape as they exited at dawn by the Rongshar Gorge. This is revealed in Tom Bourdillon's private diary recently presented to The Alpine Club by his widow, Jennifer:

> We had done about ½ mile of the 2 remaining to the frontier when a Tibetan
> armed with a sword appeared with much shouting. We went on for a while,
> Angtharkay shouting louder, till 7 more appeared. Not so good. We had to stop
> and parley. Rather anxious, in case they proved not to be venial, when an enforced
> march into Tibet and Communist hands would have ensued.
>
> However, Angtharkay presently told us to go ahead, and after about 10 mins
> came to us with the news that he had bought them off for 5Rs – about 7/6d, less
> than 1/- each. This was good.

Typical Bourdillon understatement – letting them escape with their lives
for less than 5p each in today's currency!

The diary continues:

> We went on to the frontier, crossed by a rather good bridge and lay down on a
> patch of grass in Nepal while the Sherpas cooked breakfast and the morning sun
> crept down the walls of the Gorge on the other side.

For Shipton, this exploration and the discovery of Menlungtse was the
most satisfying part of the whole trip.

Route Comparison – Nepal versus Tibet

Before they left London, Shipton had assessed their chances of finding
a feasible route, on the Nepalese side, via the Western Cwm, as 30–1
against. The odds had now shortened considerably. Murray listed five
advantages compared with the old north route in Tibet. First, the main
difficulties occurred low down, instead of at 28,000ft (8,540m). Second,
above the South Col, on the South-East Ridge, the strata dip northward,
favouring the climber, and providing better support for snow, instead of
the slippery 'tiles on a roof' formation on the north side. Third, the route

is protected from the violent north-west wind until close to the South Col. Fourth, on the north side the snow above 25,000ft (7,620m) tends not to consolidate, remaining powdery and hampering climbing until it is cleared by the wind; whereas on the south-east it does seem to consolidate better. Fifth, the South-East Ridge catches the morning sun, thus encouraging an earlier and easier start. He could have added a sixth, that the delightful approach through Nepal (if you go in the spring to avoid the monsoon) puts the climber in a far pleasanter state of mind compared to the arduous trek across the windswept Tibetan plateau.

Against these advantages, one can cite the following. First, the threat of avalanches from the walls flanking the Icefall and the Western Cwm, particularly if a party is unwise enough to be there after the monsoon breaks; a risk not present on the East Rongbuk Glacier. Second, the traverse across the face of Lhotse to the South Col could be very prone to avalanches after prolonged snow. Third, an aerial photograph of the summit shows the last 300 vertical feet of the South-East Ridge to be an exciting exposed knife-edge ridge with a little 40ft (12m) rock step to overcome partway. One must pray for a relatively windless day!

1952 – Pre-empted by the Swiss

On his return to England, Shipton was astonished by the interest in the expedition even though he regarded it as a dubious success. A lecture in Liverpool had to be repeated three times. In the 1930s, the succession of failures had made people lose interest in Everest but now the prospect of a new route seized the imagination of an adventure-seeking public who regarded Shipton almost as a cult figure. Their interest had been titivated by the huge publicity and personality cult surrounding the success in 1950 of Herzog and Lachenal on Annapurna, the first of the 8,000m peaks to be climbed. Clearly, a race was developing to climb all the other 8,000m peaks, particularly those newly opened in Nepal.

Shipton was the natural leader for a British expedition to Everest in

1952. The Joint Himalayan Committee agreed, but they got a nasty shock when they sought permission from the Nepalese Government. The Swiss had already applied and had been granted permission for both spring and autumn attempts, if necessary. The Committee had to accept that, as in the days of the Raj, the British no longer retained such a special relationship with either Tibet or Nepal, and the mountains were now open to all comers.

The Committee tried to retrieve the situation by proposing a joint expedition. As Unsworth describes more fully in his account, this didn't get very far. The Swiss politely pointed out that when they had asked for their member, René Dittert, to be included in the 1951 British Reconnaissance, they had been refused, although two New Zealanders were later admitted.

The Swiss naturally wanted their own expedition and the British, led by Shipton, had to be content with a permit for Cho Oyu, which Murray and Bourdillon had briefly reconnoitred the previous autumn.

It was about this time that I made my own very tentative entry onto the scene. As an enthusiastic member of the Cambridge University Mountaineering Club – having just been appointed President – I was kindly invited to The Alpine Club by a member to hear Eric Shipton lecture on the 1951 reconnaissance. It was the first time I had ever entered its hallowed portals at 74, South Audley Street in Mayfair. In the hallway, I was intrigued to see a pram covered by a dust sheet as if no member had need of one any longer. The lecture hall was packed; we youngsters sat cross-legged on the floor. At one side, there was a comfortable chaise longue clearly reserved for the elders. One of them used an ear trumpet. At the conclusion, Shipton mentioned that he would be selecting a team for the expedition to Cho Oyu. Several of us Cambridge climbers, with the confidence and arrogance of youth, resolved to apply although our Alpine experience was minimal and we had no more than dreamt of ever going to the Himalayas. Not surprisingly, we received polite letters of rejection.

Cho Oyu – An Abortive Dress Rehearsal?

Cho Oyu, in the spring of 1952, was intended as a dress rehearsal for a British attempt on Everest in 1953 for which permission had been hurriedly sought and granted, as with the Swiss, for both spring and autumn. The dress rehearsal proved somewhat abortive. The best route up Cho Oyu lay just over the border in Tibet. Shipton, due to his previous consular service in Kashgar and Kunming being too easily regarded by the Chinese as an 'arch spy', was loath to risk another brush with Communist soldiers, or indeed any political embarrassment to Nepal which might jeopardise their Everest permit for 1953. Therefore, he insisted on a base camp on the Nepalese side, only allowing a lightweight attempt on the Tibetan route, which inevitably failed.

As in 1951, the team broke up into smaller groups for a wonderful bout of cross-country exploration. On Hillary's recommendation, George Lowe had joined the Cho Oyu team and now the two New Zealanders made a first crossing of the very difficult Nup La Icefall to make a rapid trip into Tibet down the West Rongbuk Glacier and up the East Rongbuk to the north side of Everest. They then returned to join Shipton and Charles Evans on the Barun Glacier to the east side of Everest and found a way to the frontier ridge, overlooking the Kangshung Glacier with its stupendous views of the East Face of Everest. They were probably at the very same col reached from the Tibetan side by Howard-Bury in 1921, so completing the circumnavigation of the mountain after 31 years.

Probably the most important outcome of the Cho Oyu expedition was that it gave the British another year to plan for Everest. A field physiologist from the Medical Research Council, Dr Griffith Pugh, was attached to the party and the report of his investigations into oxygen uptake, clothing, diet, cookers and so on, proved of fundamental value. For example, he pointed out the simple fact that climbers at high altitude rarely drank enough to maintain peak physical condition. The normal daily intake of three to four pints of liquid needed to be doubled to compensate for the moisture lost by breathing in the extremely dry rarefied air. He encouraged everyone to drink a gallon a day. When all this liquid had to be melted from snow or blocks of ice, it became a serious operation requiring extra-large billies and highly efficient stoves and fuel. A small committee, including Pugh and Bourdillon, who was a research physicist as well as one of the best climbers, was also set up to develop the best-possible oxygen breathing sets, which were considered indispensable for the assault teams. This was crucial. The Swiss were later to admit that their design worked well except when the climber was moving and at low temperatures!

The Swiss – So Near to Success

The Swiss plans for Everest were, at first, modest, conceived by René Dittert and Ed Wyss-Dunant as a combined climbing and scientific expedition and involving a 'handful of friends', mostly based in Geneva but drawn from the cream of Swiss climbers. The best known outside Switzerland were Raymond Lambert and André Roch. Luckily, they were able to gain the support of the prestigious Swiss Foundation for Alpine Research which had already sponsored five previous Himalayan expeditions.

The expedition assembled in Kathmandu where they met their Sherpas and their sirdar, Tenzing Norgay. Tenzing was then 38 years old and, as with Angtharkay, Shipton's favourite sirdar, was recognised as one of the best. In the 1950s, we all thought Tenzing had been born in his parents' current home at Thame, a village near Namche Bazar, but it now seems almost certain he was born while his mother was on a short pilgrimage to a holy lake or hot spring called Tsa-chu near the monastery of Ghang La in the Kharta region east of Everest in Tibet. Therefore, although he used to claim diplomatically: 'I was born in the womb of Nepal and grew up in the lap of India,' he seemingly spent his first 15 years in the Kharta Valley before moving with his family to

Thame, and later settling in Darjeeling in India, and so by birth he was actually Tibetan or, as might even now be claimed, Chinese rather than Nepalese or Indian. He had been on three of the pre-war British expeditions to Everest and once with the 'lone' climber Earl Denman, as well as to other parts of the Himalaya and Karakoram, working his way up from a humble porter, as his sterling qualities were recognised, to be the leader of the Sherpas on an expedition, or sirdar. In 1947, he had been with a Swiss expedition to Garhwal, which included Roch and Dittert, taking over when the appointed sirdar was injured. He had done extremely well, also climbing four new peaks, so Roch and Dittert insisted he should be their sirdar in 1952, which he happily accepted.

Base Camp was established at Gorak Shep on 20 April and the attack on the Icefall begun on the 26th. They were forced to the left into a gully threatened dangerously by seracs, christened 'Suicide Passage'. At the edge of the Cwm, Roch found their way barred by a huge crevasse, as had Shipton. By lowering Asper, the youngest of the Swiss, onto a snow bridge, they were able to get a rope across and then construct a rope bridge across the chasm and so enter the Cwm. That night an avalanche swept 'Suicide Passage', but by then the climbers were safely back in camp.

Climbing the Lhotse Face

From their Camp III, at the entrance to the Cwm, they could look across the undulating but gently rising snow slopes towards the head of the Cwm, formed by the icy ramparts of Lhotse, 27,890ft (8,501m), the world's fourth highest peak, but dwarfed by the crags of Everest on the left. Between the two was the saddle known as the South Col at 25,850ft (7,879m) – almost as high as Annapurna, the highest peak yet climbed. Below the Col and to the left of the upper part of the Lhotse Face was a conspicuous outcropping rib of dark rock which they christened the Éperon des Genevois – the Geneva Spur.

From their Camp V, 22,630ft (6,900m), established at the foot of the Lhotse Face, they had now to decide how best to tackle the route to the South Col. Dittert wrote:

> Seen from the camp the Col had a gentle and deceiving appearance, all its slopes being foreshortened. But the figures proved the contrary. The Col rose more than 3,500ft above us, though one might easily reckon it as half that figure. The average slope varied between 40 and 45 degrees, almost that of the Brenva route on the south face of Mont Blanc.

Broadly, they had two choices. The most direct route was towards the Geneva Spur, then to climb the rocks of the Spur or whichever of the gullies on either side gave the easier climbing up consolidated snow or bare ice. The alternative was a more circuitous route to the right up the ice walls and shelving snow-covered ledges of the Lhotse Face, followed by a long rising traverse left until they reached the top of the Spur and could descend easily some 300ft (90m) to the Col.

It was easy to be tricked by the foreshortening that the direct route was preferable, but it was a very long way to go at that altitude without the possibility of an intermediate campsite. They were to find to their cost that there was only one small platform on the Spur, at about 24,600ft (7,500m) – not big enough for a tent – and that the gullies were mostly hard ice, climbable, but too risky for laden porters without copious fixed ropes to safeguard them. Ironically Shipton, looking across from Pumori in 1951, never even contemplated the direct route as being an alternative to the Lhotse Face.

Chevalley, Asper and the Sherpa, Da Namgyal, were the first to climb the Geneva Spur on 19 May, and next day a group of six fixed 490ft (150m) of ropes on it. Then, for two days, they were imprisoned in Camp V by a ferocious storm, which Dittert describes vividly:

With the wind came the cold. Forced to go out to see a tent-pole that was giving way, I was rendered breathless by the fearful sight that met me. The fresh dusty snow was flying in uninterrupted whirlwinds and the dark storm clouds, coming from the south-west, were racing madly across the sky. I could hear them roaring as they broke more than 3,000ft above me against the rugged bastions of Everest, then invisible in the fog. Like a fear-stricken beast I went back to hide. In a few hours the white and impalpable dust would penetrate everywhere and it was impossible to defend oneself against it. With our caps pulled down to our eyes and with our sleeping bags fastened around our necks for two nights and a day and for a further morning we cowered down and did not move. In the intervals between squalls the harsh coughs of inflamed throats could be heard in the various tents and these were the only signs of life, except that the indefatigable Sherpas, profiting by a brief calm during the first day, brought us something to drink.

On 25 May, they were ready to make a first assault. Lambert, Flory, Aubert, Tenzing and six other Sherpas left Camp V at 8.15am, aiming to establish Camp VI on the South Col, and a final Camp VII around 27,500ft (8,380m) on the South-East Ridge. After eight hours, three porters had asked to descend, fearing frostbite, and part of their loads was dumped. By 7pm they still had not reached the Col, but the slope eased and they contrived a restricted bivouac, crammed into the two tiny tents. Incredibly, Tenzing brewed some soup for everybody. They survived the bitter cold and continued to the Col next morning, the Sherpas retrieving the dumped gear, with Tenzing going down twice more for essential items.

A Gallant Failure

The expedition's momentum had virtually been shattered by the effort to reach the Col. Lambert, Tenzing, Flory and Aubert tried the South-East Ridge next morning, but they only carried food for a day and one tent, which was pitched at 27,500ft. Lambert and Tenzing were left alone for their summit bid. They had no sleeping bags, no stove to melt ice for a drink and little food, so spent a miserable night. They had three oxygen cylinders, but the demand valves of their sets were too stiff to operate while climbing and, therefore, not much help. After five hours, through a vent in the clouds they could see they were now higher than Lhotse, 27,890ft (8,501m). The top of their ridge, the South Summit of Everest at 28,700ft (8,748m), showed about 650ft (200m) above them. It is not surprising that their progress had been little more than 100ft per hour. Clearly, they weren't going to make it, and turned to go down. In round figures, they estimated they had reached 28,210ft (8,600m), just a little more than Norton's record height of 28,126ft in 1924 on the other side of the mountain, although Lambert in his account concedes: 'Was it an altitude record? No. Failure. That is what we thought.' Let's not quibble. It was still a superhuman effort.

Dittert organised a second assault on 29 May, but conditions on the Col were unbearable with intense cold and high winds. They stuck it for three nights but then withdrew, seizing their chance when the weather did improve slightly on 1 June to get down safely while they still had the strength. The expedition was over.

The Swiss tried again, with a fresh team, in the autumn, only Chevalley and Lambert coming for a second bout. Tenzing, again as sirdar, was formally declared a member of the climbing team. Curiously, Chevalley again chose the Geneva Spur route, a major tactical error, and by the time they had transferred to the Lhotse Face alternative, the winter had arrived and put an end to their aspirations. They also had an unlucky accident on the slopes below the Spur, when Mingma Dorje was hit by ice splinters in the face and neck and later died from his injuries. However, the Swiss had courageously demonstrated that the Khumbu route was possible and relatively safe and, thank God, nobody had been killed in the Icefall.

British Plans for 1953 – Shipton Bows Out

Meanwhile, back in England, the climbing establishment breathed a collective sigh of relief when the Swiss failed to climb Everest at their first attempt in the spring. It would have reflected very poorly on British climbers after their repeated failures on the north side, and the dismal performance on Cho Oyu. Hillary later expressed what most of them felt:

> I think for the first time I was really admitting to myself quite honestly that I didn't want the Swiss to climb Everest. Let them get very high – good luck to them in that but not to the summit! I wanted it left for a British party to have a crack at next year.

So the British plans for Everest in 1953 moved into high gear. On 4 July, Pugh, Secord and Gregory met with the Joint Himalayan Committee while Shipton and Evans were still in Nepal. They stressed the importance of fitness, team and equipment selection, adequate acclimatisation, and supplementary oxygen. Pugh said:

> It was clear that having regard to the lower level of fitness and mountaineering experience of any British party, that only the very best oxygen equipment could enable us to put up a better performance than the Swiss.

Clearly, the pressure for a British success in 1953 was enormous; the French were lined up for 1954 and the Swiss again in 1955. It was our last chance. It had naturally been assumed that Shipton would be the leader, but now the Committee began to question whether he was the right person in this competitive situation. When Shipton returned and met the Committee on 28 July to report on Cho Oyu and discuss the plans for Everest, these whispers of uncertainty must have reached him and he decided to make a statement of his position:

It was clear that the Committee assumed that I would lead the expedition. I had, however, given a good deal of thought to the matter, and felt it right to voice certain possible objections. Having been to Everest five times, I undoubtedly had a great deal more experience of the mountain and of climbing at extreme altitudes than anyone else; also, in the past year I had been closely connected, practically and emotionally, with the new aspect of the venture. On the other hand, long involvement with an unsolved problem can easily produce rigidity of outlook, a slow response to new ideas, and it is often the case that a man with fewer inhibitions is better equipped to tackle it than one with greater experience. I had more reason than most to take a realistic view of the big element of luck involved, and this was not conducive to bounding optimism. Was it not time, perhaps, to hand over to a younger man with a fresh outlook? Moreover, Everest had become the focus of greatly inflated publicity and of keen international competition, and there were many who regarded success in the coming attempt to be of high national importance. My well-known dislike of large expeditions and my abhorrence of a competitive element in mountaineering might well seem out of place in the present situation.

I asked the Committee to consider these points very carefully before deciding the question of leadership and then left them while they did so.

I think Shipton's statement sealed his own fate. I do not propose to recount the Committee's lengthy deliberations over this matter, which have been amply recorded in their minutes and by Walt Unsworth. It does not reflect very creditably upon them. It was not until their meeting on 11 September that Eric Shipton resigned and John Hunt was appointed leader in his place.

As the Committee must have expected, the climbing world was incredulous. Everyone knew of Shipton, very few had even heard of Hunt. The core members of the Cho Oyu team were equally astonished and several were prepared to resign and had to be persuaded – even by Shipton himself – to reconsider. The Committee was forced to reconfirm its decision at a meeting two weeks later by six votes to two. I think it was

Larry Kirwan, the Director/Secretary of the Royal Geographical Society and himself a member of the Committee, who said afterwards they had made the right decision but in the worst possible way.

I had barely met Shipton and knew nothing of Hunt, so was glad not to be involved at that stage. Shipton was badly shaken by the decision and, for some years, his personal life went through a series of crises. But his interest in lightweight mountain exploration was rekindled when he went to Patagonia and was enchanted by its possibilities. For many of us climbers, both Shipton and Tilman remain folk heroes through their outstanding achievements and their writings. Perhaps finest of all was their penetration of the Nanda Devi Sanctuary in 1934, an expedition which I was thrilled to be able to repeat in October 2000.

06

1953 – The Last Chance
To Be First

'The ultimate aim of the Expedition is the ascent of Everest during 1953.' John Hunt

Who was this new leader who only took up his duties officially on 9 October 1952, just four months before the expedition was due to sail for India?

John Hunt was 42, the elder son of an Indian Army officer who was killed early in World War I when John was only four. Following his father's career, he passed first into Sandhurst and passed out first with the King's Gold Medal and the Anson Memorial Sword, setting a personal standard of performance he was to maintain throughout his life. He was commissioned in the King's Royal Rifle Corps and served in India from 1931 until World War II when he commanded his battalion in the Italian Campaign and was awarded the DSO.

His regiment was then sent to Greece to help restore law and order following liberation from the Germans. This tense and difficult peacekeeping role earned him the CBE. After the war came several senior staff appointments and he joined the Everest expedition from the planning staff of Allied Headquarters at Fountainebleau where he was serving under Montgomery. Clearly, Hunt's military training and experience equipped him admirably for planning, organising and leading a major expedition.

His climbing experience was almost as impressive, Hunt having had the good fortune to be taken by his mother for summer and winter Alpine holidays from the age of 10. He became an enthusiastic mountaineer and skier and learned to rock climb on the Aiguilles above Chamonix.

While serving in India, he naturally gravitated to the Himalayas and reached 24,500ft (7,470m) with James Waller's party on Saltoro Kangri in 1935. He applied for Ruttledge's 1936 Everest Expedition but was turned down, so the story goes, after an RAF Medical Board detected a murmur in his cardiograph and he was warned to be careful going upstairs! Luckily, this did not seem to affect his subsequent climbing. So Hunt came to Everest in 1953 with impressive credentials despite having been outside the mainstream of Himalayan and Alpine climbing after the war.

The expedition was allocated a large office at the Royal Geographical Society (RGS) and, together with Charles Wylie, a serving officer of the brigade of Gurkhas who had already been appointed as organising secretary, Hunt got down to work. By 5 November, he had drafted the basis of a remarkably detailed plan for the assault on the mountain. It began with the self-evident fact that the 'ultimate aim of the Expedition is the ascent of Everest during 1953 by a member or members of the party'. It was to be a streamlined operation totally dedicated to this aim, cutting out any superfluous distractions, such as the need for a radio transmitter, or scientific work which did not contribute directly to reaching the summit. There would be provision for up to three assaults on successive days. This would require a team of 10 climbers, each a potential 'summitter', all supported by sufficient Sherpas.

I Meet John Hunt, Our New Leader

The selection of the team could now go ahead. The nucleus would come from the Cho Oyu team, but Hunt as a precedent decided to circulate the member clubs of the British Mountaineering Council to ensure that any worthy candidate would not be overlooked. Thus it came about that I again sent in an application, now bolstered with a lengthy list of unguided Alpine climbs that I had completed that summer although it was only my third Alpine season. This time, to my excitement, I was called to the RGS to meet John Hunt on 22 October for the first time. I came with some trepidation, prepared to expect a brusque and conventional military man. I was wrong.

He seemed a very sensitive and intensely human person. With his engaging blue eyes and confident handshake, he immediately put me at ease with his warmth and sincerity and close interest as I described my climbs of the previous summer. I had started by organizing an undergraduate meet for 16 based on Zinal, which is surrounded by some of the highest Swiss peaks over 13,120ft (4,000m). This was quite ambitious for relatively inexperienced young climbers so I had planned it carefully on the basis of a 'military appreciation' learned during my National Service training. This seemed to intrigue him. Additionally, as currency exchange controls prohibited one from taking more than £25 abroad at that time (assuming you had the money!), I had contrived to get my fare paid and $100 expenses from a wealthy American businessman, Joel E. Fisher, who was a keen amateur glaciologist. As a research project to study glacial movement, he wanted a tunnel dug and scientific measurements made in a glacier at over 4,000m on Monte Rosa above Zermatt. He had advertised in the Geography Department at Cambridge for two student volunteers but none had applied, probably because the daily walk up from the Bétemps Hut at 2,795m to the tunnel at 4,154m would be 1,359m or 4,460ft – before starting work. But I thought what a wonderful way to get fit and acclimatised, all expenses paid. So, my friend

Roger Chorley and I applied and we got the job! It enabled me to stay longer and continue climbing when our other friends had run out of cash and had to go home. In fact, it proved more of a gold mine than an ice tunnel for a few of us.

Joel E. Fisher was impressed with our energetic start, so when I wrote to him and explained that Zermatt was proving more expensive than anticipated and, therefore, we might not be able to work the planned four weeks on the tunnel, he immediately wired back 'Congratulations. Splendid start. Am cabling you 500 Swiss Francs care Manager, Mont Cervin Hotel.' Then when the main summer climbing season started in July, the two Swiss guides also working on the tunnel preferred to earn more by guiding clients up the Matterhorn – with rather less effort – so Fisher agreed I could hire two other impecunious students, Ian McNaught-Davis and Tom Patey, to replace them, and be paid no less than the guides, so they earned rather more than me! Anyway, my record of climbs in that wonderful nine-week season, including several first British or first British guideless ascents, carried out with a splendid assortment of friends, such as Roger Chorley, John Streetly, Ted Wrangham, David Fisher, Ian McNaught-Davis and Arthur Dolphin, proved enough for John Hunt to decide in my favour, even though, being only 23 at the interview, I was below the minimum age range of 25–40 that he considered desirable for an Everest climber. Just two of us, Michael Westmacott, 27, a statistician at the Rothamsted Experimental Station, who had been President of the Oxford University Mountaineering Club, and myself were chosen purely on our Alpine climbing records, neither of us having climbed in the Himalayas.

The Rest of the Team

Who were the rest of the team?

Charles Evans, 33, short but well built, was currently a Liverpool brain surgeon. Used to preparing his patients' heads, he also became the expedition barber! Despite his demanding job, he had managed to get time off to be with Tilman in the Annapurna area in 1950, in Kulu in 1951, and with Shipton to Cho Oyu.

Tom Bourdillon, 28, had been with Shipton on both the 1951 reconnaissance and to Cho Oyu. His rock climbs in the Alps, with Hamish Nicol, had inspired a new wave of young British climbers, such as myself, to repeat some of the harder routes put up by continental Alpinists. Although huge and heavily built, he could be very light on his feet. As a rocket research physicist, he was well qualified to help in the development of the experimental closed-circuit oxygen apparatus.

Alf Gregory at 39 was the oldest, apart from Hunt, and director of a Blackpool travel agency. He was small and wiry but toughened with long Alpine experience and had acclimatised well on Cho Oyu.

Wilfrid Noyce, 34, a schoolmaster at Charterhouse, had been one of our finest pre-war climbers. During the war, he had worked for some time at an aircrew mountain training centre in Kashmir and then had climbed Pauhunri, 23,400ft (7,132m), in the Sikkim Himalayas.

Charles Wylie, 32, was British Pentathlon Champion in 1939. A serving Gurkha officer, he had survived a Japanese prison camp during the war and then climbed in the Alps and Garhwal. Both his father and grandfather had served in Nepal and his fluent Urdu and Nepali would be a great asset in working with the Sherpas and porters.

The two New Zealanders, Ed Hillary and George Lowe, completed the team of 10 climbers. They were both tall and lanky. George's New Zealand Alpine experience pre-dated Ed's, to whom he introduced some of the best climbs, which were almost entirely on snow and ice, so their ice technique was of a high standard. George, 28, was teaching in a primary school in Hastings, New Zealand, whereas Hillary, 33, with his father and brother ran a family bee-keeping business near Auckland. He was once asked how he managed to take so much time off for climbing and replied that he had several thousand workers who needed no supervision. Luckily the time of year when the bees went to sleep also coincided with the Himalayan climbing season!

Hunt did not know the New Zealanders beforehand, and had intended to meet all candidates personally to form his own view as to whether they would fit in the team. However, they had both been with Shipton in 1952, and Hillary on the 1951 reconnaissance. So strong were their claims that Hunt accepted a reflected view for these two, given by those whose judgement he respected.

In addition to the ten climbers, we had three specialists: Michael Ward, 27, was our doctor, studying to qualify as a surgeon. We all respected him as a fine climber too, and it was his initiative that had sparked the 1951 reconnaissance. In fact, several of us rated him a better climber than an expedition doctor! It can be a frustrating task. In a normal surgery, the patient is given some pills or medicine and told to come back next week. However, on an expedition, the doctor is literally living with his patients and gets no respite from impromptu consultations. Mike's three words of Nepali with which he opened the porters' morning surgery were 'Yo hospital ho!' translated as 'I am a hospital!'

Griffith Pugh, another qualified doctor, was the field physiologist sponsored by the Medical Research Council whose work on the Cho Oyu expedition had been so valuable, and he was to continue his research. He had been an Olympic skier in 1936.

Finally, Tom Stobart, a first-class honours zoologist, who had become a professional cameraman, came to make a film of the expedition. He was a wonderful raconteur on the trail with stories of climbing Nun Kun, filming whales in Antarctica, on safari in Africa with Armand and Michaela Denis, or shooting crocodiles in Northern Queensland. Unfortunately, he returned from this last trip with amoebic dysentery and had trouble convincing the doctors he was capable of going to Everest. To do so, he tried running upstairs, but an over-zealous publicity agent distorted the story: 'Desperate to prove he was fit for Everest, Photographer Tom Stobart swept up the Sister and carried her up four flights of stairs. Then he turned to the doctor. "What do you mean, too weak to climb ...".'

This now made a total of 13, but to John Hunt's relief he could avoid this unlucky figure when, after arriving in Nepal, he invited Tenzing to join the climbing party. After all, with Raymond Lambert, Tenzing had already been several thousand feet higher on his two feet than any of us.

Not that any of us were really superstitious, but one had to consider the possibility that one might not return. Charles Wylie mentioned the Sherpas were covered by an insurance policy. 'But what about us "Sahibs"?' somebody murmured. 'Oh! That's up to you to arrange your own policy,' was the official reply.

It wasn't normal to take out climbing insurance in those days, but one of us enquired and was offered £1,000 cover for death (with a compensatory 25 per cent per lost limb or 5 per cent per lost finger, I recall). All this for a modest £100 premium – just for the period of the expedition. 'But that's a chance of one in ten of not returning, and there are ten of us!' I gasped. 'It's outrageous.' Griff Pugh looked up some statistics and conceded it was not far wrong. 'You remember that German expedition to Nanga Parbat,' he said, 'when a huge avalanche destroyed a whole campsite with all its occupants.' Wilf Noyce was married with several children, so felt he should be covered and through a broker was quoted a lower premium of £50, reducing the odds to 1 in 20. Mike Westmacott, hurriedly reading the small print, sent off a cheque for just £5, so he had insured his life for a mere £100. The rest of us decided to live at risk, so we joked that if there was a particularly fragile-looking snowbridge over a large crevasse in the Western Cwm, we would push Wilf in front to test it, belayed and followed by Mike, so that if the bridge held we could reasonably risk following in their footsteps!

Our First Team Meeting

However, I am getting ahead of myself. I still remember the date of

17 November 1952 when all the UK members of the team were summoned to the Royal Geographical Society, close to the Albert Hall. After greeting each other, we sat around a huge boardroom table, the like of which I had only seen previously in Hollywood films, and John Hunt assigned to each of us various tasks in addition to our role as climbers. Several members were already fully involved: Charles Wylie as Organising Secretary; Tom Bourdillon with closed-circuit oxygen; Gregory, or Greg as he was always known, was a natural to deal with our travel arrangements by sea or air, and probably earn a useful commission for his firm at the same time. Michael Westmacott was just old enough to have served in the Bengal Sappers and Miners at the end of the war, so he took on responsibility for tents and bridging equipment. I wondered what I might usefully do, until John Hunt said we needed walkie-talkie radios to be developed for communication between camps on the mountain, and also a short-wave radio or two to receive high altitude weather forecasts to be prepared specially for us by the Met. Office which would be broadcast daily by the BBC, and relayed by All India Radio, as we moved progressively up the mountain. These forecasts would help us to time the assaults during predicted periods of fine weather, expected during the second half of May, and also give us early warning of the approach of the summer monsoon which builds up in the Bay of Bengal. When it hits the high Himalayas, bringing heavy snowfalls and dangerous avalanches, you need to be off the mountain. I mentioned that during my National Service I had been in the Royal Corps of Signals and learned a little about radios, so Hunt said: 'You're just the chap.' But I protested gently, saying that most of my time after completing training I had been a messing officer at the HQ School of Signals in charge of catering. 'Better still,' he said, 'then you can also help Griff Pugh with the food!' This is never a very popular task, but at least I could help ensure we had plenty. On a live radio interview after the 1951 Reconnaissance, Tom Bourdillon was asked about the food. Never one to cause offence, after a long pause, he hesitantly conceded: 'I think the main thing

is to have some!' He was built like a second-row rugby forward and had lost about 30lb (13.6kg) in weight during that trip because he didn't like rice, which Shipton, who could live on anything, had included as their staple diet.

Preparations and Equipment

Once all tasks were assigned, we were carefully measured up to ensure that all the special high altitude clothing and equipment being designed for us would be a perfect fit. A new windproof material had been devised called 'Wyncol', with cotton threads as the warp and fine nylon fibres as the weft. So-called 'breathable materials' such as Gore-tex had not yet been invented. Both our windproof clothing and mountain tents would be of Wyncol, which had been tested in the wind tunnel at the Royal Aircraft Establishment at Farnborough. In a simulated 100mph gale, there was only a 3mph 'breeze' inside the tent.

Our high altitude boots were also to be of a totally innovative design. Griff Pugh established that a pound's weight on the feet was physically equivalent to 5lb (2.25kg) on the shoulders, so the boots' weight was reduced at the expense of durability, as they were only needed above, say, 20,000ft (6,100m) for the one expedition, but they also needed to be warm enough to protect against frostbite. In the days before plastic shell boots, they were conceived from first principles by a physicist, Dr Bradley, who was the Director of the British Boot, Shoe and Allied Trades Research Association of Kettering. The sole was of low-conductivity micro-cellular rubber and the uppers made on a vapour-barrier principle, the kapok insulating material being kept dry within a waterproof envelope designed to exclude wet snow from outside and perspiration from the inside. An average pair weighed 4¼lb (1.9kg). Thirty different firms were involved in their manufacture or providing materials. Special lasts were made to accommodate Sherpa feet. Some Sherpas taking size 6 boots had wider feet than Hillary's size 12! The boots proved very popular and nobody got frostbite, although they were not very practicable for safe climbing on steep or difficult ground. In fact, since the climbing was almost entirely on snow or ice, they were usually used in combination with crampons.

Griff Pugh was pleased that our high-altitude protective clothing of windproofs, eiderdown jacket and trousers, which were of the latest French design, and Bradley boots together weighed less than 9lb (4kg), which is probably no heavier than today's equipment. There is a public perception now that our 1953 equipment was very primitive, but we had, in fact, progressed considerably from the Norfolk jacket, tweed breeches, puttees and nailed leather boots of the 1920s and 1930s.

We were also strongly committed to using supplementary oxygen for all the summit attempts, unlike some of the earlier Everest expeditions. We had learned from the Swiss that the poor performance of their oxygen equipment was one reason for their failure.

Peter Lloyd, a member of the Committee, who had used oxygen on Everest in 1938, took responsibility for development of the open-circuit apparatus on which we would mainly be relying. At that time, nobody knew whether, or for how long, a human being could survive at 29,000ft (8,840m) without extra oxygen. To help convince us of its importance we were taken to Farnborough, the team fitted with oxygen masks and shut into a decompression chamber. The air was then pumped out until we were at a simulated 30,000ft (9,144m). 'George,' said the instructor, 'I'd like you to take your mask off to see how well you can cope at this altitude. To give you something to do, just keep signing your name on this clipboard.'

I was rather pleased; I seemed to have no problem. Halfway down the page, I was scrawling a bit, but then continued towards the bottom, totally conscious the whole time. 'You realise you've now got your mask on, don't you?' he said. 'That's strange, you took it off,' I said. 'What's the time?' he said. I looked at my wrist – no watch. 'Where's your tie?' That had gone too. Everyone was laughing at me. I had actually collapsed, until he had slapped the mask on again, and then I had continued signings blissfully unaware. 'That's the problem with altitude,' he told us all. 'You slip into unconsciousness gradually, insidiously, without knowing anything is wrong.' Griff Pugh was the second guinea pig, a more alarming demonstration. He began spasmodic twitchings and sank to the floor, trying to fight off the mask as the instructor put it back on. It showed the dangerous over-confidence of the anoxic, and a lesson to us all to be careful on Everest. Although not relevant to assessing performance on the mountain after one had acclimatised, Tom Stobart commented the test had shown one thing: 'like a lie-detector, decompression had shown the team was made up of most ruthlessly determined characters, filled with an intense spirit of one-upmanship – competitive – a sort of commando. From that moment I was rather alarmed at the sort of people I had come amongst.'

John Hunt had never forgotten being turned down for Everest in 1936 because he was said to have failed certain laboratory tests which he thought irrelevant, so he arranged for Lord Horder, the Queen's physician, to see all the short-listed candidates. Nobody would question his decision. Horder took my height and weight but didn't seem particularly interested in testing my physique or poor eye-sight. If I had been climbing actively, surely that was enough? We had a pleasant chat. He was looking for what he called the 'Excelsior Spirit' – a determination to press on, however adverse the circumstances: I passed.

Time seemed to fly by, all of us busy with our respective tasks. We decided to entrust Pye Telecommunications Ltd with the responsibility for our radio equipment. Their headquarters was very conveniently in Cambridge and I liaised closely with their Director, Brigadier Moppett, recently retired from the Royal Corps of Signals. As well as visits to their assembly plant, this involved several excellent lunches at his London club – much enjoyed by a hungry student! We took eight 'walkie-talkies' adapted from their 'Walkie-Phone' PTC 122, a VHF set with crystal control on both transmit and receive, with a fixed frequency of 72 megacycles. They had flexible tape aerials, and weighed 5lb (2.25kg) each. We were concerned that in very cold conditions the dry batteries, supplied by Vidor Ltd, would fade, so they were carried separately in a 'waistcoat' which could be worn beneath a duvet jacket or in a sleeping bag, kept warm by body heat to prevent loss of efficiency. They gave good service in a net between Camps I, II and III, and up to Camp VII (24,000ft/7,315m), but one taken to the South Col was, unfortunately, damaged in transit.

In January, Charles Evans, who had the important role of quarter-master, organised a packing plan which was carried out by Andrew Lusk at Wapping Wall, close to 'The Prospect of Whitby', a famous old pub. As one walked past the ranks of warehouses, one could savour the exotic smells of ginger, cloves and spices from the Far East mingled with the stale sweat of the dockers. Everyone was wonderfully co-operative, including John Hunt's wife, Joy, and two friends, sewing name tapes on to all our garments so they would not get mixed up on the mountain!

A last role for John Hunt before leaving for India was to consider the extra men and material needed for a repeat autumn expedition in case ours was unsuccessful. As the Swiss discovered, it was too late to defer such decisions until June. Hunt had appointed four reserve climbers in case of need and they had selflessly given us great assistance, in particular Emlyn Jones who took over from Wylie as Organising Secretary and would probably have led the autumn attempt. The others were Hamish Nicol, Anthony Rawlinson and John Jackson.

We Sail for India

Eventually, on 12 February, the main party and most of the baggage embarked at Tilbury on SS *Stratheden* bound for Bombay. Greg was there to see us off, and again to meet us in Bombay, having meanwhile flown out by Comet, the pride of BOAC. A handful of us accompanied our 7½ tons of baggage by rail across India, carefully watching coolies unloading and reloading our 473 packages into freight cars as we twice changed trains from one rail gauge to another, before entering Nepal. As the train made its leisurely progress, I remember sitting in the open doorway of our carriage as the sun set, watching the water buffaloes being herded for milking and girls in their colourful saris gracefully carrying earthenware waterpots home on their heads. As night fell, we had been warned to lock ourselves securely into our private reserved compartment. Then in the early hours, there was a loud hammering on the door when we stopped at a station. Obligingly, but mistakenly, Wilf Noyce opened it. In a trice, it was flung back and hordes poured in: men, women, children, babies, cases, pots, pans and live chickens. We got little sleep for the rest of that night!

In those days there was no road into Kathmandu, the capital of Nepal. You either flew, landing on the grass airfield, or walked the last 18 miles (29km) from the roadhead, crossing two 10,000ft (3,050m) passes. At the first pass, George Lowe exclaimed: 'Look, George, your first view of the Himalayas!' 'Where?' I asked, seeing nothing but haze above the near hills. 'Look again, higher!' There indeed it was; a chain of glistening snow and ice, impossibly high, across the sky.

Our 473 packages were conveyed that last stage into the valley of Kathmandu by an aerial ropeway, but it could only carry modest loads of 1cwt (50kg) or so. In the city itself there were much heavier cars moving smoothly about, and even an equestrian statue weighing 2½ tons. All of those had literally been carried on wooden frames over the 18-mile (29km) track by relays of coolies, or porters as we more politely call them nowadays, maybe 40 or more struggling with each vehicle.

Arrival in Kathmandu

Dirty and dusty, we met the other members of the team, who had flown in, and duly presented ourselves to the British Ambassador, Mr Christopher Summerhayes. He had kindly arranged billets for us all with the various Embassy staff. As very few foreigners were allowed into Nepal at that time, there were no hotels to cater for them. Some years later, one of the old Royal Palaces was converted into an hotel by an enterprising Russian, Boris Lissanevitch, who had once been a ballet dancer and later ran an exclusive club in Calcutta. He reputedly kept a panda in one of the bathrooms, and created the first 'Yak and Yeti' bar in Kathmandu where he served the products of his own distillery: 'Tiger', a pseudo-whisky, and 'Rhinoceros', an even stronger gin.

We now met Ed Hillary and George Lowe, arriving from New Zealand, and our Sherpa contingent headed by Tenzing. By his exploits with Lambert in 1952, he had become the best-known Sherpa climber and a mountaineer of world standing. The Sherpas were wearing an assortment of clothing mostly from previous expeditions: green berets, blue ski caps, balaclavas, brightly coloured sweaters and outsize boots. Some were well known to John Hunt and others, and had been specially asked for: Thondup, the cook; two brothers, Annullu and Dawa Tensing with his traditional pigtail; and Da Namgyal, who had done well with the Swiss in 1952. They all came forward grinning shyly to be introduced to us in the Embassy garden. Some of the Sherpanis, their wives and girlfriends, were with them, hoping to be engaged as porters for the return journey to their homeland of Sola Khumbu.

The Trek to Thyangboche

To save a day on the trek, our baggage had been moved by truck to a parade ground at Bhadgaon, 8 miles east of Kathmandu. Charles Wylie mustered 350 porters to carry it all, too many for one baggage train, so we moved off in two separate caravans a day apart on 10 and 11 March. We had to take money with us to pay off the porters. They were suspicious of flimsy paper notes and wanted at least half in hard rupee coins, so heavy that we needed 12 porters just to carry them!

What a wonderful experience this was for me, an impressionable

24-year-old, on my first visit to the greatest mountain range in the world. We were walking through a sort of super-Switzerland, initially quite cultivated on narrow terraces that had been cut into the hillside. Fruit trees were in bloom and the farmers were busy with their spring ploughing. We were travelling east, crossing the grain of the country, up one hillside, down the next and crossing the rivers which drained from the glaciers and snow peaks to the north.

At Risingo, we entered Buddhist country. There was a small monastery on the pass surrounded by long bamboo poles on which prayer flags fluttered. On each flag was written many times over the eternal Buddhist prayer, 'Om mani padme hum!': Hail to the Jewel in the Lotus. Every time the wind flaps the flags, so the prayers go up to Heaven. A typical day on the march would begin with a call around 5.30am when a Sherpa would thrust a mug of hot tea into your tent, to be followed shortly after by a basin of warm water for a perfunctory wash. In fact, you would probably already have been woken up by that traditional sound of Himalayan travel, a raucous clearing of the throat followed by a loud spit – the porters' substitute for brushing the teeth. One could hardly sleep through that, so you were glad to get on the trail, soon after 6am, aiming to complete a good part of the march in the cool of the morning. Thondup, the cook, and his assistants, would have gone ahead to find a good breakfast spot, perhaps beside a river, so that when you arrived around 10 o'clock, the meal was nearly ready. You might fill in the time with a refreshing bathe in the ice-cold river before tucking in to porridge, scrambled egg, coffee, biscuits and marmalade. Continuing on our way, in the foothills we would all be wearing the same strange adopted uniform: plimsolls, nowadays replaced by expensive trainers, shorts, T-shirt, a stubbly beard and an umbrella to keep the sun off during those hot valley marches and the rain off on our return in June after the monsoon had broken. Individuality was expressed in our hats: Hillary's – a blue-striped Foreign Legion style protecting the nape of the neck; Gregory's – a purple woolly with a bobble on top; Lowe's – a white broad-brimmed sunhat of the kind sold at cricket matches; mine – a black-banded Italian straw hat I had bought cheaply in Cambridge. By mid-afternoon, we would reach our campsite; Thondup would soon produce a cup of tea and we could rest, read a book, write up our diaries, practise a little bouldering or look for interesting birds. Mike Westmacott had brought a butterfly net, offering to collect for the Natural History Museum. Hillary would either borrow it to race after elusive specimens, or would adopt what later came to be known as the 'Everest position' – lying flat out on his air mattress, preferably with eyes closed.

Soon after dusk, supper would be served, before we retired early to bed around 9 o'clock. We were too large a group to try 'living off the country' and had brought all our own food. For consumption up to 20,000ft, we had adapted Army 'compo' rations, each box weighing 42lb (19kg) and containing 14 men's rations for one day. There were seven menus, one for each day of the week, so if it were steak and kidney, baked beans and rich fruit cake, we knew it was Tuesday!

Above 20,000ft (6,100m) we had special assault rations, in single man-day units weighing 2½lb (1.1kg), specially vacuum packed to save bulk and weight. At high altitude, one tends to lose appetite and reject fatty foods, so much of the calorie intake consisted of sugar in tea, lemonade or other drinks, or taken with cereal and reconstituted milk. One could pick and choose and augment it with some items from the five Luxury Boxes for which, back in the UK, each climber had been allowed to select several items. Popular choices were: tinned fruit, juices, Marmite, Ovosport, Cheddar cheese and saucisson.

Based on Griff Pugh's research on Cho Oyu, 14oz (400g) of sugar were included in each daily assault ration – an astonishing amount. This may have been the quantity Griff recorded as being consumed per Sahib daily, but I think most of it went surreptitiously to the Sherpas to sweeten their tea. Previously, with no access to sugar, they had drunk tea 'Tibetan style', flavoured with yak butter and salt, which was just acceptable if you thought of it as more like beef consommé, rather than a cup of tea.

As we climbed higher, around 8,000ft (2,440m), we entered the rhododendron belt, which in springtime can be one of the great sights of the Himalayas. The flowers can be blood red, salmon pink, yellow and white. Many varieties were collected in Sikkim, further east, by Joseph Hooker in the 19th century and brought back to Kew Gardens to provide the stock for the numerous hybrids we enjoy in our gardens today. Slightly higher, we came across the incredible magnolia (M. *campbellii*), a 40ft (12m) tree without any leaves but instead huge white blossoms, each the size of a soup plate.

One of the great pleasures of the trek was just chatting as we went along, getting to know each other better. Tom Stobart had a fund of knowledge about game and wildlife. One day Bourdillon saw a bird with a red crest, catching flies by a river. 'What do you think it's called?' he asked Stobart. Tom paused and then announced: 'That's almost certainly the Himalayan red-crested fly catcher.' Bourdillon was sceptical and on return looked it up at the Natural History Museum. Sure enough, it was!

Griff Pugh, in his role as a field physiologist, had done fascinating experiments to research how people survive in extreme conditions. He attached thermocouples to the various orifices of an Egyptian Channel swimmer, and followed him with all the instrumentation in a rowing boat, to try to determine the rate of heat loss from his body, and explain how he could withstand the near-freezing water for so many hours.

Griff's fair skin suffered on the trail from the tropical sun, so to cover his exposed flesh he wore a pair of blue cotton pyjamas. In the evenings, he would twirl a special thermometer rather like a Buddhist prayer wheel. With his unruly thatch of red hair, horn-rimmed spectacles, studious and slightly absent-minded air, he was considered a very special person by the Sherpas, possibly accompanying the expedition in the role of a holy man or lama.

Let me quote some excerpts from my diary – the first dramatic view of Everest and my first taste of the Sherpas' staple alcoholic drink, 'chang':

Tuesday, 17.3.53

A long plug uphill culminating in a race for the top of the pass. Then scrambled up a tree and saw Everest for the first time. I saw it first! Bearing 59 degrees. North Ridge on left and bulk of South Face – snow covered – on right. Lhotse was not too obvious so some argument about it. I took many photos. Exultant! Sunlight emphasized the South-East Ridge and the crest between north and south summits. West Ridge invisible. Soon clouded over.

Friday, 20.3.53

Da Tensing brought Charles some 'chang' and I had my first taste. It has the colour of tea and consistency of buttermilk; a strange smell of banana essence comes from it. It tastes at first milky and then of a characteristic slightly sour fermented quality. It has flecks of grain and husk in it which spoil the butter-milky texture. This chang was prepared from a mixture of grains – barley, rice, maize and was of superior quality. An acquired taste; pleasant in small quantities.

On the 12th day, we descended into the gorge of the Dudh Kosi – or Milk River – flowing down from the mountains west of Everest. We now turned northwards along the east side of the gorge, then climbed up to reach Namche Bazar at 12,000ft (3,660m), the chief village of Khumbu. Before entering the village a small deputation, relatives of our Sherpa team, met us with a barrel of milky-coloured chang, a charming gesture. The 17th day, 26 March, was the climax, arriving at the Buddhist monastery of Thyangboche, on a shoulder of mountain at about 12,000ft. The slopes below were covered in fir trees and scrubby rhododendron, and all around us were magnificent virgin peaks over 20,000ft (6,100m). At the head of the valley to the north lay the Everest massif, its summit pyramid just appearing above the 25,000ft (7,620m) serrated ridge joining the high peaks of Lhotse and Nuptse. In the forests around us, if we were observant, were glimpses of musk deer and the national bird of Nepal, the iridescent-blue monal pheasant.

In front of the monastery was a grazing ground for yaks and here we put up our colourful acclimatisation camp. We paid off most of the porters and started unpacking and sorting out our gear. Let me quote from the next day's diary, 28 March:

Got up to pass water for 2 mins 40 secs! Effect of altitude? Blacksmith came to fit crampons and fitted one of mine to Wilf Noyce's boot! Good fit obtained eventually with two odd ones. Unfortunately, the Bhend-bindings are not designed to fit the Grivel-ringed crampons! Oxygen practice.

Invited to monastery at midday. One approaches the entrance in a clockwise fashion. Taken into room full of idols where John presents our Expedition's 1953 flag and a silk scarf. The Head Lama's throne on right of Buddhas, and throne on left reserved for the Head Lama of Rongbuk. The old Lama died recently and his successor is a young lad now being taught at Lhasa. His mother lives here. One religious hand printed book unwrapped from its cloth binding and shown to us – most are in Tibetan, some in Sanskrit. Shirrup (one of our Sherpas, a former monk) in great form. Then upstairs (we had taken our shoes off) for tea, fried potatoes, and chapattis with the acting Head Lama.

John and Charles Wylie chatted with him while Tenzing translated. Conversation about Yeti – one came 4 years ago across the hill opposite. Also a story of Tibetan Yetis copying men who were eventually trapped by drinking poisoned chang set out for them, since when Yetis have been protected by Tibetan government! Afterwards visited holy of holies where ashes of the previous Head Lama were kept and also the ceremonial masks used in devil dances – about 15ins long, lurid and gaily coloured. Drums were beating meanwhile in the courtyard. They asked for 4,000 rupees to mend the monastery roof! Back for lunch. Dishing out food and packing up wireless after. At 5.30 listened to the boat race. Cambridge won by 19 lengths in 19 minutes 54.5 seconds. Hurray! Tom set off a magnesium fuse during supper. Wrote home and to Brig. Moppett after sorting out my kit for tomorrow. Bed 9.30. My red jersey and two Shetland pullovers missing and therefore pinched in England probably. A poor show.

The above yeti story was the closest I have been to meeting one. Our host pointed out of the window to where he had seen it clearly visible against the snow during the hard winter a few years previously (1947?). It was scratching itself (and here our host paused to demonstrate vigorously on himself) and combing the bushes for berries. They regard yetis as unclean, so got out their drums, trumpets and long horns to scare it away. In the wilder stories, Sherpas say the yeti has its feet on back to front, so that when you follow its trail, you are going the wrong way. At that time, many of us genuinely believed that there quite likely was such a creature. There are many miles of unpopulated high valleys where it could live virtually undetected in the company of other rarely seen creatures, such as leopards, bears, wolves, foxes and small rodents. After 1953, several expeditions were mounted just to look for it, but without confirmed success, so if it ever did exist it is probably now extinct. The monastery at Pangboche had a scalp of one used in devil dances which Ed Hillary was later allowed to take to Europe and to the USA to be examined by zoologists. They concluded it was most likely a fake, probably cut from the back of a serow, a rare goat-antelope, *Capricornis sumatraensis*, and shaped so that the short red-brown hairs parted naturally from a central ridge, corresponding to the serow's spine. The scalp was returned to Pangboche but has since sadly been lost.

Acclimatisation

We now divided into three parties to test our equipment by climbing modest peaks or passes up to about 20,000ft (6,100m). I was with Charles Evans, Tom Bourdillon and Mike Westmacott. Our objective, apart from testing the oxygen equipment, was to explore the Mingbo Valley to the south of the spectacular peak of Ama Dablam and try to reach the Mera La at over 19,000ft (5,790m), the pass leading into the Hongu Valley to the east. After a couple of days' trying out both the open- and closed-circuit oxygen, on one of the southern spurs of Ama Dablam and also teaching our Sherpas how to use it, we tried the pass – without the benefit of oxygen – to encourage further acclimatisation. The first time, I just seemed to flake out at about 500ft (150m) below the pass and had to turn back. Going downhill was no problem, but uphill one just seemed to run out of puff. However, after a day's rest, we tried again. Quoting from my diary:

Going much better this time. Started breathing faster on purpose and this seemed to do the trick. A breath for each step. Up a hard snow slope to the Col, about 50 degrees at the steepest part. Roped with Charles, Dawa Tensing and Kirken. Just managed to stand the pace – up in about five hours.

We camped on the Col, my first night sleeping at over 19,000ft. Pemmican for supper. It is quite pleasant and unrecognizable from the previous brand I have had. It contains herbs and has a meaty granular consistency – good for eating raw and makes a good soup. Talking about Alpine climbs with Tom until 8.15. Developed a tickling cough during the night. Just a little cold in outer sleeping bag and without duvet jacket, so put on the latter and pyjama trousers over windproof and breeches and then slept soundly.

Next day, we returned to Thyangboche, all feeling much fitter. I realised it was Easter Sunday. Meanwhile, the Sherpas had found a box with flags and bunting so, as well as putting a Welsh flag on John Hunt's tent, they had made a flagpole and run up the Union Jack where it fluttered for three days upside down before anybody noticed!

We now split up into three different parties, to continue the acclimatisation training. It was during this second trip that Charles Evans' group made the first ascent of a fine peak some 3 miles (5km) due south of Lhotse to which Shipton in 1952 had already given the name 'Island Peak', because from one direction it resembled a rocky island in a sea of ice. It now has a local name, Imja Tse, and has become one of the most popular 'trekking peaks' in the Everest area.

To the Khumbu Icefall

John Hunt decided to give one party the special privilege of having a first crack at the Khumbu Icefall. A thorough reconnaissance was required in order to find the safest possible route up it. This would save precious days when the whole expedition moved up to Base Camp at the foot of Everest. He selected Ed Hillary, whose previous experience in the Icefall in 1951 would be invaluable; George Lowe, by virtue of his outstanding ice-craft; and the two youngsters, Mike Westmacott and myself. Mike, in charge of the bridging equipment, would be in his element. At Thyangboche, he had already tried out three sections of our light aluminium ladder bolted together to make an 18ft (5.5m) bridge. Suspended between two boulders, it sagged alarmingly in the middle when his Sherpa assistant crawled gingerly across but it held.

The Icefall party began to swell in numbers, as we had to be self-sufficient from 9 April until the others joined us on 22 April. Griff Pugh and Tom Stobart – with the prospect of some exciting filming – decided to come along too, so, with five Sherpas and 39 porters, we were 50 in all.

We made four short stages with three camps which have become regular sites for Everest trekkers: a yak pasture at Phalong Karpo, 14,600ft (4,450m); Lobuje, 16,400ft (5,000m); Lake Camp or Gorak Shep, 17,350ft (5,290m); (the 1952 Swiss Base Camp); and then on to our Base Camp at 17,900ft (5,455m) on the Khumbu Glacier itself. The first afternoon it unexpectedly began to snow and 4ft (1.2m) fell overnight. Next day was gloriously sunny, and the snow squealed underfoot; very beautiful but serious for the porters without snow goggles. We only had a few spare pairs to lend them. Their usual trick of tying strands of hair from their pigtails across their eyes was hardly adequate protection against snow-blindness. Then Tom Stobart had a bright idea. He cut up some yellow and orange photographic filters and with black plastic sticky tape we made up 15 pairs of makeshift goggles. We could carry on. At Lake Camp it grew colder, 15°F/–9°C at 6pm, but there were stone walls and crannies to provide some shelter for the porters. From there, it was only two hours the next morning to our Base Camp site (the Swiss Camp I), with plenty of firewood left. Our way led through the maze of vast ice pinnacles up to 35ft (11m) high, similar to those encountered by the pre-war Everesters on the East Rongbuk Glacier. It felt exceedingly hot in the sunshine. After clearing a level site for the big mess tent, we all seemed very lethargic until sun-down but recovered after a fine stewed steak supper supervised by Tom. I set up the short-wave wireless and aerial and let the jingles on Radio Ceylon cheer us up: 'When you're feeling – ENOs!'

The 13 April was our first exciting day in the Khumbu Icefall. At last, after all the days and weeks of anticipation, we were getting to grips with the first great problem on the mountain. Sadly George Lowe was not well – we nearly all had bouts of tummy trouble or vomiting occasionally which would lay us low for a day or two – so there were just the three of us. My diary for the day:

Off by 9. Aimed to left by curious winding lanes between ice pinnacles. At 9.30 waited for Sherpas; Tom and Griff arrived as well. Icefall looked too complicated to allow for a camp so sent Sherpas back and the 3 of us went on together for a recce while Griff, Tom and Gyaljen followed filming. Met occasional Swiss marker flags. Easy going at first but tiring up and down. Took turns leading until Ed only had sufficient energy left for the task. Mostly powder snow on ice, wearing crampons. Mike cut up a nice little wall. Eventually going rather intricate in amongst fallen blocks and by a few seracs.

Keeping to the left centre. At 1.45 impasse. In view of a saddle above and remains of Swiss Camp II below on right. Rested and left at 2.10. Back into camp in 2 hours unfortunately soaking my feet in a stream which now runs down the lanes between pinnacles. Took 12 photos. Next time will aim to right, up sunken lane to right of our impasse or perhaps further left. Quite tired and slight headache on return although fit during the day, if not energetic. Ed went strongly.

That afternoon, Ralph Izzard, a journalist with the Daily Mail, visited our camp. He had the considerable initiative to walk from Kathmandu and earned his scoop. 'Nightmare march across the slopes of Everest' was the headline. Most other journalists had been quite content to prop up the bars in Kathmandu, picking up what rumours they could about our progress. The Times had paid £10,000 for the exclusive copyright to the Expedition's despatches and photographs – about half the out-of-pocket cost of the whole expedition – so did not take kindly to other rival newspapers trying to horn in. We were not supposed to talk to other journalists, but at least we gave him a cup of tea! This incident may have rattled The Times and our Joint Himalayan Committee, and made them realise that it was a considerable burden on John Hunt to both lead the expedition and write detailed despatches. So it was agreed that The Times would send out a young journalist to assist John Hunt and provide a first-hand account of our doings. The choice fell on their engaging boyish-looking Middle East Correspondent, James Morris, 26, for which Everest was to provide a sudden startling contrast to riding a camel across the sands of the Sultanate of Oman. He had never been on a serious mountain before but he took it in his stride, saying to John Hunt when he met him at 17,000ft (5,180m) that he was feeling a little short of breath and was this unusual? Most of us had felt very much worse initially!

Next day, we set off for the Icefall in two groups: Ed, Mike and Ang Namgyal; George and I, but George was still unwell and I continued cautiously alone. I found a short cut, which would also be a useful route for attacking the right-hand part of the Icefall. The others had done well, reaching a potential campsite in a hollow.

Two days later, Ed, George and I with three Sherpas put up the temporary Camp II at 19,400ft (5,910m), halfway up the Icefall. The site was free from seracs but more exposed to wind. We had started giving names to awkward features on the route, particularly ice walls close to yawning crevasses, which were named after the original climber:

'Mike's Horror' and 'Hillary's Horror'. Later came the 'Atom Bomb Area', an unstable section liable to collapse, and the 'Nutcracker', where you had to clamber over blocks jammed in the gap between two impending walls of ice.

Next day, we continued through the upper half of the Icefall where great strips of ice – the size of a row of cottages – had split off from the more level floor of the Western Cwm. The route became very involved amongst tottering seracs with the issue always in doubt. Finally, Ed led up a vertical 20ft (6m) crack in an ice wall and we had almost reached the plateau of the Cwm, although barred from it by the final huge crevasse. This was no route for porters yet. Later on, the crack was by-passed using a rope ladder presented by the Yorkshire Ramblers' Club. But for the present, we had created a route through the Icefall and our mission was accomplished. We turned to descend. To our surprise, near Camp II we met John Hunt coming up with Ang Namgyal, keen to see for himself how we had got on. He awarded us two days' rest at Lobuje; a very satisfying conclusion to our week, and my first experience above 20,000ft. I was coping but still nowhere near fully acclimatised. At Base Camp, the mail had arrived — 18 letters for me!

While we were resting, the others moved up to Base Camp, and then a team consisting of Ward, Westmacott, Noyce and Hunt started improving the route, chopping more steps, fixing the occasional rope, putting ladder bridges in place and, when these ran out, replacing them with simple log bridges so the ladders could be used higher up. On 22 April, my diary records:

The Sherpas brought up kit for Camp III (20,200ft) at the top of the Icefall, and in a short recce with John and Ed we found a shallow depression on the left leading well into the Cwm with few crevasses. We were separated from it by a 16ft gap. Just the place for Mike's 18ft ladder!

This may well have been the spot where in 1952, for want of such ladders, the Swiss had contrived their ingenious but very strenuous aerial ropeway although, of course, the character of the Icefall is continually changing with the glacial movement. Earlier on, we had seen some of the Swiss marker flags which were now in totally inaccessible or dangerously threatened positions.

A Change of Diet

Back at Base Camp, we had an unusual diversion. To vary our daily 'Compo' diet we had planned occasional 'meat on hoof' as the Army call it. This duly arrived in the form of a yak, tethered to an ice pinnacle, looking rather forlorn. This is the moment when the Sherpas remembered that, as strict Buddhists, they should not take life and that I, George Band, was in charge of the food, so I timidly held the halter! We had a light 0.22 rifle and George Lowe, whose father had once been in the butchery trade, agreed to be marksman. Just as I was expecting the yak to charge me, George fired and the yak dropped like a stone. Then followed the gruesome business of skinning, gutting and chopping it up into joints. At least there was no shortage of cold storage around us. To celebrate, we had scones for tea and then a tremendous supper of yak brains and liver, followed by jam omelette. The following night it was yak tongue.

Cooking the flesh so that it was sufficiently tender was more of a problem. A yak does not get the lush grazing of an Aberdeen Angus! At high altitude, the boiling point of water is depressed well below 212°F (only 185°F/85°C at 21,000ft/6,400m), which exacerbates the problem. Pressure cookers came to the rescue. We had taken a couple. The Sherpa cooks, initially sceptical, adopted them enthusiastically and even devised their own: a biscuit tin with the lid forced on and a small hole stoppered with a stick acting as the safety valve!

On 1 May, we were due to receive our first daily weather forecast from the Met. Office. In return, and later to help check their accuracy, I had agreed to set up a mini weather station with a recording thermograph which I sheltered from the direct sun under a perforated cardboard box rather like a Stephenson screen. For a month, it must have been the highest station in the world! High up on the mountain we could expect temperatures down to –40°F or °C – as predicted from balloon data from Indian hill stations in 1933. It would feel worse with wind chill. Our protective clothing, sleeping bags and air mattresses were designed to combat this. At Base Camp, the temperature would drop to around 10–15°F/–12 to –9°C during the night, but in the Western Cwm in the midday sunshine, sheltered from the wind, the temperature could soar above 100°F/36°C. (On Cho Oyu in May 1952, Griff Pugh recorded sun temperatures of 156°F/65°C at 19,000ft/5,790m) Then as soon as the cloud shut out the sun, within moments it was near freezing! So when the Met. Office forecast winds of 30 knots and temperatures of 20°F (6.66°C) at 21,000ft in the Western Cwm, we might, in fact, be suffering from near heat exhaustion and crying out for more iced lemonade. You get the same sort of effect in an Alpine ski resort, although not as pronounced.

The Build-up

We now had a rather more mundane period of nine days during the last week of April and early May in which we all took turns escorting teams of Sherpas carrying up stores to stock the higher camps. The Low Level Ferry operated from Base up the Icefall to Camp III and the High Level Ferry operated on to Camp IV at 21,200ft (6,460m), near the head of the Western Cwm. This was near the Swiss Camp IV site, and the first reconnaissance party to reach it on 26 April, consisting of John Hunt, Charles Evans, Ed Hillary and Tenzing, were delighted to find some abandoned delicacies: Swiss cheese, chocolate and Knäckerbröt amongst many discarded tins of pemmican! Noyce and Gregory were close behind leading the first High Level Ferry, a fine crew: fat little Gombu (Tenzing's 17-year-old nephew), Kancha (meaning 'younger brother'), who was my 'personal' Sherpa, Pasang Dawa, quiet, experienced and sensible, Tashi Phutar, Ang Tharke, Pemba Norbu and Phu Dorji.

Each day fresh snow fell, so the track, wiped out overnight, had to be remade. It was terribly exacting work, floundering in loose snow, the Sherpas struggling with a 40lb (18kg) load. By 2 May, 90 loads – a total of 1½ tons – had been lifted up to Camp III and half of them onto Camp IV, which became our Advance Base.

The next great barrier was the Lhotse Face, 4,000ft (1,220m) of steep ice walls alternating with shelving snow-covered ledges, leading to the South Col at nearly 26,000ft (7,925m), the saddle between Everest and Lhotse. As the Swiss had learned by bitter experience, it was essential to have at least one intermediate campsite which could be found by deviating onto the Lhotse Face rather than trying to climb directly up to the South Col. On 4 May, a reconnaissance party led by John Hunt, with Evans, Bourdillon, joined by Wylie and Ward, started up the Face in dismally bad weather. This vital recce was also a dress rehearsal for Everest. It would be trying out both the open- and closed-circuit oxygen equipment and would enable John Hunt to finalise the plans for the assault. They occupied Camp V, 22,000ft (6,710m) at the foot of the Face, found the beginning of the Swiss autumn route and pitched a temporary Camp VI at 23,000ft (7,010m). Next day Tom Bourdillon and Charles Evans using closed-circuit oxygen struggled upwards in atrocious snow and weather conditions to close on 24,000ft (7,315m) but, in poor visibility, there was no point in going further. At least it showed that the Lhotse Face would be as tough a problem as had been expected, and much time would have to be devoted to making a route, establishing a good intermediate camp, and getting all the stores needed up to the South Col and above. Fortunately, the experimental closed-circuit oxygen had performed satisfactorily in these colder conditions at higher altitude.

The Assault Plan

These results confirmed John in his plans and he called a meeting at Base Camp on the 7 May to outline them to the team. Almost inevitably not everyone could be present. George Lowe and I were at the time at Camp III conducting the High Level Ferry parties to Camp IV, so I will draw on Ed Hillary's account of that important meeting:

Most of the night John Hunt's light was shining and his typewriter was tapping. But when he called Evans and myself together for a conference next morning, May 7th, he was his usual drawn-faced but positive self. He invited our comments on a list he'd drawn up apportioning certain tasks in the assault to certain people. We agreed with all his selections. We crossed over to the large tent where the whole expedition was gathered, and as we went inside it was impossible not to feel the air of suppressed excitement and anticipation. Hunt started talking, and there was a sudden hush in the tent as everyone concentrated on his words. He explained his view of the problems ahead; the Lhotse Face, the establishing of a substantial camp on the South Col, the putting in of a very high camp at 28,000ft and finally the two assaults with different types of oxygen apparatus. There was nothing new about this, and on every face I could read the same thought. 'Hurry up, John! Tell us what job you've given to me!' John Hunt picked up his list and started reading, and as each name appeared with its selected task, I could hear tense lungs relaxing with a quiet hiss of satisfaction.

The tough problem of the Lhotse Face had been given to Lowe, Westmacott, and Band; the vital job of getting a large number of Sherpa porters to the South Col to Noyce and Wylie; the first assault party, using the powerful closed-circuit oxygen apparatus was to be Evans and Bourdillon; Hunt and Gregory were the support party to establish Camp IX at 28,000ft; Tenzing and I were the second assault party using the open-circuit oxygen set.

Tenzing was in the tent with us, and Hunt explained to him in his fluent Hindustani the details of the plan and the allocation of tasks. When Hunt came to his name, Tenzing smiled as though well satisfied. In fact, I think there was general satisfaction except perhaps for poor Mike Ward, who had been asked to act as a reserve. He was finding the responsibilities of being medical officer an unhappy restriction on his climbing activities.

We didn't waste any time putting the plan into operation but right from the start the Lhotse Face party became depleted. Band developed a cold and had to return to Base, and Westmacott though he tried again and again, seemed unable to drive himself much over 22,000 feet. So the burden of the task fell on the shoulders of George Lowe.

A Personal Setback

Returning to Camp III on 7 May from the High Level Ferry, I retired to my sleeping bag:

Thursday, 7.5.53
Developed sore throat, cold and headache in evening quite suddenly and felt like hell. Still managed to eat supper and slept well with some APCs (Aspirin, Phenacetin, Codeine).

I had caught a bout of 'flu, not getting better at this height, and next day agreed over the radio with John that I should descend for a day or two to recover at Lobuje where several of the others had just had a short break. I was desperately disappointed not to be able to fulfil my appointed task, and I am sure Mike Westmacott was too. Fortunately, we were a large enough team that other members, such as Noyce and Ward, were able to take over some of the work on the Lhotse Face assisting George Lowe in his Herculean task.

From my diary, I recalled that two nights previously on the Low Level Ferry, I had happily shared a tent with Tenzing at Camp II adjacent to the 'Atom Bomb Area' in the Icefall. During breakfast a large area close by had collapsed and subsided with a loud 'wurrumph'! I certainly finished off my Grapenuts quickly that morning!

With hindsight, I have occasionally wondered if while sleeping beside Tenzing in such a restricted space, we may have exchanged virulent 'flu germs of a kind that I had never previously encountered. However, there was nothing I could do about it except to recover as quickly as possible and rejoin the fray.

Lobuje was a delightful break: short grass with tiny primulae in flower; choughs, plumbeous redstarts and a rose finch hopping about. Charles Evans, the brain surgeon, gave me a haircut. Five other 'sahibs' were there, including Tom Stobart recovering from pneumonia, so after supper conversation ranged widely: 'Kingdon Ward asked me to go to Assam last summer'; 'Haven't smelt a musk deer since I was in Siam'; 'Of course, there are two sorts of African rhino . . .'

The Trials of the Lhotse Face

By 11 May, George Lowe was established at Camp VI, 23,000ft (7,010m), his only companion a tough, strong Sherpa, Ang Nyima. The two of them cut hundreds of steps, fixing ropes on the trickier sections, so the route would be possible for heavily laden porters. Noyce went up to relieve Ang Nyima and they established Camp VII at 24,000ft (7,320m), halfway up the face. One night George Lowe took sleeping pills but underestimated their effect. Noyce struggled to wake him in the morning to get going, but he kept falling asleep in his steps on the steep ice. They stopped for a bite, but with a sardine half out of his mouth, George fell asleep again. A whole day wasted!

We were now in the second phase of the build-up, continuing to escort the daily Low Level and High Level Ferries. I was back on form. On my way up, I set up the short-wave radio and aerial at Camp III on the lip of the Western Cwm and had the most marvellous reception of the BBC World Service from the Free Trade Hall, Manchester. John Barbirolli was conducting the Hallé Orchestra playing Beethoven's Leonora Overture No. 3. I think the walls of the Western Cwm and the

Lhotse Face were acting as one huge satellite dish focusing the radio waves perfectly onto my aerial. John Hunt joined me in our little tent and after receiving the Met. bulletins we listened to Scrapbook for 1929. It was the year I was born, during the Great Depression. John was 19 at the time, and very impressionable, he recalled. He was the Senior Under Officer at Sandhurst and it was his fifth Alpine climbing season. We were both almost weeping with emotion.

Most of us were now moving up to live at Camp IV, which became our Advance Base and gave a grandstand view of the Lhotse Face. Every morning we looked anxiously upwards to see if there was any activity, none more anxious than John Hunt himself. My abiding memory is of him sitting on a packing case, elbows resting on knees, smears of sun-block cream giving him an unnaturally pale face, only partly shaded by a floppy hat, eyes peering through binoculars up at the highest point reached so far. He had driven himself hard; at 42 he was the oldest of us climbers and one wondered about the extent of his reserves.

One day I strolled to the nearest moraine to pick up some geological specimens. I nearly fell into a hidden crevasse after 40 yards and could hear some running water below. Coming back again, this time accompanied by Ed, we discovered a small glacier-dammed pool with beautiful fresh water. From then on we used it for drinking and cooking instead of having to melt blocks of ice, and it saved us a lot of kerosene.

Back on the Lhotse Face, Ward and Da Tensing went up to relieve Noyce, but the wind and the cold seemed to prevent them getting any higher. I was now feeling quite fit and was glad to have a break from organising food boxes, dishing out rations, trying to repair portable radios, monitoring the Met. broadcasts and, for relaxation, reading Tolstoy's War and Peace. I welcomed the opportunity to escort a group of Sherpas up to Camp VII. I commanded a 7am start from Camp V but was inevitably delayed over breakfast when Ang Temba suddenly produced some fresh eggs brought to Base Camp by his wife. What a treat! Camp VII, 24,000ft (7,320m), was the highest I had been and pretty exhausting without oxygen, but it was exciting to be there. One was now leaving the shelter of the Western Cwm and beginning to feel the strength of the north-west wind battering the summit pyramid 5,000ft (1,510m) above, with its plume of condensation, cloud and spindrift. George and Mike gave me a cheery welcome, having a rest day after being wind-battered the day before and both getting a nip of frostbite. They planned a final bash next day in the hope of reaching the traverse line towards the top of the Geneva Spur, before descending the same evening. The radio at Camp VII had packed up, so when I got back down to IV, in two hours dead, everyone was anxious about George and Mike. Why weren't they out? It was easy to criticise from the comfort of Advance Base about lack of drive or that George Lowe had been up high for too long, despite all he had done, but in fact the momentum of our attack was slowing down and time was running out.

The South Col Carry

Drastic action was required. John Hunt decided to start the South Col 'carry' even though the route to it had not been proven. On 19 May, the first party of seven Sherpas, led by Noyce, would go up to Camp V, then on to VII on 20 May. Wylie and the second team would follow a day behind. John said to Wilf: 'If George and Michael don't manage to prepare the Traverse before they come down tomorrow, you will have to decide at Camp VII whether to carry straight on with the Sherpas next day, or go up yourself first and prepare the track.'

On 21 May, we looked up anxiously from Camp IV. Nothing happened until 10am. Then only two dots emerged from VII; it was Wilf and Annullu, using oxygen to help pave the way. They passed the previous highest point and commenced the traverse – two specks against that dazzling backcloth of whiteness – heading for the South Col.

As they topped the Geneva Spur at 26,000ft (7,925m), our mood of despair at possible failure changed to one of great excitement and hope.

They had reached the objective we had been striving to attain for 12 days. Noyce and Annullu returned, still quite fresh, but now Wylie was charged to escort both groups of Sherpas with their loads. This would be a well nigh impossible task. Hunt decided to reinforce the 'carry' by sending up Hillary and Tenzing that afternoon – the only pair that could be spared – to lead the Sherpa party across next day. Who better than Tenzing to raise their morale and inspire them?

They had a difficult night crammed into tents insufficient for so large a party, nor could they manage a proper breakfast before starting, just a mug of tea and no nourishment at all for some. On 22 May from 8.30am, the entire caravan of 17 was spread out along the Traverse. One Sherpa faltered, but Wylie took over his load. In one go, nearly all our required supplies had been lifted to the Col over the Spur at 26,000ft, equivalent to the height of Annapurna, the highest peak yet climbed. It was the Sherpas' finest hour. The assault was on!

The First Assault

Next day, the first assault pair, Bourdillon and Evans, with their support, John Hunt, Da Namgyal and Ang Tensing, climbed up to Camp VII on the Lhotse Face, meeting and congratulating the South Col Sherpas as they descended. The following day, at a snail's pace, they repeated the climb and long traverse upwards, not topping the Geneva Spur until 4pm. From there, they could gaze up at the South Summit of Everest, 'an elegant snow spire', no longer appearing so foreshortened but rising like a new mountain 3,000ft (915m) above them. Just below them were the icy wind-blown wastes of the South Col, a place the Swiss climbers said 'smelt of death'. They moved towards some crushed remnants of the Swiss tents and tried to erect their own Pyramid tent, but the wind was blowing so fiercely. They struggled for over an hour before collapsing exhausted inside, to make a brew of four mugfuls each, lemonade, soup, tea and cocoa, before settling down for the night. It was clear next morning, but they were not ready to start. Ang Tensing was sick. The oxygen had to be prepared, so they spent the day sorting themselves out and resting.

Although the route up to the South Col had been prepared mostly without using oxygen, it was the principle for the assault parties to use oxygen from Advance Base, so as to conserve their energy. At night, two climbers could also share oxygen at a low rate of 1 litre per minute each, splitting the supply at a T-piece and using soft, pliable masks. This enabled them to sleep much better, waking automatically when the shared cylinder was exhausted.

The 26 May was Bourdillon and Evans' great day. To describe it in some detail, I have had privileged access to Tom's personal report which he wrote for John Hunt and which, in addition to his diary, his widow, Jennifer, has just donated to The Alpine Club.

They slept well, and woke as they had planned at 5am. They had reduced their early morning preparations to a minimum – in Tom's case no more than tightening the lacing of his boots and putting on sun goggles – and last-minute checks of their oxygen apparatus. Breakfast consisted of two Thermos flasks of lemon juice. At 6am, they were ready to start, but as soon as Charles began moving he found his oxygen set to be faulty. The conditions were very difficult, intense cold and a high wind – one could not remove gloves for more than a few seconds without risking frostbitten fingers – and it took them one and a half hours to find and cure the fault. Tom had to replace the continuously variable oxygen supply valve on Charles's set with a fixed aperture, giving a nominal 2 litres a minute. This was a major disadvantage, being much less economical in the use of oxygen, and hence limiting their endurance, and also limiting the maximum effort Charles could make over short periods. Their earlier excitement was now tempered with some gloom, for the combinaton of the loss of 90 minutes, the use of some of their oxygen, and a reduction in their endurance, severely reduced their chances of reaching the summit.

However, they were soon cheered by the excellent pace they were able to make over the first easy ground. John Hunt had started some 20 minutes before them with Da Namgyal to establish a high camp for use by the second assault party. Tom and Charles passed them on the first steepening of the snow slopes of the great couloir below and to the left of the Ridge proper – they were wearing open-circuit apparatus and were clearly putting forth a magnificent effort. The incident served to show the superiority at this altitude of the closed-circuit apparatus which Tom and Charles were using, in which one breathes nearly pure oxygen, over the open-circuit, in which one breathes air with some added oxygen. At about 27,350ft (8,340m), John and Da Namgyal reached the limit of their powers – John not realising until later that ice had probably been partially blocking the flow of oxygen to his mask – so they left their loads and descended as Bourdillon and Evans pressed on upward above the Snow Shoulder.

The couloir steepened, but fortunately the snow continued to be mostly good, and they made rapid progress up its bed until it became too steep, when they broke out over the rock wall on the right. There followed some mixed rock and snow, and they arrived on the crest of the ridge at the place where Lambert and Tenzing had camped before their very gallant climb last spring.

For a few minutes, they sat on the tattered remains of the Swiss tent and rested. The situation seemed promising. They had climbed from 25,800ft (7,860m) to 27,300ft (8,320m) in 1½ hours over ground not at all easy, but were still reasonably fresh. Before them lay 1,400ft (425m) of climbing to the South Peak, and then a rise of 330ft (100m) along 1,115ft (340m) of torturous ridge to the true summit.

From that camp, conditions became much worse. They were moving part of the time on hard snow covered with ankle-deep powder snow, the ground was very slow and tiring to cover, particularly with their short pointed crampons, and part of the time they were on rock, again covered with powder snow, which is almost as bad.

After two hours' going, they were no more than halfway between Lambert's camp and the South Peak, and on finding a reasonably secure place decided to change their canisters and cylinders. They were carrying one oxygen cylinder and absorbent canister for the first half of the day and a second pair for the latter half. As Tom said, this was a nervous business, for on previous occasions they had found that the sudden introduction of the cold canister to the circuit caused the valves to freeze up. While lower down this might have been no more than a nuisance, at this altitude they were not at all sure how drastic the sudden cessation of the oxygen supply might be in its effects.

However, they had spent the night with the second canisters in their sleeping bags and had since taken what care they could to keep them from getting too cold. All went well. They set off again up the ridge, which was a fine, narrow, snow knife-edge, with considerably lighter burdens – about 25lb (11kg) each instead of 45lb (20kg).

Charles soon began to experience an abnormally high ventilation rate. This grew worse, and it became clear that his second canister had been damaged, and that severe channelling was occurring. This was a bitter blow. He was able to continue climbing, but only at a low rate, and with greatly disproportionate effort.

For the next two hours, they climbed on steep snow. As Tom said later: 'In the Alps, at a reasonable altitude and in warmer conditions, it would have been very enjoyable.' The South Peak of Everest seen from the Col is a slender snow spire which is very different from the brutal rock massif that is Everest from the north.

As it was, they were both becoming tired. At the top end of the rope, Tom was obsessed with the need for speed if they were to stretch their fast-expiring time limit to allow them to cover the summit ridge, and Evans at the lower end was having to put forth Herculean effort to keep going with his defective canister.

At last the angle eased and, with surprising suddenness, they were on the top of the South Summit. It was a great moment. They were higher than anyone on earth had been before, and now that the labour of ascent had stopped, the beauty of their surroundings staggered even their tired brains. Before them, the final summit ridge was a wonderful sight; mixed rock and snow lines sweeping up from the left and great ice cornices overhanging the very steep right edge. It was a wilder and more fantastic ridge than either of them had seen before in the Himalayas or the Alps. Below and behind, the Cwm looked like nothing so much as a plaster relief model. All the country they had covered in 1951 and 1952 lay exposed save for occasional cloud wreaths.

Tom said he found it impossible to describe. He was only grateful for having experienced it, and hoped that the photographs would show something, although probably, as in the aerial photographs, they would fail to convey depth.

For a while, they sat and ate sugar. Charles had expended himself in climbing the last stretch while breathing a high percentage of carbon dioxide. Whilst this was a wonderful effort, he and Tom both knew that now there was no possibility of his going on. Tom was in slightly better shape, but realised that if he went on alone he should not have enough oxygen for the descent. They had already had an alarming experience of the deacclimatising effect of the high oxygen pressures obtained with the closed-circuit apparatus, and they did not expect to be able to get down without oxygen. So, reluctantly, they turned back down. Later, they were to be shown how correct this decision was by their dramatic descent to the South Col.

The descent proved a nightmare that Tom hoped he would forget. At first, he was able to protect Charles from the effects of minor slips on the difficult ground. He, of course, was still breathing a high percentage of carbon dioxide, and since the apparatus was capable of conversion to open circuit, they tried this. However, the high carbon dioxide pressure was found preferable to the low oxygen pressure and they soon changed back. Towards the end, they were both far too tired to be safe on ground of that difficulty, and they were very lucky to get down without injury, if not without some spectacular slides. It was a very great relief to be welcomed onto the safe ground of the South Col by the party there.

John had been very careful in briefing Tom and Charles. He had told them to make the South Summit at 28,700ft (8,750m) their primary objective, and only carry on if three things held true: first, the weather was reasonable; second, their oxygen was working properly; and third, they were both feeling able to tackle the final ridge and return safely. As we have seen, all was not in their favour. Having made the difficult but correct decision to turn back, on their way down they were able to leave two partly filled cylinders of oxygen behind for later use by Hillary and Tenzing. Tom and Charles reached the tents on the South Col at 4.30pm, utterly weary, ice caking their eyebrows and hair, looking in their bulky clothing like two creatures from another planet. It was a prodigious effort and an historic achievement.

The Second Assault

The day before, Hillary and Tenzing had started from Advance Base for the second assault. Greg had given me a roll of his best Kodachrome film for my borrowed Contax, so I took pictures of the pair, both on their departure and return. You can see in the photograph, wrapped around Tenzing's ice axe, tightly furled, the flags which he was hoping to wave on the summit: the United Nations, the Union Jack, and the flags of India and Nepal. (The small Union Jack, incidentally, had come from the Embassy's official car: a gift from the Ambassador to John Hunt, as we had not thought of bringing one.) Also note that Tenzing preferred to use his Swiss high altitude boots, incorporating reindeer fur, rather than our 'Bradley' boots, which Hillary was wearing.

Greg and three Sherpas accompanied them in support. George Lowe, always ready for another job, had persuaded John Hunt that he should join them, escorting another small group of Sherpas taking additional stores to the South Col. Shortly before the group reached the South

Col, through a gap in the clouds, one of the Sherpas saw two tiny figures – Evans and Bourdillon – approaching the highest point: higher than anyone had ever trodden before. 'Everest khatm hogya, Sahib,' he shoute; 'Everest has had it.' But he did not realise that this was just the South Summit. You could not see the main summit from there – along a further 370 (340m) yards of sheer-sided ridge.

It was an overcrowded camp on the South Col that night, both first and second assault parties and their support teams squeezed into three tents: the Pyramid, the Meade and the tiny 'Blister' tent. Buffeted by a gale, they had little sleep. It was still blowing like mad in the morning so the next assault was postponed a day. In a brief interval, Evans, Bourdillon and Ang Temba, who was sick, descended with the support of John Hunt, as Tom was in a critical state after trying to get over the hump of the Geneva Spur. Charles Evans seemed the only rational member of the party. Hillary whispered in his ear, 'For God's sake, Charles, keep an eye on John! He's out on his feet but doesn't realise it!' Charles turned on him his warm and friendly smile and said, 'Don't worry, Ed – I'll get them down!' The four of them moved off. Now those of us who would be remaining at Advance Base had little to do except await the outcome of the second assault, on which all our hopes rested.

To the Top!

Back on the South Col on 28 May, the wind eased and they decided to start. Pemba was ill and only one Sherpa, Ang Nyima, who had worked with George Lowe on the Lhotse Face, was fit to continue out of the original band of three. So it was good that George Lowe was there and able to help carry the camp. He had also learned how to use a small Bell and Howell movie camera brought by Tom Stobart, and George did all the filming above 22,000ft (6,710m), capturing some of the most moving sequences in the expedition's film. At 8.45am, Lowe, Gregory and Ang Nyima set off, carrying 40lb (18kg) each and breathing oxygen at 4 litres per minute, Hillary and Tenzing following later up the freshly cut steps to save their energy. They reached the ridge at noon and joined the other party close to the bare skeleton and tattered yellow shreds of the tent shared by Lambert and Tenzing a year previously. They moved on confidently another 150ft (45m) to the dump left by Hunt and Da Namgyal, which they had to add to their already heavy loads. Hillary was now carrying 63lb (29kg) and the others around 50lb (23kg) each, so they continued more slowly but steadily, looking for a suitable ledge for the tent. Growing a little desperate, Tenzing remembering the ground suggested a traverse to the left where there was a relatively flat spot. It was 2.30pm, at an estimated 27,900ft (8,500m). Lowe, Gregory and Ang Nyima dropped their loads with relief and hurried off down the mountainside.

Hillary and Tenzing pitched their tent on a sort of double ledge; Tenzing heated soup and Ed checked the oxygen for the morrow. They drank lots of liquid and munched sardines on biscuits, tinned apricots, dates, jam and honey. They had four hours' sleeping with oxygen. Looking out at 4am, it was very still. Down at Thyangboche, even now the monks might be praying for the expedition's safety. On a thermometer I had lent to Hillary, he noticed the temperature was –27°C. After more liquid – lemon juice and sugar – and the last tin of sardines and biscuits, they crawled out of their tent into the sunshine and hoisted on their 30lb (14kg) of oxygen, which amounted to two cylinders each – one full, the other only two-thirds full. They were ready to go on 3 litres per minute.

They reached their first objective, the South Peak, at 9am and for the first time had a clear view of the final ridge, certainly impressive, even rather frightening. On the left or west side, mixed terrain of rock and ice plunged 8,000ft (2,440m) down to the Western Cwm. On the right, a long ice slope, overhung by fragile-looking cornices, swept 9,000ft (2,740m) down to the Kangshung Glacier in Tibet. They could take their choice! Keeping on the west side close to the junction between the rock and ice, Hillary led off, cutting steps, Tenzing belaying him on the rope.

They moved one at a time, each protecting the other. To Hillary's relief, the snow was crystalline and firm. After 40ft (12m), he brought Tenzing along and they continued. In an hour, they had reached the 40ft rock step which we had seen from aerial photographs. The rock itself seemed smooth and almost holdless but between it and the icy cornice to the right, there was a wide crack. Hillary was able to jam himself in it; his back on the ice, hands searching for every little hold, crampons scrabbling below, and somehow, with all the energy he could muster, force his way up. Breathless at the top, but triumphant, he felt that nothing could stop them now. He gave Tenzing a tight rope and he, in turn, 'collapsed at the top like a giant fish just hauled from the sea'. Tenzing later took exception to that phrase, but I can just imagine how he felt at the time! They continued as before, their original zest gone. It was becoming a grim struggle but then Hillary realised that the ridge ahead, instead of continuing to rise, now dropped sharply away. I can't improve on his words:

I looked upwards to see a narrow snow ridge running up to a snowy summit. A few more whacks of the ice axe in the firm snow and we stood on top.

My initial feelings were of relief – relief that there were no more steps to cut, no more ridges to traverse and no more humps to tantalize us with hopes of success. I looked at Tenzing and in spite of the balaclava, goggles and oxygen mask that concealed his face, there was no disguising his infectious grin of pure delight. It was 11.30am. The ridge had taken us two and a half hours, but it seemed like a lifetime.

We shook hands and then Tenzing threw his arms around my shoulders and we thumped each other on the back until we were almost breathless. I turned off the oxygen and removed my set. I had carried my camera, loaded with colour film, inside my shirt to keep it warm, so I now produced it and got Tenzing to pose for me on the top, waving his ice axe on which was a string of flags – British, Nepalese, United Nations and Indian. Then I turned my attention to the great stretch of country lying below us. To the east was our giant neighbour Makalu, unexplored and unclimbed. Far away across the clouds the great bulk of Kangchenjunga loomed on the horizon. To the west, Cho Oyu dominated the scene. The most important photograph, I felt, was a shot down the North Ridge showing the route made famous by those great climbers of the 1920s and 1930s.

Meanwhile, Tenzing had made a little hole in the snow and in it he placed various articles of food together with the flags. Small offerings, indeed, but at least a token gift to the Gods; all devout Buddhists believe they have their home on this lofty summit. Two days before, Hunt had given me a small crucifix which he asked me to take to the top. I placed it beside Tenzing's gifts.

People often ask: 'Why is there no photograph of Hillary standing on the summit of Everest?' He replies: 'Well in those days, Tenzing didn't know how to operate a camera and I felt this wasn't quite the place to start teaching him!'

After 15 minutes they turned to descend. Their oxygen lasted back to their tent, where Tenzing made a lemon drink while Hillary changed to the cylinders left by Evans and Bourdillon which, in turn, lasted them almost to the South Col camp. George Lowe and Wilf Noyce were there in support and came to meet them with hot soup and spare oxygen.

'Well,' said Ed to George in their New Zealand slang, 'We knocked the bastard off!' He was striking, I think, a friendly adversarial note, not a triumphant one. Many people talk about the 'conquest' of Everest but we, in our team, do not, counting ourselves very lucky to have been the first to succeed. The great mountain has hardly been subdued. It is still there, in fair weather or foul, ready to accept or casually brush off the challenge of future mountaineers.

Next day, after a more leisurely start, the four descended to Camp VII where Wylie and several Sherpas plied them with hot drinks before they carried on down to Advance Base, where the rest of the team was waiting. Our radios were not working then, so we would not know of their success or failure until we actually met them, so you can imagine the fever pitch of excitement and anticipation in camp. Hoping to catch it live on film, Tom Stobart had gone up some way with his heavy camera and tripod. Earlier I had turned on the radio and picked up an Indian news bulletin that said the expedition had failed and was withdrawing from the mountain before the monsoon broke. All sorts of totally unfounded rumours were flying around!

Then, 100 yards or more from camp, the returning party appeared over the crest of a snow slope. Sahibs and Sherpas all emerged from the tents and we quickened our pace towards them. Mike Westmacott was well ahead. None of us could muster the strength to run! It was an emotional meeting superbly captured by Stobart: handshakes all round but unrestrained hugs by John for Hillary and Tenzing – a victory both for himself and for his people. One veteran Sherpa, his pigtail flowing behind him, bowed gravely to touch Tenzing's hand with his forehead. Others bent forward with respect, their hands clasped as if in prayer. Joyfully, we strolled back together and sat them down for a lemon drink, munching salmon omelette as they talked. Then, quite naturally, Tenzing slipped into the Sherpas' tent and Hillary into our mess tent to tell us the whole story.

James Morris's Scoop

James Morris, with consummate timing, had arrived at Advance Base that morning, to earn the scoop of his life for The Times. To get a message off to Namche next morning, he had to start down again that afternoon, so Mike Westmacott led him down through the now thawing and crumbling Icefall in an epic race with the darkness.

By the light of a flickering hurricane lamp, James typed out the short message in a deliberately misleading code, pre-arranged with John Hunt and the editors of The Times to confuse their competitors, but still hopefully acceptable for transmission by the Indian Army radio station we had discovered at Namche. This message would be passed to their Embassy in Kathmandu who, in turn, would convey it to the British Embassy. It read: 'SNOW CONDITIONS BAD STOP ADVANCE BASE ABANDONED YESTERDAY STOP AWAITING IM-

PROVEMENT STOP ALL WELL', which being interpreted would mean: 'summit of Everest reached on May 29 by Hillary and Tenzing'. The first three words – 'Snow conditions bad'– meant that Everest had been climbed. The rest referred to Hillary and Tenzing. Each climber was identified by a phrase which could reasonably refer to events on the mountain:

BAND:	SOUTH COL UNTENABLE
BOURDILLON:	LHOTSE FACE IMPOSSIBLE
EVANS:	RIDGE CAMP UNTENABLE
GREGORY:	WITHDRAWAL TO WEST BASIN
HILLARY:	ADVANCE BASE ABANDONED
HUNT:	CAMP FIVE ABANDONED
LOWE:	CAMP SIX ABANDONED
NOYCE:	CAMP SEVEN ABANDONED
TENZING:	AWAITING IMPROVEMENT
WARD:	FURTHER NEWS FOLLOWS
WESTMACOTT:	ASSAULT POSTPONED
WYLIE:	WEATHER DETERIORATING
SHERPA:	AWAITING OXYGEN SUPPLIES.

Back in Advance Base that evening, we talked and talked, scarcely daring to believe that Everest had at last been climbed after so many gallant failures. The sun set after a perfect day, making the face of Lhotse glow like fire and gilding the crags of Everest high on the left. A full moon rose overhead. We began to realise that although we had formed a wonderful team, we had grown sick and tired of life at high altitude and would be glad to descend. We were leaving behind us not an enemy we had conquered but a mountain that had been a friend. A friend in allowing two members of our party – it did not really matter which two – to ascend for a few privileged moments to its summit and now for all of us – Sherpas and climbers – to return to our homes.

Three days later we were safely off the mountain and gathered at Base Camp, all thanks to Mike Westmacott and his group of Sherpas who had done a great job keeping the perilous route down the Icefall open to ensure we would not be cut off.

It was 2 June. I tuned in the radio and on the Overseas Service we picked up fragments of the Coronation Service. Then shortly after came the staid formal tones of the BBC announcer reading the news:

> Her Majesty the Queen was crowned today in Westminster Abbey. Crowds waiting in the Mall also heard that Mount Everest had been climbed by the British Expedition. Messages of congratulations have been sent to the Leader, Colonel Hunt, by Her Majesty and the Prime Minister, Sir Winston Churchill.

The news of our achievement had hit the world. We were dumbfounded that it had got back so soon. James Morris had earned his scoop. It was just the official confirmation we needed to believe it ourselves! 'A lively evening', is the terse note in my diary. 'Finished off the rum. Sick as a dog!'

The next evening just after the BBC news broadcast, we received a special message from Sir Edwin Herbert, President of the Joint Himalayan Committee, followed by one from Joy Hunt to her husband, our leader; 'Hallo, darling,' she said, 'we are all so thrilled by the great news . . .' But none of us, even John Hunt, can remember what followed, we were so overcome by this very personal link with home.

Next day, we used our avalanche gun for the first time, firing off all the bombs we had brought, as a salute to the Queen. The Sherpas loved it and the mighty peaks around us reverberated to our tribute.

Over the years, the myth has grown up that the news of our success was deliberately held back a few days to add an extra sense of triumph to the Coronation. On the contrary, it was sent back as fast as possible. James's messenger ran with it 20 miles (32km) to the radio station on 31 May. The Indian Vice-Consul forwarded it on 1 June to our

Ambassador, Sir Christopher Summerhayes, who scribbled in the margin 'arr. 17.45 hrs' before he sent a confidential telegram to the Foreign Office in London. The Foreign Office informed *The Times*, where the news was received 'around tea time', still on 1 June. So the Queen was given the news on the eve of the Coronation and it was in all the newspapers the next day.

Why Did We Succeed?

What were the reasons for our success? One can cite several factors, all of which contributed:

- Building on the experience and determination of those who had tried before us.
- The extra impetus of competition, knowing that if we failed, the Swiss, the French, the Americans and others were burning to beat us to it.
- The research of those, such as Griff Pugh, Dr Bradley, and the developers of our oxygen sets, who all helped to ensure that our acclimatisation, clothing and equipment were better than ever before.
- The meticulous preparations, planning and inspired leadership of John Hunt in choosing a strong team of both climbers and Sherpas who worked superbly together and have remained good friends.
- Finally, one might add the thoughts and prayers of all those who followed us in spirit and hoped for our success.

Was it worthwhile? John Hunt expressed it for the whole team:

> For us who took part in the venture, it was so beyond doubt. We have shared a high endeavour; we have witnessed scenes of beauty and grandeur; we have built up a lasting comradeship among ourselves and we have seen the fruits of that

comradeship ripen into achievement. We shall not forget those moments of great living upon that mountain.

The two poems below were written by Wilfrid Noyce.

THE SOUTH COL
In retrospect from the plains

Great hill above
And cloud below;
Reckless of love
The fast winds blow.
But all between
Is space beyond dead;
Spirits unseen
Here make their bed
In blackened rock-rift
And ice rubbed bare,
Crusted snow-drift
That blizzards tear.
Long ago
These were the same,
Never small, never slow,
Never soft, never tame.
What are men here?
What have they done?
A heap of rags here,
Yellow and brown.

BREATHLESS
Written at 21,200ft on 23 May, 1953

Heart aches,
Lungs pant
The dry air
Sorry, scant.
Legs lift
And why at all?
Loose drift,
Heavy fall.
Prod the snow
Its easiest way;
A flat step
Is holiday.
Look up,
The far stone
Is many miles
Far and alone.
Grind the breath
Once more and on;
Don't look up
Till journey's done.

Must look up,
Glasses are dim.
Wrench of hand
Is breathless limb.
Pause one step,
Breath swings back;
Swallow once,
Dry throat is slack.
Then on
To the far stone;
Don't look up,
Count the steps done.
One step,
One heart-beat,
Stone no nearer
Dragging feet.
Heart aches,
Lungs pant
The dry air
Sorry, scant.

07

Aftermath – The Other Everest

'Everest – The Crowning Glory.'   Daily Mail, Tuesday, June 2nd 1953

Coming down from the mountain, we now had to face what Wilf Noyce called 'The Other Everest', an avalanche of publicity and razzmatazz far beyond anything we could have imagined.

The 4 June was our last night together as an expedition. In the afternoon, we had enjoyed a display of 'Devil Dancing' by the monks at Thyangboche Monastery. After supper our own Sherpas began dancing beside the camp fire, in a long line, arms linked, men at one end, women at the other, swaying and stomping their feet in a regular rhythm to the accompaniment of rather sad and mournful singing. We sang our songs in between the dances and then joined in.

Charles Evans had always planned to stay in Khumbu for further exploration and survey and, being strong-minded, saw no reason to change his plans. John, Greg and Tom Bourdillon formed an advance party to get to Kathmandu as quickly as possible while the rest of us would start as soon as enough porters had been mustered to carry all the expedition's equipment.

During the walk back the monsoon had broken and, as we traipsed over the misty mountains, our umbrellas became indispensable. One afternoon, I was walking with Ed and George when the dak runner arrived with our mail. On top was a handwritten note from John addressed to Sir Edmund Hillary, KBE, the last three letters heavily underlined. George, wearing his broad-brimmed hat with a long feather in it, bowed low like an Elizabethan courtier and, with a deferential flourish, proffered the letter: 'Your mail, Sir Edmund.' 'What's this,' snorted Ed, 'some kind of a joke?. But it was true! In the upsurge of emotion, in the days following the Coronation, the Queen had approved a Knighthood for John Hunt, and the KBE for Ed, which in protocol ranked marginally higher than John's award but had, I believe, been pressed for by the New Zealand Government, and a George Medal for Tenzing, who was not, of course, a British subject, so did not qualify for an 'Order of the British Empire', but instead received this highest award for valour.

It was only then we began to realise that for a week, after the receipt of James Morris's coded telegram, the world press knew nothing about the details of our success except the bare names of Hillary and Tenzing. The press had to wait for John Hunt's detailed story, carried by a runner for six days to Kathmandu, to be published exclusively by The Times on 8 June, and Ed Hillary's personal account not until 26 and 27 June. So it was not surprising that the reporting in the interim was somewhat unbalanced, giving special prominence to Hillary and Tenzing for their wonderful feat rather than to the total success of the team. If the Honours Committee had had the time or inclination to consult us, we would have fully supported the knighthood for John Hunt, as leader, with some more modest award for each of the team members. In fact, the Queen later presented Coronation Medals to each of us at Buckingham Palace with 'Mount Everest Expedition' engraved on the rim, at her request, which makes them a very special award. Fortunately, both Ed and Tenzing took the Honours in their stride. 'I think I'll have to buy a new pair of dungarees,' said Ed, 'when I go out to deliver my honey.'

Within days, the dak runner was bringing copies of the Coronation Day newspapers with their banner headlines 'EVEREST – THE

CROWNING GLORY'; 'ALL THIS AND EVEREST TOO', together with mail from our loved ones, congratulating us and telling how the news broke to the crowds waiting in the Mall and all along the procession route on that rainy summer morning.

At our last camp, John came out to join us, together with his wife Joy, who had flown from England. They warned us of the reception we would be receiving in Kathmandu.

Return to Kathmandu

As we came closer to the city, reporters from Indian and Nepali newspapers came out to meet us, together with some politically minded gentlemen keen to see Tenzing before anybody else did. At the pass near Banepa, we were met by Colonel Proud of the British Embassy with beer, plums and cake! Then soon we were caught up in the crowds, with people cheering, chanting and pressing around. Tenzing, John and Ed, all garlanded and smeared with red Holi powder, were segregated in a state coach filled with flowers, and pulled by four horses; Tenzing, seated high in the centre, facing forward, looked bewildered but exalted, with his wife and daughters below him; John and Ed were seated in a sort of pit below Tenzing, facing to the rear. The crowd surged around them. 'Tenzing Zindabad,' they shouted. 'Hail Tenzing, first man to conquer the Everest!' The procession slowed as we entered the narrow streets adorned with triumphal arches, graffiti and placards. There was a banner depicting Tenzing on top of Everest waving an ice axe and Hillary on his knees in the bottom right-hand corner being hauled up by the rope. They paused at the Town Hall, opposite a five-storey pagoda, for speeches and then pressed on. The rest of us got separated and were given lifts by our kind Embassy staff. Somehow, two or three of us missed out but the others ended up at the Royal Palace around 7pm. Wilf Noyce described the scene:

Were we to go up dirty, unshaven, in our shorts? Uniformed Nepalis seemed to be expecting us; up we went. We were in a lofty hall with decorated roof and chandeliers on the pattern of the Victorian 1850s. Men and women in a variety of costumes were taking their seats along the sides; we did likewise, finding ourselves opposite the Ministers in their black frock-coats and tight white trousers. I was near Griff, who still wore the now very grey pyjamas in which he always walked, because the sun on his legs burned him, he said. His spectacles surveyed the scene with interest: the first time surely that an investiture has been attended, or a king had his hand shaken, by a man clad in pyjamas.

All at last took their places. The three red-smeared figures, looking even less reputable than before, were seated in the centre of the left-hand wall. They now seemed very weary; they had in fact had no food or drink since the meeting with Colonel Proud at eleven that morning. Tenzing was conducted to the King at the end of the hall and decorated with the Star of Nepal, first-class. John and Ed received very portly medals. Finally the whole assembly moved back to the fresh air under the pillars. The King shook hands with each of us, and the whole expedition was photographed, with the Ministers beside. This greeting was pleasantly unceremonious, the King being dressed in simple Nepali costume and wearing the national hat; Griff, of course, in pyjamas.

After 7.30 in the evening a group of very tired men with grateful hearts was conveyed to the British Embassy; to food, to a bath, to sleep between the sheets of a bed.

Who Got to the Top First?

We were quite glad to escape from some aspects of Kathmandu, eventually. In the minds of the more political journalists, Tenzing, a son of Nepal, had shown the world the way up Everest. To them it was most important that Tenzing had reached the top first, rather than Hillary, and they pressured Tenzing into signing a statement that he had done so. This was unfair on Tenzing and unfortunate for him. It had never occurred to us that this might be an issue; a pair of roped climbers climb as a team and which one makes the final step onto the summit is totally irrelevant. It had been John Hunt's special wish, which we all supported, to include an outstanding Sherpa in one of the assault parties, to give recognition and to pay tribute to the work and achievement of all the Sherpas on the expedition which contributed so much to our success. It was wonderful that Tenzing was able to fulfil this role. John Hunt was able to help defuse the issue by producing a statement jointly agreed by Hillary and Tenzing that they reached the summit 'almost together'.

It was a whirlwind journey back, meeting the President of India and the Prime Minister, Mr Nehru, in Delhi. The Times kindly paid for our air passages instead of us having to return by sea. Tenzing and his wife Ang Lamu and their two teenage daughters, Nima and Pem Pem, came with us. Looking down as we flew over the Suez Canal, I remember George Lowe explaining to the two girls about this great man-made ditch dug by hundreds of workers to connect two seas together. 'Yes,' observed Pem Pem, 'wasn't it built by Ferdinand de Lesseps?'

High Life in London

On 3 July, we landed at London Airport. After meeting our friends and loved ones, an investiture of a rather different kind awaited us at Buckingham Palace. Griff Pugh had changed from his pyjamas to immaculate morning dress. That evening there was a Government reception at the newly refurbished Lancaster House, followed by dinner hosted by Lord Woolton in place of Sir Winston Churchill, who was indisposed. Sadly, I never had another chance to meet him. We finished off the Government's last and best 1929 Bordeaux, which Tenzing imbibed with gusto, causing an aged peer to exclaim, 'I can see that your Mr Tenzing appreciates a really good claret!'

One of the popular questions we would be asked on these occasions was 'How high did you get?' Gregory would reply that he helped to carry the final camp to 27,900ft (8,500m), where Hillary and Tenzing spent the night below the South Summit which earlier had been reached only by Evans and Bourdillon. 'Ah,' said the questioner, perhaps imagining that when John Hunt fired a starting gun at Base Camp, we would all rush for the top, 'that means you came fifth!'

Slotted in between dinners and receptions, we all travelled by train to the Lake District to spend the weekend with Eric Shipton who was then Warden of the Outward Bound Centre at Eskdale. We wanted to pay tribute to all his earlier achievements on Everest. He was a generous host; after a fine day's climbing, we had a wet day on the River Esk borrowing the Centre's canoes. Tom Bourdillon, George Lowe and I shared an open Canadian canoe but we capsised at almost the first opportunity. In the ensuing rapids, George was floundering and shouting incoherently, 'I've lost my teeth!' He had to phone the Expedition Office to make a dental appointment on the Monday instead of having lunch with the Lord Mayor of London at the Guildhall, where he couldn't have got past the soup course. The story had a happy ending. Some days later, a lady was walking beside the River Esk with her dog which stopped to retrieve something unusual amongst the pebbles. It was George's set of false teeth, washed ashore but still firmly locked together! Having read about the incident in the local paper, she was able to return them only slightly chipped in a neat parcel addressed to the Royal Geographical Society.

The following winter, and indeed for many years after, we responded to the popular demand for lectures, initially in all the major cities and later to schools and societies. I myself spoke on six occasions in the Royal Festival Hall. In the larger concert halls, we were able to charge the same ticket prices as if Barbirolli were conducting the Hallé Orchestra, so within a year, together with receipts from the Everest film and John Hunt's book The Ascent of Everest, we were able to raise sufficient funds to set up the charitable Mount Everest Foundation to support exploration and research in mountain regions.

⬆ Jack Longland crossing a Tibetan river in 1933

⬇ The 1938 team: Warren, Lloyd, Tilman, Oliver, Smythe, Odell, Shipton

↑ Shipton's 1951 Everest panorama from 20,000ft (6,100m) on Pumori. Hillary stands bottom right

→ The 1951 team: Shipton, Murray, Bourdillon, Riddiford, with Ward and Hillary seated

← Cooling off in the Arun River during the monsoon – Shipton, Ward and Murray

↑ The Swiss enter the Western Cwm, 1952

← A crevasse bars entry to the Western Cwm, 1951

↓ Shipton's snapshot of a yeti footprint, with ice axe, 1951

← Glaciologist Maynard M. Miller sample profiling the great crevasse, 1963

↓ Sunset over Lhotse; full moon overhead, 1953

↑ Everest's South Summit from the top of the Geneva Spur, 1952

↑ The terrifying Hindu god Black Bhairab in Old Kathmandu

↑ Band instructs Hunt on the 'walkie-talkie'

↑ A Sherpani combs and greases her boyfriend's hair

↑ Thyangboche Camp under snow, 1953, with the monastery behind

↑ Indian Air Force photograph, with our 1953 route and camps

↑ The great Khumbu Icefall. Three climbers
at top centre

↓ Low Level Ferry – Band leading

↑ Evans on first ascent of
South Summit, 26 May 1953

↓ The whole team (except
Westmacott) in the
Western Cwm

↑ Tenzing on top! 11.30am,
29 May 1953

↑ The final ridge from the South Summit, with the 'Hillary Step' halfway along

← Tenzing and Hillary leave Camp IV for the second assault

↑ Haston climbing the
Hillary Step, banked in snow,
24 September 1975

↓ Junko Tabei, first woman
on top, 16 May 1975

→ Webster climbs the 'Jaws
of Doom', 1988

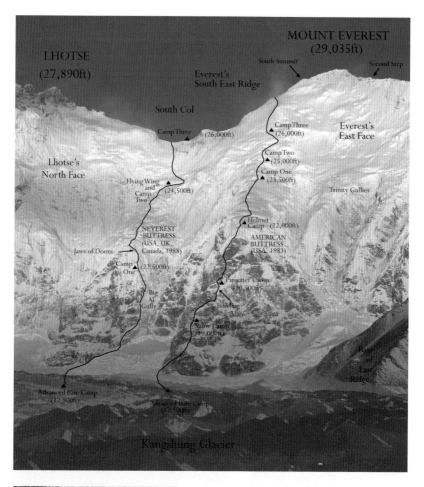

LHOTSE
(27,890ft)

MOUNT EVEREST
(29,035ft)

South Summit

Second Step

Everest's
South East Ridge

South Col

Camp Three
(26,000ft)

Camp Three
(26,000ft)

Everest's
East Face

Lhotse's
North Face

Camp Two
(25,000ft)
Camp One
(23,500ft)

Flying Wing
and
Camp Two
(24,500ft)

Trinity Gullies

NEVEREST
BUTTRESS
(USA, UK,
Canada, 1988)

Helmet
Camp (22,000ft)

AMERICAN
BUTTRESS
(USA, 1983)

Jaws of Doom

Camp
One
(22,500ft)

Big
Al
Gully

Pinsetter Camp
(20,500ft)

Bowling
Alley

Snow Camp
(19,000ft)

Base
of
East
Ridge

Advanced Base Camp
(17,800ft)

Advanced Base Camp
(17,500ft)

Kangshung Glacier

↑ Kangshung Face showing the 1983 and 1988 routes

← Venables iced up after summitting

↓ Venables' frostbitten toes

↓↑←→↖↘↗↙

↑ Band, Westmacott, Lowe, Wylie of the 1953 team meet the Queen and Duke of Edinburgh at the 50th Anniversary, 29 May 2003

↑ Hillary and Hunt at the 45th Anniversary Reunion, Pen-y-Gwryd, 1998

Life Goes On

Certainly Everest changed all our lives to a greater or lesser degree. Seven of us survived to celebrate the 50th Anniversary of that first ascent. I would like to pay my personal repects to those who have passed on.

Tom Bourdillon was sadly killed, together with Dick Viney, in a climbing accident on the ascent of the East Buttress of the Jägihorn in the Bernese Oberland in 1956.

Wilfrid Noyce, after the success of his book *South Col*, was able to give up teaching modern languages at Charterhouse to devote himself to writing prose and poetry. He also was killed, with Robin Smith, while descending Peak Garmo in the Russian Pamirs in 1962.

Tom Stobart, after the great success of his Everest film, continued his adventurous life as a cameraman, being shot in the leg in Ethiopia when an armed guard ran amok. He was not an easy person to contact as he was never keen to let the Inland Revenue know his exact whereabouts, but I think he died in 1978. When, during the trek back to Kathmandu, we were reading a sheaf of congratulatory telegrams, he told Griff: 'Do you know, the producers of the film say I can have a bath in champagne!' Always interested in gourmet food and drink, Tom was a keen cook and wrote a book on herbs.

Tenzing Norgay had every reason to have his head turned by the god-like adulation he received after the climb. But his innate strength of character, and qualities as a natural gentleman, and his flashing smile, enabled him to pull through. He became Chief Instructor and then Director of Field Training at the Himalayan Mountaineering Institute in Darjeeling set up by Nehru to 'train a thousand Tenzings'. During his international travels he was a splendid ambassador for his race, although in his last few years, due to family and financial pressures, he was not so happy. He told Hillary he was often lonely and felt insecure. He died in Darjeeling on 9 May 1986 in his 74th year. Both his son Jamling, from his third wife Daku, and his grandson Tashi, by his daughter Pem Pem, have since climbed Everest. His nephew Gombu, our youngest high altitude Sherpa in 1953, was the first person to climb Everest twice: in 1963 with the Americans and in 1965 with the third Indian expedition.

Griffith Pugh continued his research in high altitude physiology and adaptation to cold climates, advising the Americans at the South Pole. On retirement he brought his analytical mind to bear on various entrepreneurial projects. Growing rather lame after a number of car accidents which, of course, were never his fault, he attended our 40th Anniversary celebrations in his wheelchair. He died in 1994.

Charles Evans was clearly going to have difficulty in combining his love of Himalayan exploration with the demanding profession of brain surgeon. Two years after Everest, he led the British expedition to climb Kangchenjunga, 28,169ft (8,586m), the third highest peak. Then after performing as Chief Druid at the Llangollen Eisteddfod – he had spoken Welsh since childhood – a new career opened up as Principal of the University College at Bangor, part of the University of Wales. Sadly, within a few years he developed multiple sclerosis and became confined to a wheelchair, although with his intellect unimpaired he was still able to continue his academic career until retirement. We were delighted that he was able to attend the 40th anniversary of our Kangchenjunga climb in 1995 in Snowdonia, but he died later that year.

One cannot do justice to John Hunt's career in a few lines. After Everest, he was increasingly in demand to lecture or respond to invitations to work with young people, so he decided to give up a promising military career to become the first Director of the newly created Duke of Edinburgh's Award Scheme, which gave him rather more time to indulge in interesting expeditions. He must have inspired thousands to take up and enjoy challenging outdoor pursuits. He was created a Life Peer in 1966 and began an exceptional period of public service: advising on relief after the Nigerian civil war; first Chairman of the Parole Board and of the Advisory Committee on Police in Northern Ireland; and President of the Council for National Parks and for

Voluntary Service Overseas. The list seems endless. In 1979, he was appointed one of the 24 Knights of the Garter. He became President of both The Alpine Club and the Royal Geographical Society. In 1995, I interviewed him on his life for the Oral History archive of the British Empire and Commonwealth Museum in Bristol. At last beginning to show his age, he presided over our 'Everest family' 45th anniversary reunion in 1998 but died on 7 November that year. Among the numerous press tributes, one by Lord Longford struck me especially: 'In my eyes, Lord Hunt was the greatest Englishman of his time.' He was certainly the greatest that I could call a close friend.

Seven Survivors

And now for the 'magnificent seven' survivors in order of age.

Alfred Gregory returned to his travel agency but gradually converted to a career as a professional photographer. Through being responsible for the still photography in 1953, he developed a strong association with Kodak and lectured widely on their behalf. He also led treks and tours to exotic locations, particularly for keen photographers. He and his wife, Sue, now live in a delightful rural retreat in the Dandenong Hills, near Melbourne, where my wife and I visited them last year. He still enjoys travelling and taking dramatic photographs in the Australian outback.

Edmund Hillary had the most dramatic change in life style of any of us. Luckily, his brother was able to take over management of the bees! In between expeditions, his life seemed to revolve around a continuous series of lectures and public appearances. Although originally dropping out of university, he now confesses to being awarded five honorary degrees, and his face graces the New Zealand 5 dollar bill. He led a team of tractors to the South Pole as part of Sir Vivian Fuchs's Commonwealth Trans-Antarctic expedition, and jet-boated up the Ganges 'from the Ocean to the Sky'. He was an unlikely but ideal diplomat to represent his country as New Zealand's High Commissioner in India, Pakistan, Nepal and Bhutan. He was also made a Knight of the Garter. But perhaps the achievement which has given him the greatest satisfaction over the last 40 years is his work in creating and running his Himalayan Trust which has helped to improve the lives of the Sherpas in their remote homeland in north-east Nepal. His first wife, Louise, died tragically in a plane crash in Nepal with their third child, Belinda. He is now married to June, widow of his Antarctic partner, Peter Mulgrew, and they live in Auckland. A special exhibition to celebrate his life was opened in Auckland on 24 October 2002 by the New Zealand Prime Minister.

Charles Wylie was British Military Attaché in Kathmandu from 1961 to 1964, becoming the third generation of his family to be involved with Nepal. His grandfather was British Resident in the 1890s. His father was commissioned in the 4th Gurkhas and became Chief Recruiting Officer for all the Gurkhas, who in those days numbered 20 battalions. After retirement from the Gurkas, Charles worked for many years on behalf of charities such as the Britain Nepal Medical Trust and the Gurkha Welfare Trust. He was Chairman of the Britain Nepal Society for five years. In 1956, he was a member of Jimmy Roberts' expedition to climb Machapuchare, 22,940ft (6,992m), the supremely beautiful 'Fish Tail Peak' dominating Pokhara in central Nepal. Wilf Noyce and David Cox got to within 150ft (45m) of the summit, which was very steep sheer ice and decided, having nine children between them, to exercise discretion and leave it virgin. Roberts, reporting back to the Minister, General Khattri, suggested it should remain unclimbed, so to this day no other expedition has been permitted to try it and the mountain remains inviolate. Incidentally, Roberts, a fellow Gurkha Officer, renowned Himalayan climber and the founder of Mountain Travel, the first trekking agency in Nepal, was extremely helpful to us in 1953, escorting a third convoy of porters to Thyangboche with 60 loads of oxygen cylinders flown out from England to Kathmandu.

During the 1953 Expedition, Charles's wife bore him a son and this joyful news was sent over the Indian Army wireless link to Namche

Bazar. The Indian Commander of the station sent the message by runner with a covering note which read, as follows: 'I am transported with exultation at this wonderful news. May God grant you a similar blessing at least once each year. Please pay the bearer one rupee backsheesh.'

George Lowe's life changed as much as anybody's. His filming at high altitude added greatly to the success of Stobart's Everest film. He flew back to England with the team and later became a member of the crossing party in Fuchs's Trans-Antarctic Expedition. Afterwards, he resumed teaching, first in England and then accepted a headmaster-ship in Chile. Returning to England, he became an HM Inspector of Schools. He and his wife, Mary, have settled in Derbyshire and George became the first Chairman and Secretary of the UK Branch of Sir Edmund Hillary's Himalayan Trust. He was recently appointed a Companion of the New Zealand Order of Merit (CNZM) for this work.

Michael Ward was one of the few who didn't lecture much after the expedition; he was too busy qualifying as a surgeon and he became a consultant at the Royal London Hospital. He also developed a special interest in high-altitude physiology, and while wintering at 19,000ft (5,790m) on the Silver Hut expedition made an unofficial first ascent of the spectacular peak of Ama Dablam, 22,402ft (6,828m), near Everest. He published an autobiography and *Mountain Medicine* and collaborated on other books. One book he threatened to write in 1953 was to be called 'Tibetans Prefer Tins', which began 'The Yak belched lustily ...' but he never got any further! One interesting diversion in the 1960s was to look after the health of the King of Bhutan, which enabled him to do some original exploration in the north of that country. He later accompanied a Royal Society expedition in a traverse across Tibet and in recent years he has written about the early travellers and explorers in Central Asia. He became a member of the Apothecaries' City Livery Company and recently served as its Master.

Michael Westmacott returned to his work as an agricultural statistician at Rothamsted – for example, analysing the effect of feeding penicillin to pigs – but it was the sort of establishment where you really needed a private income, so he applied for a job with Shell. They astutely offered him one as an economist at the minimum salary level he had mentally thought of accepting, and he remained with the group mostly in London, but with a spell in the USA, until retirement. He has continued mountaineering and rock-climbing longer and at a higher standard than any of us, possibly spurred on by his wife Sally, who was the first lady to join The Alpine Club when it opened its doors to the fair sex. Michael has rendered great service to the Club, first as Chairman of its unique library and then as President. He also developed the Himalayan Index, a computerised database that lists 2,500 peaks over 6,000m (19,680ft) in height, 5,000 attempts or ascents, 4,300 references and 30,000 climbers' names. It is a great asset for research and expedition planning, and is now available on the Internet.

James Morris was the 'anonymous' Special Correspondent of The Times attached to the expedition. He was not a climber, but deserves to be 'mentioned in despatches'. He had been a journalist since he was 16 years old and became a brilliant and very successful writer. He was married with one son and, like Charles Wylie, received news of the birth of another during the expedition. I took him on his first journey up the Khumbu Icefall and his description of this experience is one of the highlights of Tom Stobart's Everest film. He spent 1954 as a Commonwealth Fund Fellow in the USA and wrote *Coast to Coast*. His magnum opus was the *Pax Britannica* trilogy about the rise and decline of Queen Victoria's Empire. 'As an aesthetic concept of imperialism it has no peer,' said The *Times Literary Supplement*.

Although we never realised it in the 1950s, as he described in his book *Conundrum*, James increasingly felt he was a female imprisoned in a male body. After his children had reached maturity, he therefore took the brave and bold step to change gender, and now lives and writes as Jan Morris, and is always welcomed to our Welsh reunions. She continues to write prolifically and I envy the ease with which she does so, although

A *Writer's World*, published in 2003, may be her swansong. She was recently awarded the CBE.

Finally, myself, George Band, although the publisher will doubtless have something to say about me on the dust jacket! In 1953 I was still a student and had a final year to complete at Cambridge while giving, someone joked, as many public lectures as any two dons. The modest fees from lecturing and writing enabled me to be independent for four years with an interesting expedition each year, notably with Charles Evans to Kangchenjunga in 1955, when four of us completed the first ascent. Initially, the names were withheld in Charles Evans's first cable, deliberately to emphasise the team effort, which became clear in his full despatch. Joe Brown and I summitted on 25 May; Norman Hardie and Tony Streather the following day. For me it was a much more satisfying climb than Everest as nobody had previously been above 20,000ft (6,100m) on the South-West Face by which we climbed it.

My parents were always asking, 'When are you going to start a proper job?', so they were probably quite pleased when I began a career with Shell in 1957, initially as a petroleum engineer concerned with oil and gas exploration and production. This was on an international basis working in seven different countries from Venezuela to Borneo until finally, after oil was discovered in the North Sea, many of us returned to the UK or the Netherlands to help in its development. This provided a very interesting and satisfying career although it meant that mountaineering became merely an occasional recreational pastime. Now, in retirement, like Michael Westmacott, I have been fully involved in bodies such as The Alpine Club, the Royal Geographical Society, the British Mountaineering Council, the Mount Everest Foundation, Ed Hillary's Himalayan Trust and occasional lecturing, but still find time as Chairman of 'Far Frontiers' to lead one or two adventurous treks each year in the Himalayas, and to write this book, so I am still enjoying life. How long can one keep it up? Belarius put it well in Shakespeare's *Cymbeline*, 'Now for our mountain sport. Up to yond hill; Your legs are young; I'll tread these flats!'

08

So Many Ways to the Top

'The wind – always the wind – was viciously asserting its authority.'   Dougal Haston

So at last Everest was climbed! 'Now,' thought a lot of climbers, 'we can get back to some sensible mountaineering on the host of other unclimbed peaks where you can enjoy some technical problems without always fighting for breath in the thin cold air.' Some non-climbers even wondered if it meant the end of Himalayan mountaineering. Wilfrid Noyce responded with his rhetorical question: 'Did the ascent of Mont Blanc in 1786 kill the interest in Alpine mountaineering?' Everest, being the highest of all, still clearly exerts a magnetic attraction both for the true mountaineer and the egocentric and for the wide range of persons with mixed motives somewhere in between.

In the 50 years since 1953, 15 different routes have been made to the summit, with a total number of 1,501 ascents to the end of 2001. On a single day in May 2002, 56 people reached the top!

In the course of the next two chapters, I pay tribute to some of the most outstanding and innovative ascents, with only a slight bias to those made by my fellow Britons, and finally, a few words on the quickest, quirkiest and craziest!

We were happy that a Swiss team, after their hard-won experience in 1952 and the help they had given us, were able to make the second ascent in the spring of 1956. Albert Eggler's ten-man team reached the South

Col in mid-May, and then completed a bold double. Fritz Luchsinger and Ernst Reiss made the first ascent of Lhotse, 27,890ft (8,501m), the world's fourth highest peak, by its North Ridge on 18 May. Then from a camp at 27,550ft (8,400m) on the South-East Ridge of Everest, first Ernst Schmied and Juerg Marmet on 23 May, and then Adolf Reist and Hans Rudolph von Gunten on the following day, climbed Everest. They were the first Europeans to do so.

Everest from Tibet

Meanwhile, what was happening behind the Iron and Bamboo Curtains? When an informal English Climbers' Club party, including John Hunt and myself, were permitted to climb in the Russian Caucasus in 1958, and met several of the top Soviet climbers in Moscow, we were surprised how much they knew about our climbs on Everest and Kangchenjunga. In contrast, we knew very little about Soviet achievements. In 1953, various European newspapers reported a Russian attempt on Everest from the north side in November 1952 in which lives had been lost. This report was denied by Russians who came to lecture at The Alpine Club in 1955, and I believed them. In 1958, we learned the Russians were planning a joint Russian–Chinese reconnaissance in 1959, and a full-scale assault in 1960. I think the recce did take place, but because of political problems in Tibet and the increasing animosity between the Russians and Chinese, the joint expedition was called off and the Chinese decided to go it alone. In a few years, they had learned a lot from the more experienced Soviet climbers. It was a massive expedition, 214 men and women, a third of them Tibetan. Details are rather sparse, but they managed to establish a top camp at 27,900ft (8,500m) from which on 24 May a party of four made the final assault, Wang Fu-chou, Chu Yin-hua, Konbu and Liu Lien-man. They were trying the North-East Ridge direct – not Norton's lower traverse line – and soon came to the sheer rock precipice of the Second Step, where they were stopped by the final 5m (16ft) wall. Liu Lien-man made four attempts to scale it but each time fell back. Chu Yin-hua took over, removing his boots and stockings to try barefoot, but also failed. Then by combined tactics, Liu gave Chu a shoulder and he finally made it. Giving the three others a tight rope, in turn they joined Chu. Together it had taken them three hours to climb this crux. Liu was too exhausted to continue, so the other three pressed on in the gathering darkness. They had no torches and, at about 28,970ft (8,830m), their oxygen ran out. They discarded the sets and continued, sometimes crawling on all fours, until at 4.20am (Peking time) on 25 May, they staggered onto the summit. It had taken them 19 hours from their final camp. They had a small cine camera with them, but it was too dark to take any shots. When they rejoined Liu at 28,540ft (8,700m) it was light enough so Chu took a few shots. They returned safely to Base Camp by 30 May. Shih Chan-chun's account in the *Alpine Journal* of May 1961 reports as follows: 'Summing up our conquest of Everest, we must in the first place attribute our victory to the leadership of the Communist Party and the unrivalled superiority of the socialist system of our country. Without all this, we, the ordinary workers, peasants and soldiers, could never have succeeded in climbing the world's highest peak.'

This was such an incredible achievement that it was regarded with some scepticism in the West, but is now generally regarded to be true. The Chinese made a better-documented ascent in 1975, by nine climbers, leaving a survey tripod on the summit which was discovered by a British party later that year.

The West Ridge and the First Traverse

Back on the south side of Everest, the Indians, with their considerable experience from amongst the armed forces and from the creation of the Himalayan Mountaineering Institute in Darjeeling and the Indian Mountaineering Foundation in Delhi, had launched two expeditions to Everest in 1960 and 1962, which reached heights of 28,300ft (8,625m) and 28,600ft (8,720m), respectively, but their time had not yet come.

It was up to the Americans in 1963 to make the next significant step. Sadly, they also had the first casualty in the Khumbu Icefall – Jake Breitenbach – with whom I had climbed the Grand Teton in Wyoming in 1960 while I was working for Shell Oil in the USA. He was killed instantly when a whole section of ice cliff – 'about the size of two rail-road cars one on top of the other' – broke away and buried him. The expedition was conceived by Norman Dyhrenfurth, 44 years old, a film producer of Swiss origin whose father had led international expeditions to Kangchenjunga and the Baltoro in the 1930s. The American media and corporate world were not particularly interested in mountaineering, so Dyhrenfurth realised he had to think big in order to attract financial support. It was not enough just to repeat the South Col route – rapidly becoming known as the Yak Route. The Swiss had climbed Lhotse as well; why not add Nuptse – the third peak in the Everest massif? But his potential team of climbers had another idea: why not tackle the unclimbed West Ridge of Everest? The National Geographic Society agreed to back the expedition but only if there were to be a strong scientific element as well. Dyhrenfurth's team fulfilled this dual role by combining scientific and mountaineering ability; of the 19 members, five had doctorates and eight had master's degrees.

As they got closer to the mountain and intensified their debate, the objective evolved into a two-pronged attack: a West Ridge attempt combined with an ascent of the Yak Route, with the possibility of completing the first-ever traverse of the mountain – the safest way being up the West Ridge and down the South-East where a supporting team could receive the traversing party. This was so ambitious that some felt the team's resources would get so stretched that they could fail on both routes. Was it not more prudent to satisfy their sponsors and give priority to the South-East Ridge? Factions developed, based on old friendships. Tom Hornbein and Willi Unsoeld plumped strongly for the much greater mountaineering challenge of the West Ridge; big Jim

Whittaker and Lute Jerstad for the more certain South-East. Advance Base was set up in the Cwm on 2 April, designated Camp II, but in much the same location as our Camp IV in 1953. From there the two factions separated and immediately competition developed for manpower and resources. Dyhrenfurth compromised that a reconnaissance of the West Ridge could have priority, but Hornbein was firmly committed to recceing all the way to the top! He and Unsoeld were a very determined pair. Tom Hornbein, 32, ex-Naval Lieutenant Commander, was a practising physician at the University of Washington. Willi Unsoeld, 36, was an Assistant Professor in Philosophy and Religion at Oregon State University, and a Teton mountain guide.

With the help of Barry Bishop, a climber and photographer seconded from the *National Geographic*, and David Dingman, a surgeon, they climbed slopes of 35° to 45° snow and ice and opened the way to the West Shoulder where they were able to set up a safe Camp 3W (W for West Ridge) at 23,800ft (7,250m). Among the seven Sherpas who helped establish their camp was Tashi, my 'personal Sherpa' on Kangchenjunga in 1955, who was now in his mid-fifties. The West Ridge above them was a daunting prospect. Hornbein wrote: 'The cloud cauldron of the great South Face boiled, accentuating the black, twisting harshness of the West Ridge ... Our eyes climbed a mile of sloping sedimentary shingles, black rock, yellow rock, grey rock to the summit. The North Col was a thousand feet below us across this vast glacier amphitheatre.' If the Ridge itself proved too difficult, they would be forced onto the less steep North Face, with its treacherous overlapping slabs. From photographs, they had seen a snow-streaked gully cutting up through the slabs, now christened 'Hornbein's Couloir'. On 12 April they reconnoitred further, finding an ideal site for Camp 4W at the foot of the rock ridge at 25,100ft (7,650m), and noting a 'Diagonal Ditch' to the left of the ridge which might lead to the foot of the Hornbein Couloir. Their recce had been a brilliant success. They returned to Advance Base only to find that in their absence Dyhrenfurth had decided to give top priority to the

South Col route. Hornbein and Unsoeld were furious and felt betrayed.

Camp V was set up on the South Col on 29 April, and Camp VI on the South-East Ridge at 27,450ft (8,370m), rather lower than intended. The following day, Whittaker and Gombu were the lead assault pair: Whittaker, a 6ft 5in guide on Mount Rainier and sports equipment shop manager from Seattle; Gombu, Tenzing's chubby nephew who in 1953 at the age of 17 had carried a load to the South Col. Dyhrenfurth and his personal Sherpa, Ang Dawa, formed the second pair. Dyhrenfurth was keen to have movie film of the summit and he was the only fit cameraman, but he did not have the strength and had to return to Camp VI. Whittaker and Gombu had made an early start on 1 May, the Hillary Step was largely under snow so without technical difficulty they reached the summit at 1pm where Whittaker planted a large American Stars and Stripes. It was the earliest Everest had been climbed.

More assaults were planned, and even a plan for Lhotse was resuscitated, but there was not nearly enough oxygen available on the Col, which together with illness and a change in the weather, led to a general withdrawal to Base Camp for rest and recuperation. Personal relations were also on a knife edge. This can very easily happen at high altitude when there is difficulty in agreeing multiple objectives within a group containing strong, articulate individuals. Fortunately, they still had a month before the monsoon. They regrouped and made a new plan. They would simultaneously tackle both the West Ridge and the South-East Ridge and hopefully the parties would meet on the summit. If so, all would descend the South-East Ridge to the South Col so that the West Ridge party would have traversed the mountain. The West Ridge team comprised two pairs: Unsoeld and Hornbein, Corbet and Emerson, with Auten in support. The South-East Ridge party were Bishop and Jerstad, with Dingman, Jimmy Roberts and Girmi Dorje in support. Maynard M. Miller, a glaciologist and my friend from Cambridge days, managed Advance Base. Target date for the summit was 18 May.

Meanwhile, while the others rested, Corbet and Emerson had been steadily restocking Camp 3W, making use of winches. By 15 May, Unsoeld and Hornbein were again established at Camp 4W at 25,100ft. Prospecting the next day, they found the Diagonal Ditch was easy and did indeed give access to the Hornbein Couloir; above that they were unable to see. Next day, the West Ridge team was nearly wiped out by a high altitude storm. Around midnight, two of the Camp 4W tents and their occupants were literally blown 50 yards into Tibet, miraculously coming to rest on a shallow ledge. At the height of the gale and close to exhaustion, they were able to retreat to Camp 3W. After rest, they conceived a simpler plan; just one camp above 4W instead of two. Of the three remaining fittest, Corbet agreed to stand down so that Hornbein and Unsoeld, as a pair, would have the best chance. Dyhrenfurth agreed over the radio. They decided to stake everything on the Hornbein Couloir. Corbet, Auten, Emerson and five Sherpas made the carry to Camp 5W on a tiny platform at 27,250ft (8,310m) at the foot of the Yellow Band and left Hornbein and Unsoeld in their eyrie.

The pair set off on 22 May soon after 6am, cutting steps in the bed of the Couloir which narrowed to 10–15ft (3–4.5m) and steepened to 50° as it cut through the crumbling limestone of the Yellow Band. They moved singly and the first 400ft (120m) took four hours. Hornbein jibbed over a 60ft (18m) wall – possibly his oxygen was not working properly – but Unsoeld managed to climb it with a supreme effort. Not wishing to descend the same rotten way, when there were no rappel points, they were now irrevocably committed to traversing the mountain. They could now move together. They veered right to the crest of the Ridge, first on clean rock – 'almost like a day in the Rockies' – and then cramponning up the snowy summit slopes. Suddenly, ahead of them was Whittaker's American flag. 'It was 6.15. The sun's rays sheered horizontally across the summit. We hugged each other as tears welled up, ran down across our oxygen masks and turned to ice.'

Beginning their descent of the South-East Ridge, they were encouraged by the fresh footprints of Lute Jerstad and Barry Bishop, who had summitted three hours previously. Bishop had not been well and they were going very slowly. Hearing the shouts of Hornbein and Unsoeld, they waited and joined forces. Going very slowly, after midnight, they endured an open bivouac on the Ridge while waiting for dawn – the highest in mountaineering history at that time. It cost Unsoeld nine of his toes, and Bishop all ten of his. 'Yet for me,' wrote Hornbein, 'survival was hardly a conscious thought. Nothing to plan, nothing to push or, nothing to do but shiver and wait for the sun to rise. I floated in a dreamlike eternity, devoid of plans, fears, regrets.'

Next morning, Dingman and Sherpa Girmi appeared, searching for the bodies of Jerstad and Bishop but finding to their amazement all four were still alive. The West Ridge had been climbed and Everest traversed, a triumph for the Americans and particularly for that very determined and insistent pair – ex-Navy doctor Thomas Hornbein and his hyperactive climbing companion, Willi Unsoeld.

The Challenge of the South-West Face

The Indians came back for a third attempt on the South-East Ridge in 1965 and this time were brilliantly successful under the leadership of Naval Officer Lt Cdr Mohan Kohli. On 20 May, Captain A.S. Cheema summitted with Nawang Gombu. So the chubby, cheerful Gombu became the first person to climb Everest twice. He came to our anniversary celebrations in Britain in 1993, 1995 and 2003 and we have made him an honorary member of The Alpine Club. On four separate days, the Indians put a total of nine climbers on the summit, showing that given reasonable weather the technique was now well established for climbers of many other nations to follow suit.

As climbing techniques developed and the main ridges of Everest had been climbed, interest turned towards tackling harder routes, in particular the huge South-West Face rising 8,000ft (2,440m) from the floor of the Western Cwm. The Japanese were particularly active, being granted permission for three consecutive expeditions in 1969 and 1970.

The lower two-thirds of the Face consists of steep snow-slopes, while the upper part forms a steeper wall called the Rock Band. There is a break in the middle – called the Central Gully – which trends right in a sort of snow-covered ramp extending towards the South-East Ridge. On the left, the Band is cut by a narrow gully. Above the Rock Band the angle relents, forming an upper snowfield below the final rocky summit pyramid. The climb starts from the same Advance Base area at around 21,000ft (6,400m) used for the South Col route, now generally called Camp 2. The early part of the expedition therefore repeats the climb through the Khumbu Icefall and consists of building up supplies in the Cwm.

The autumn 1969 expedition set up three camps on the Face below the Rock Band: Camp 3 at 23,000ft (7,010m), 4 at the mouth of the Central Gully at 24,600ft (7,500m) and 5 at 25,600ft (7,800m), the last two on very restricted sites which meant that portable tent platforms would be needed in future. They opened the way for a full-scale expedition to try to penetrate the Rock Band in spring 1970. This massive group also wanted to satisfy their sponsors and supporters with a near-certain success on the South Col route, so, like Dyhrenfurth, they split their forces, but didn't have the same degree of luck. They were joined in the Cwm by a totally separate Japanese ski expedition, so there must have been some 150 people passing through the Icefall. Sadly, six Sherpas from the ski expedition were killed in an Icefall avalanche, and one of the Japanese climbers died from a sudden heart attack. The climbing leader, Ohtsuka, decided to give priority to the South Col route and their star climber, Naomi Uemura, did what he was told and, with Teruo Matsuura, summitted on 11 May. The winter of 1969 had been very dry, so the South-West Face had unusually little snow cover, and some unexpected stonefall. It was more of a formidable rock climb than they had anticipated. After reaching 26,400ft (8,047m) below the left-hand gully, they withdrew. Meanwhile, from the ski group, perhaps the first of the 'odd ball' expeditions, their star, Yuichiro Miura, skied down from the South Col, reaching 100mph before opening a parachute brake. Losing his balance, he slid the last 600ft (180m), coming to rest just before a crevasse. Cameras with huge telephoto lenses captured it all for television. Watching it in a Somerset farmhouse, I remember it particularly vividly, as I had had a spectacular head-on crash and almost written off my new Mercedes earlier that day and was feeling very sorry for myself!

The failure of the Japanese on the South-West Face had created worldwide interest. This had now become 'the last great unsolved problem', and was bound to attract the acknowledged 'star' climbers from other nations. Those from France, Italy, Germany and Austria had yet to summit by any route. Out of this mêlée who should arise as the potential leader for an international expedition in spring 1971 but the idealist Norman Dyhrenfurth, again assisted by the down-to-earth Gurkha soldier Jimmy Roberts. Dyhrenfurth had had enough trouble exerting leadership over a purely American team in 1963, but he seemed a demon for punishment, as he also assumed the main responsibility for fund raising. Once again, to keep all his climbers happy he sought refuge in multiple objectives – the main one would be the South-West Face, another the West Ridge direct – clearly setbacks on these would encourage some climbers to fall back on the more certain South Col route. Rusty Baillie, before he resigned from the expedition, wrote: 'All expeditions are a strain on inter-relationships, an international one even more so ... an international one with a divided aim may well spend its energy solving problems of personality rather than of mountaineering.'

By the time the expedition reached Nepal, there were 33 members from 13 different countries – including the media men. One could almost predict a shambles, comparable with building the Tower of Babel. Not surprisingly, it was unsuccessful, so the less said about it the better.

There was an initial tragedy when the popular Indian climber Harsh Bahuguna was left to die of exposure on the Face during an unprecedented ten-day storm, despite determined and united attempts to rescue him.

The two British stars on the expedition were Don Whillans and Dougal Haston, who had reached the summit of Annapurna by the South Face in 1970 on Chris Bonington's landmark expedition. One of the main sponsors was the BBC, who bought the TV and newspaper rights. When the two Brits spent a long time out in the front on the Face as lead climbers, actually 21 days continuously above 24,000ft (7,315m), supported only by the two Japanese, Ito and Uemera, they were criticised and suspected of colluding with the BBC to hog the limelight and thereby ensure the success of their film. Needless to say, it was not true.

I will only tell one apocryphal story which may not previously have found its way into print. Dyhrenfurth had asked Wolfgang Axt, a 35-year-old schoolmaster, to organise the food, not realising he was a vegetarian and health-food fanatic, so his choice of diet did not receive universal approval. One evening, they heard over the radio the results of an international football match, England v Germany. 'Vot you say, Don,' said Wolfgang, 'we Germans have beaten you English at your national game!' Don flashed back: 'Just remember, Wolfgang, we beat you Germans twice at your national game in 1918 and 1945!' Before he sues me, I assume the story cannot be true because I have just discovered Axt was from Austria, not Germany!

Whereas the Japanese had tried to tackle the Rock Band by a gully on the left, the Britons rejected this as too steep and tried to the right along the ramp, placing Camp 6 at the far end, at 27,200ft (8,290m). Above them was a formidable 800ft (240m) buttress split by a steep gully. Whillans climbed part way and then saw, to his surprise, that it would be possible to break out right over slabs to join the 'Yak' route on the South-East Ridge; but this would be deemed a cop out, and they did not have the resources and backing to complete the route up the Face. 'How about buggering off?' said Whillans. And they did.

The 1971 Expedition to the South-West Face had shown that for success on an unclimbed route of this magnitude, it was essential to have a cohesive fully united team with a clear purpose and a single objective. Even then, they had to be favoured with fair weather. Several more expeditions were to founder on the Face before this message got through.

Dr Karl Herrligkoffer's European Everest Expedition 1972 got to about the same height as in 1971, but also ended in acrimony and arguments.

Then came Chris Bonington with expeditions in 1972 and 1975, both post-monsoon. The 1972 venture was organised in a rush after Herrligkoffer's failure. At least all the climbers were from one nation and had mostly climbed together previously, and they had the one objective of the South-West Face. But the weather did not co-operate. 'The wind – always the wind – was viciously asserting its authority,' said Haston. The chimney line that he and Whillans had discovered in 1971 was now stripped of its snow and ice and revealed as steep, difficult rock climbing – too hard at 28,000ft (8,530m).

In between these two expeditions, the Japanese tried again in autumn 1973. Again they failed at around 27,000ft (8,230m), but a South-East Ridge party did make the first post-monsoon ascent of Everest, and it was also climbed directly from the South Col for the first time without an intermediate camp. These were both important successes.

Everest – The Hard Way

In the 1970s, the Nepalese government allowed only two expeditions a year on Everest, either pre- or post-monsoon, so they were booked up years ahead. In late 1973, Bonington was able to get permission for post-monsoon 1975 after Canadians withdrew their application. With the help of the explorer's favourite agent, George Greenfield, he was able to persuade Barclays Bank to underwrite the expedition, which would cost at least £100,000, from their advertising account. This enabled him to concentrate in the year available on much more detailed planning than in

1972. The logistics, or flow of supplies up the mountain, were initially analysed on a mainframe computer by a programmer, Stephen Taylor, provided by Ian McNaught-Davis of Comshare. This enabled Chris to identify critical points in the plan. There probably had not been such thorough preparation since John Hunt's memorandum 'Basis for Planning' in 1953.

From the Annapurna South Face climb of 1970 and Everest 1972, Chris Bonington was able to assemble a strong core of British climbers: Hamish MacInnes, Dougal Haston, Doug Scott, Mick Burke, Nick Estcourt, Martin Boyson and Mike Thompson. With others, he built up a team of 18 climbers, with a corps of 66 high-altitude Sherpas led by Pertemba as sirdar. Chris was the undoubted leader of this talented group through his own climbing exploits, such as the first British ascent of the North Face of the Eiger with Ian Clough in 1962. By his additional abilities as a photographer, lecturer, writer and television presenter, he had shown himself to be a great communicator and he continues as Britain's 'ambassador for mountaineering' to this day. One omission from the 1975 team was the inimitable Don Whillans with whom he had snatched the first ascent of the Central Pillar of Frêney on Mont Blanc in 1961, and who had designed the Whillans' Box for high-altitude camps, able to withstand gales of Patagonian ferocity. Between their two forceful personalities, Bonington felt there was room for only one leader.

He planned to begin the climb in late August just as the monsoon was ending so as to complete it before the winter cold and wind became too severe. To avoid transporting all the gear during the monsoon they sensibly sent it out in the spring and stored it at Khunde, only a few days from Base Camp.

Studying the route to be followed on the Face, they decided to reject the Whillans' Chimney, and try the deep gully to the left looked at by the Japanese in 1969. If this enabled them to cut through the Rock Band, they would set up Camp 6 above it, and then traverse the long snowy shelf leading to the final ridge of Everest just beyond the South Summit. Base Camp was set up on 22 August and Advance Base (their Camp 2) in the Cwm at 21,700ft (6,610m) on 2 September. Camp 5 was set at 25,500ft (7,770m), 500ft (150m) lower than previously and in a better position for the left-hand route.

The weather was good; all was going well. Chris reflected that he led democratically, consulting others throughout the expedition, but when a decision was required he made it. Not everyone saw it that way. 'It's a very strong hierarchy set-up here,' said Doug. Dr Charles Clarke commented shrewdly:

> Chris is desperate that the master plan unfolds smoothly. He really is a great leader in spite of all the criticism levelled at him. Nobody else has the personality to command us and deep down we respect him. I have a very good relationship with him particularly as I, thank God, am not in the raffle – i.e. the great decision of who goes to the top. This sadly alienates him from most of the lead climbers. Even a little is enough and it's just beginning to show itself. No splits, no factions, no nastiness, but it's all there in their hearts.

Ropes were fixed from Camp 5 to the Rock Band, and Estcourt and 'Tut' Braithwaite were the first to tackle the deep gully leading to virgin ground. There was good snow in the bed, and crampons bit firmly. They led alternately. It was about Scottish Grade III, but at 27,000ft (8,230m). Suddenly their oxygen ran out and it all seemed a lot harder. Just above, a ramp led right to the upper icefield. It narrowed, sloping outwards and an impending wall above pushed one out of balance. Estcourt was in a desperately precarious position but just had to keep going. Eventually, he reached a good crack, hammered in a secure piton, and gasped with relief! 'Given the conditions, it was the hardest pitch I've ever led.' They had overcome the Rock Band.

Bonington designated Haston and Scott as the first pair to try for the summit, as widely expected, but as the expedition was ahead of schedule there would be time for a second or even third attempt.

On 22 September, with the help of three Sherpas, Bonington, Burke and Thompson, Haston and Scott set up Camp 6 at 27,300ft (8,320m), just above the gully exit, and next day fixed 1,500ft (460m) of rope across the upper snowfield in preparation for their summit attempt. One difficult rock pitch required five pitons to surmount. On 24 September they set off at 3.30am in the dark, reaching the end of their fixed rope at dawn. Suddenly Haston's oxygen failed. Ice had blocked the junction of the mouthpiece tube. They lost an hour repairing it. Below the South Summit, they floundered in waist-deep powder snow up to an angle of 60° but at 3pm, after 11½ hours, they emerged onto the ridge. Should they bivouac and complete the climb next morning? Scott made a brew while Haston started a snow hole. But the weather could change and they would lose their chance, so they decided to continue over the Hillary Step, which was banked with snow. At 6pm, they were on the summit, actually the first Britons to climb it. On top was the survey tripod left on 25 May by the Chinese. Scott stood beside it and handed his camera to Dougal. 'Here you are, youth,' he said, 'take a snap for my mother.'

There was no moon and it was soon considered too risky to try to return to Camp 6. They enlarged the snow hole at the South Summit – the highest ever bivouac – and tried to keep warm by rubbing and shuffling their limbs. They began to hallucinate. Dougal had a long conversation with somebody else. Doug found himself talking to his feet. But they survived and, at first light, moved continuously down, reaching their Camp at 9am, after 30 hours away. They only suffered frost-nipped toes and fingers.

On 26 September, the second team of four climbers had their turn. Leaving Camp 6 at 4.30am, they set off individually, clipping in to the fixed rope: Boysen first, then Boardman and Pertemba, with Burke bringing up the rear. Almost immediately Boysen's oxygen packed up and then he lost a crampon. He limped back to the tent in utter frustration.

At the end of the fixed rope, the snow was in better condition so Boardman and Pertemba continued climbing solo and they reached the South Summit at 11am and, after correcting a similar ice blockage in Pertemba's oxygen set, they continued, reaching the main summit at 1pm. Pertemba fixed a Nepalese flag to the Chinese tripod but they were denied a view; cloud had been boiling up around them.

On the descent, they were amazed to meet Burke sitting in the snow just above the Hillary Step; they thought he had rejoined Boysen. Although going rather slowly, he was determined to film on the summit and they agreed to wait for him at the South Summit, but then the weather really began to deteriorate. They waited 1½ hours; Mick should have rejoined them three-quarters of an hour ago but there was no sign of him. Visibility was now down to 10ft; the sky and the cornices and swirling snow merged into a single whiteout. Something must have happened to Mick. Wearing his thick glasses and blinded by spindrift, it would be all too easy to put a foot wrong on fragile wind slab or through a cornice into Tibet. They still had a very tricky three-hour descent ahead and, in these conditions, would not have survived a bivouac like Doug and Dougal. They were already freezing cold. At 4.30pm, the 24-year-old Boardman decided they must descend. It was an epic. Pertemba was not used to climbing without a fixed rope, and was shaken by Burke's disappearance. By a miracle, they found the end of the fixed rope in the dark and stumbled into their 'summit box' at half past seven, where Boysen awaited them. For 30 hours, the three were trapped by the raging storm.

So the South-West Face had at last been climbed, but at a price. Bonington had told them over the radio to stick together but afterwards conceded that if any of them had been in Burke's position – with the summit so close – they would have gone for the top. He reflected:

Once again we had had tragedy and triumph, that painful mixture of grief at the death of a friend and yet real satisfaction at a climb that had not only been successful in reaching the top, but in human terms as well. This very diverse group of nearly a hundred people had merged as a single team. From my point of view, leading the South-West Face Expedition was the most complex, demanding and rewarding organizational challenge I have faced.

Young Peter Boardman reflected, 'For a mountaineer, surely a Bonington Everest Expedition is one of the last great Imperial experiences that life can offer!'

Even the computer programmer had the personal satisfaction that he had helped Chris in managing to take the biggest expedition by the hardest route in the shortest time – to the top of Everest!

Women on Top!

The year 1975 was also remarkable for two less epic events: the first women to stand on the summit of Everest. On 16 May with a Japanese Ladies' Expedition, a 35-year-old school teacher from Tokyo, Mrs Junko Tabei, climbed the South-East Ridge, in deep soft-snow conditions, led by Sherpa Sirdar Ang Tshering. Only 11 days later, on 27 May, the 37-year-old Tibetan housewife and mother of three, Phantog, reached the summit by the North-East Ridge in a group of nine climbers from the huge Chinese expedition that left the survey tripod on the summit. Phantog was the deputy leader and had previously climbed Muztagh Ata and Kongur Tiube Tagh, both over 24,000ft (7,315m).

Will it Go without Oxygen?

Everest's three main ridges and the great face between the West and South-East Ridges had now been climbed. Until the Chinese opened Tibet to foreigners to give access to the great North and East (or Kangshung) Faces, there was little scope for major new routes, except as variants to the existing ones. However, Everest had so far only been climbed with the aid of supplementary oxygen, although the Chinese claimed not to have used it continuously while climbing but only during their rest periods.

As far back as 1924, Norton had reached 28,126ft (8,570m) without oxygen, and several others had subsequently been within 1,000ft (300m) of the summit without it. Indeed, I think one of the reasons why Everest took over 30 years to climb was that the early climbers got so close that, given the right weather and snow conditions, it was felt that a fully fit climber could manage without oxygen. It was only the successive failures that convinced the planners and organisers of our 1953 Expedition that full commitment had to be given both to the development of efficient apparatus and to its use on the mountain. Until Hillary took off his mask on the summit, it wasn't known whether a fully acclimatised person could survive above 29,000ft (8,840m) without supplementary oxygen. Even so, after some 10 minutes of taking photographs, he recalled: 'I was becoming rather clumsy-fingered and slow-moving, so I quickly replaced my oxygen set and experienced once more the stimulating effect of even a few litres of oxygen.' And so for the next 20 years, the use of oxygen to scale at least the three highest peaks was considered standard practice. Back in the 1950s, with a few exceptions, we British Alpinists were not athletes in the modern sense; we didn't go on training runs, or pump weights. Indoor climbing walls were not invented until the 1960s. We just climbed in any spare holiday time because we enjoyed it and that was our recreation; we didn't think of it as 'training'. I got into trouble once drawing an analogy with rugby football by saying that we were just club players – like the London Irish – rather than internationals. Roger Bannister invited some of our team to his physical fitness testing laboratory at Oxford and was, I believe, quite surprised at our relatively low level of performance. On a Himalayan expedition, the customary 10–20 day approach march to the mountains was considered sufficient to tone up the muscles.

The better professional Alpine guides were doubtless much fitter than we were, but even so probably not of an Olympic medal standard of fitness. As more and more people were attracted to take up high-altitude mountaineering, and it became more competitive, so inevitably a few of that 'sample population' would statistically have the determination and lung power to climb Everest without extra oxygen. There was a greater risk in doing so, as we had learned in the decompression chamber at Farnborough, but sooner or later somebody was bound to try.

Everest without Extra Oxygen

The year was 1978 and the two were Reinhold Messner and Peter Habeler, both from the Tyrol. Messner, 34 years old, had established a reputation in his twenties for solo ascents of hard rock climbs with the minimum use of pitons. In 1970, he went to Nanga Parbat and made the first traverse of the mountain up the Rupal Flank and down the Diamir Face with his brother Günther, who sadly was killed on the descent. Peter Habeler, 36 years old, was a guide from Mayrhofen, quiet and unassuming compared to the more outgoing and flamboyant Messner. They began a remarkable partnership in 1974, specialising in extremely rapid ascents. They climbed the North Face of the Matterhorn in 8 hours and halved the previous best time on the Eiger to ten hours. Although they were not particularly close friends, when climbing together they developed an instinctive rapport. They were both keen to break away from the major-expedition concept current in the Himalayas and to return to the simpler style of A.F. Mummery, who was the first to tackle Nanga Parbat in 1895. They achieved this in 1975 in the Karakoram by making the second ascent of Gasherbrum I (Hidden Peak), 26,470ft (8,068m), in a single push in three days, without using oxygen. Habeler wrote:

> Reinhold and I sat happily in the plane on the way home. We ordered a gin and tonic – the height of luxury – and toasted each other, as if we were speaking in unison: 'To Mount Everest.' 'Without oxygen,' I said. 'Without oxygen,' came Reinhold's echo. Then we laughed like two small boys hatching some mad prank.

Everest was booked for several years ahead, so the only way they could get permission was to join an expedition already approved. Fortunately, the Austrian Alpine Club had secured spring 1978, hopefully to make the first Austrian ascent via the South Col. The leader, Wolfgang Nairz, agreed they could join and generously allowed them to try first without oxygen. On the way up on 23 April, Habeler became ill with food poisoning while on the Lhotse Face and had to descend. Messner pushed on with two Sherpas to establish a camp on the South Col, but they were caught in a raging storm for two days and were lucky to escape with their lives. This left Nairz to go ahead, and four of his team summitted on 3 May with three more a week later, including Reinhard Karl making the first German ascent. In between these two successful groups, Messner and Habeler were able to make history.

Possibly affected by his illness, Habeler became plagued by doubts. Was it too risky without oxygen? Might he suffer permanent brain damage? In the end, he decided to go but, as a psychological and emergency back-up, they took with them two oxygen cylinders and a face mask.

On 7 May, Messner and Habeler, together with the Welsh camera-man Eric Jones, reached the South Col. At 5.30am next day, Messner and Habeler left for the summit. It was a misty, gusty day. They climbed unroped, pausing for a brew at the tent on the ridge, and changing the lead at intervals. Habeler dumped his rucksack at the South Summit and they broke through the clouds into sunshine. There were big cornices on the final ridge, so they roped up and Messner filmed Habeler coming up the Hillary Step which was completely covered in soft snow and most exhausting to climb. But they pressed on, with the rope snagging occasionally on the cornices until they reached the top at 1.15pm – just over an hour from the South Summit. They were clearly very close to the limit. 'It was a very personal, lonely victory in a struggle which each of us fought alone,' wrote Habeler afterwards. 'In spite of all my euphoria, I was physically completely finished. I was no longer walking of my own free will, but mechanically, like an automaton. I seemed to step outside myself, and had the illusion that another person was walking in my place.'

They cut off a metre of their yellow rope and tied it to the Chinese tripod to prove they had been there. Reinhard Karl brought it back several days later.

After 15 minutes, Habeler descended, leaving Messner filming on top. He asked Habeler to fix the rope at the Hillary Step, but there was no anchor, so they both had to climb down solo. The gentle slope up to the South Summit was particularly exhausting. Habeler continued down, jumping into the final gully leading to the Col. The snow gave way beneath him and he tumbled down, losing his ice axe and goggles, and hurting his right ankle. Eric Jones saw him and, fearing the worst, came up to help him down. He was bleeding from a cut in the forehead, his nose almost black from cold and his beard snow white. Emaciated and hollow-cheeked, he looked like a living corpse. Reinhold was much the same when he staggered down half an hour later. Habeler had come down in an hour from the summit compared with almost eight hours for the ascent.

That night, Messner was in great pain from snow-blindness as he had been removing his goggles frequently for filming, but he refused to take any oxygen. Struggling down to Camp 3 next day, they met Dr Oswald Ölz on his way up for his summit climb and he treated Messner's eyes. Back at base, the Sherpas could hardly believe they had succeeded without oxygen. Calling in at the hospital at Khunde, Habeler had a surprise.

Ed Hillary was visiting on an inspection tour and offered his hearty congratulations. 'I have always believed,' he said, 'that one day the mountain would be conquered without oxygen. I am proud to be able to shake your hand.' It had taken 25 years since the first ascent in 1953.

Tibet Reopened

On 20 September 1979, the Chinese reopened the north side of Everest to mountaineers. The depredations of the Cultural Revolution had reached as far as Rongbuk, and the monastery, which had been an historic centre of worship and pilgrimage, was in total ruins. However, instead of having to make the three-week journey from Sikkim across the windswept Tibetan plateau, expeditions could drive with the bulk of their equipment up the new road from Kathmandu, transferring to Chinese lorries at the Nepalese border. The huge 1975 Chinese expedition had even put a rough road in from the main Kathmandu–Lhasa highway so that one could drive right up to Base Camp! The Chinese saw this reopening as an excellent opportunity to earn foreign currency, imposing high charges, so not surprisingly the Japanese were the first to receive permission – for a reconnaissance in autumn 1979 to be followed by a major joint expedition with the Chinese in spring 1980 which altogether may have cost around a million pounds. They actually split into two teams: one on the North-East Ridge and the other on the right-hand side of the North Face taking a new line up the whole length of the Hornbein Couloir and onto the upper West Ridge as the Americans had done in 1963. Both were successful.

Messner Solo

Not far behind the Japanese in seeking permission came Reinhold Messner. His ascent of Everest, without oxygen, together with Peter Habeler on 8 May 1978 had been a tremendous achievement, but to Messner it lacked purity. They were attached to Wolfgang Nairz's Austrian expedition so if anything had gone seriously wrong, the Austrians would surely have come to their assistance. The following August, climbing the Diamir Face, Messner had made the first solo ascent of Nanga Parbat – the first of any 8,000m (26,240ft) peak. Surely, the ultimate aesthetic achievement would be to climb Everest solo all the way, unsupported and without oxygen. He proposed this to the Chinese and, so as not to interfere with the pre- and post-monsoon slots already allocated to conventional expeditions, he proposed to climb during the monsoon. For a charge of $50,000, the Chinese promptly agreed. At the end of June 1980, his girlfriend Nena Holguin, plus the statutory interpreter and liaison officer, accompanied him to the foot of the North Col. As the pre-war British climbers had found at this time of year, the snow was soft and deep and the slopes to the North Col ready to avalanche. They withdrew. Returning two weeks later, they had luckily hit a weather window and the snow had consolidated. On 17 August, he made a preliminary trip to just below the North Col, leaving there his 44lb (20kg) rucksack containing the bare essentials for his climb: a bivouac tent, sleeping bag and mattress, a stove and food; dried beef, dried fruit, chocolate, sardines, soup and tea.

Next morning at 5am, he set off again from Advance Base, retrieved his gear, but before reaching the Col he was suddenly 26ft (8m) down in a concealed crevasse! Luckily, he was able to climb out by a narrow ramp, but it was a close thing. He made good progress, despite softening snow, climbing some 5,000ft (1,520m) that day before bivouacking. Starting at 9am as the sun hit the crags above, he soon realised the snow was too deep and soft below the North-East Ridge to allow him to climb that way. Instead he traversed across the great North Face until he reached the Great Couloir and camped on a little promontory, safe from avalanches, at about 26,900ft (8,200m). He was depressed as he had only gained 1,300ft (400m) in height.

Next day, 20 August, the weather began to change, it clouded over, light snow began to fall and visibility decreased to 165ft (50m). He abandoned everything, taking only his ice axe and camera. He crossed the Great Couloir – probably close to where Norton had been 56 years previously – and broke out to the right and upwards. The last part seemed to take forever; a few paces, then resting on his axe. At last, he spotted just the top section of the Chinese tripod poking above the monsoon snow. He crawled the last few feet on hands and knees. It was 3pm. He just sat there for an hour: 'I knew I was physically at the end of my tether,' he said. Retracing his steps, he was back at his little tent in 3½ hours and flopped into his sleeping bag, too tired to do anything else. At first light, he forced himself back over the traverse, abandoning everything except his camera and climbing gear, until at last he stumbled into the arms of Nena.

> It was only when I reached the foot of the mountain and the ordeal was over, when I no longer had to worry about falling, or dying of exhaustion, or freezing to death, that I collapsed. I no longer had to grope forwards in the mist; no longer summon my whole will to take another step forward – and with that, all will left me.

Chris Bonington paid tribute: 'The very speed, sureness and efficiency of his ascent of the world's highest mountain masks the size of the barrier through which he was breaking.' Not surprisingly, after this climb, Reinhold's mother asked him to give up extreme mountaineering. He did not. He went on to become the first person to summit all 14 of the world's peaks above 8,000m (26,240ft), and he is still alive today!

Filling in the North Face

Messner's solo climb of Everest was such an incredible achievement that nothing seemed impossible any longer – given reasonable weather conditions. On the North Face, an Australian group made the first ascent of the Great Couloir direct when Tim McCartney-Snape and Greg Mortimer summitted on 3 October 1984 without using oxygen. Climbing conditions were perfect; the snow had frozen hard so crampons bit firmly into the slope. However, perhaps the most astonishing climb on the North Face was in 1986 when Jean Troillet and Erhard Loretan climbed the Hornbein Couloir direct without any intermediate camps, no oxygen and even no ropes. On 28 August, they skied from their camp to the foot of the Face, then started the ascent at 11pm using head-torches. At daylight, after a good rest, they pressed on, again continuing overnight, and reached the summit at 2pm on 30 August after 31 hours of actual climbing. After an hour on top, they descended mostly by glissading for which conditions were ideal, and reached the foot of the Face in an astonishing 3½ hours. The whole excursion took an un-believable 43½ hours! They were tough to keep up with; Pierre Beghin had set off with them but had to turn back exhausted. Erhard Loretan, a Swiss, went on to be the third climber to complete all the 8,000m peaks. His 14th and last was Kangchenjunga and we passed him on the trail coming out on 10 October 1995 when I was leading a nostalgic trek to the Base Camp on the 40th anniversary of our first ascent.

Two more distinct lines remained to be completed on the north side of Everest, both to the east of the originally attempted route from the North Col. Both of these join the old route at the North-East Shoulder and continue from there up the North-East Ridge to the summit.

The most recent of these two to be attempted was by a typically modern concept: a bold line just straight up the North-East Wall, or what Unsworth suggests should be called the 'Secondary North Face', to the east of the North Ridge. It was spotted in 1994 by the Russians as a possible route, and climbed without ceremony at their first attempt in May 1996. Previously Russell Brice had given up at 24,600ft (7,500m). After camps at 23,030ft (7,020m) and 24,600ft on the Face, the route takes a 3,300ft (1,000m) north-north-east couloir at 45° to 60°, now known as Zakharov's Couloir, after Nikolai Zakharov, the leader of the expedition, consisting of 15 very tough Alpinists from Krasnoyarsk. The Couloir leads onto the North Ridge where they had their final camp at about 27,230ft (8,300m). The route so far was tricky; difficult to arrange adequate protection and hampered by heavy snow and occasional rockfall rather than avalanches. 'There was always a strong wind,' said Zakharov. It came from different directions and sometimes swirled around us like a washing machine filled with small chips of ice. Often it was hard to balance or even stand at all.' Finally, on 20 May, there was just the classical ridge: the First and Second Steps climbed in decreasing visibility and eventually a full blizzard. So when the first three had returned from the summit, and Zakharov was just 15–20minutes away, at 6pm, he gave up his own attempt so that they could regroup and descend immediately in zero visibility, keeping close together. They reached their top tent at 10pm. Descending by the North Col route, they heard someone say 'crazy Russians'. But they did keep together as a team, and they all came back home safely after summitting on the precise day anticipated in their plan! Not many, if any, Everest expeditions can make that claim.

Across the Pinnacles

The other route to complete the lines on the north side was the full North-East Ridge starting from the Rapiu La at 21,360ft (6,510m), and undulating over 3 miles to the summit at 29,035ft (8,850m). In the 1920s this had always been rejected as far too long and difficult. The classical route from the North Col was a much easier short-cut to the North-East Shoulder at some 27,500ft (8,380m).

A key feature of the North-East Ridge, shortly before the Shoulder, was a series of three rocky pinnacles which, at over 27,000ft (8,230m), would be a serious technical problem. Few climbers thought of it as an interesting route, partly because the upper part was so well known, but then Chris Bonington decided to assemble a small team to have a go at it in 1982; Peter Boardman, Joe Tasker, Dick Renshaw, with Dr Charles Clarke and Adrian Gordon in support at base. Flushed with success on Kongur in western Xinjiang, they decided to make several forays onto the ridge, to gain a jumping off point at about 26,250ft (8,000m) from where they could make a continuous push for the summit, carrying bivouac gear. However, with the huge scale of the mountain, the wind and the cold and the altitude, this began to seem rather optimistic for such a small team. They used snug snow caves instead of tents and, after 17 days, had caves at 22,503ft (6,859m), 23,806ft (7,256m) and 25,755ft (7,850m). It was exhausting digging as the ice was rock-hard; the second one took 14 hours, spread over three days, but the warmth of friendship, wrote Chris, was one of the factors that made the struggle worthwhile.

> Of all the expeditions I have been on, this was the most closely united, one in which I don't think there was a serious spark of anger through its course. We did have differences of opinion on tactics, discussions that became heated, but there was a holding back born from a mutual respect and liking.

On 4 May, Pete, Joe and Chris set out for the Pinnacles. Pete was going particularly strongly; Chris, pushing 50, was beginning to feel his age. Next day, it was the turn of Dick and Joe, while the others carried rope and tentage. During the climb, Dick had experienced a strange sense of numbness down one side of his body. It had worn off, but they had spent four nights at close on 26,250ft, so it was sensible to go down for a rest. Later Charles feared that Dick had suffered a stroke and should probably go home. It was agreed Charles should escort Dick to Chengdu, where he could catch a plane. Charles would then rejoin the team. This left Pete and Joe as the strongest pair to try to complete the traverse of the Pinnacles – only 980ft (300m) in height gain but nearly a mile in distance. It was agreed that Chris and Adrian should climb up to the North Col, from where they could observe Pete and Joe from time to time and meet them as they came down the North Ridge to the Col. Realistically, without supplementary oxygen, they were unlikely to have the strength and resources to go for the summit of Everest as well. Pete and Joe left for the snow caves on 15 May. By radio, they reported reaching the top cave on the 16th and would go for the Pinnacles next day. That evening just before dark, after a 14-hour day, they were seen at the foot of the second Pinnacle, but no light shone from their bivouac and next morning there was no sign of them. They were never seen again.

Chris and Adrian spent three days on the North Col gazing across at the ridge, waiting, hoping, willing Pete and Joe to reappear, but there was no sign. Beyond the First Pinnacle, it was later learned, the ridge was knife-edged, with cornices on either side, and awkward steps to negotiate. They must have fallen or collapsed from sheer exhaustion.

On 21 May, Chris and Adrian rejoined Charlie at Advance Base. It was unrealistic to try to ascend the ridge itself to look for Pete and Joe. Charlie suggested he and Chris should go right round to the Kangshung Valley to examine the other side of the ridge by telescope, while Adrian remained in lonely vigil at Advance Base, but there was no sign of life or tracks. They had done all they could, except to break the sad news to their families.

In May 1992, Kazakh climbers found Pete's body, sitting 'looking like he was asleep', close to the Second Pinnacle near where the two had last been seen ten years before. There was no sign of Joe. Possibly he had fallen, and Pete died of exhaustion while trying to descend alone.

Both Pete and Joe had become successful writers about their earlier expeditions, so their memory has been wonderfully perpetuated in the Boardman–Tasker Award, an annual prize for mountaineering literature, which celebrated its 20th anniversary in 2002 with a memorable evening of lectures at the Royal Geographical Society on 8 November.

Several more expeditions were launched at the North-East Ridge before it was finally climbed in totality by a Japanese team. In 1985, in a party led by Mal Duff, Rick Allen found Tasker's movie camera at about 26,900ft (8,200m). British parties tried again in 1986, led by 'Brummie' Stokes, and in 1987 with joint-leaders Doug Scott and Rick Allen, but all three were turned back by foul weather. Then, in 1988, Brummie Stokes assembled a large team nicknamed 'The Golden Oldies' Expedition' because it included my old friends, Joe Brown, Mo Antoine, with whom I climbed the Old Man of Hoy, Philip Horniblow and several other very mature climbers. Stokes suffered three strokes and had to hand over to Paul Moores. This was Mo's impression of Everest, told to Al Alvarez:

You see these huge expanses of rock and ice and you think, that one small flank is
bigger than any of the mountains I've ever been on ... On the North-East Ridge
route, everyone talks about the pinnacles: once you're up them, you've cracked it,
they say. Not true. You're still 1,700ft vertical feet and three-quarters of a mile in
distance from the summit, and that's a long, long way when you're above 28,000.
I mean, there are only a couple of other places in the world that high. So it's by
no means over when you've done the pinnacles. You've still got a full day to go.

Harry Taylor and Russell Brice succeeded in traversing the Pinnacles to
the North-East Shoulder with the benefit of oxygen. They bivouacked
before the Third Pinnacle, but that night it snowed heavily. Next
morning it was a virtual whiteout, but after crossing the last Pinnacle
they heard over the radio from Joe Brown that the weather was clearing
and they should sit tight until they could see their way down the North
Ridge. So it was prudent to retreat via the North Col. Bonington
commented: 'It was a bold necky push and a fine piece of
mountaineering. But they haven't climbed the North-East Ridge, because
you've got to get to the summit to do that.'

Five years later, on 10 May 1993, Harry Taylor did reach the summit
of Everest by the South Col route, the second Briton to do so without
oxygen, as a member of Peter Earle's DHL Expedition commemorating
the 40th Anniversary of the first ascent of Everest. John Barry was the
climbing leader and the expedition was also notable because the only
other team member to summit was Rebecca Stephens on 17 May together
with two Sherpas, Ang Pasang and Kami Tschering, thus earning a place
in history as the first British woman to climb Everest.

It was left to a large Japanese expedition from Nihon University to
administer the coup de grâce on the North-East Ridge in spring 1995.
They used full siege tactics, employing a team of 13 climbers and
31 Sherpas, headed by Kiyoshi Furono, fixing ropes for much of the route
to their Camp 5 at 25,750ft (7,850m) at the foot of the First Pinnacle.
Switching teams, between April 25 and 29, they climbed the three

Pinnacles and pitched Camp VI on the ridge just beyond. They then retreated to Base Camp for a rest while others restocked the camps. On 9 May, Furono, Shigeki Imoto and ten Sherpas re-climbed the Pinnacles using oxygen, and slept at Camp VI. Next day, they continued to the Second Step; finding the Chinese ladder had collapsed, they repaired it that night. Leaving at 4am, the two Japanese and four Sherpas reached the summit at 7.15am. After an hour, they raced back through the Pinnacles all the way to Advance Base, which they reached at 6.15pm just before sunset. Congratulations!

The Virgin Kangshung Face

When the Chinese reopened the north side of Everest in 1979, the immediate reaction was to apply for routes up the great North Face which I have described, but the whole East Face of Everest stretching from the Rapiu La at the foot of the North-East Ridge round to the South Col also lay in Tibet and was totally virgin. It is known as the Kangshung Face, because it forms the catchment area for the Kangshung Glacier which flows down into the Kama Valley. It had been left severely alone since the 1921 Reconnaissance when Mallory first entered the valley, saw the stupendous Face and uttered his famous phrase: 'Other men, less wise, might attempt this way if they would, but, emphatically, it was not for us.'

Nearly 60 years on, the Face was clearly due for re-examination. In autumn 1980, an American climber, Andrew Harvard, accompanied by a veteran Chinese climber, Cheng Rong Chan, and an interpreter, travelled by jeep from Lhasa to Kharta and made the four-day trek in to Pethang Ringmo below what he called 'The Forgotten Face of Everest'.

Between the North-East and the South-East Ridges, the upper 8,000ft (2,440m) consisted of snow, ice and hanging glaciers. The lower 3,000ft (900m) is a series of ice-draped rock buttresses like giant claws with an extra-large buttress in the centre capped by a broad ice ridge leading right to the South Summit. For two days, Harvard watched the avalanches pouring down the Face; but he also noted the big buttress and its protective ridge above. Was this a feasible route?

A year later, a largely American team, led by Richard Blum, with Lou Reichardt as climbing leader, came to try it. The team included the Americans John Roskelley and George Lowe (not the New Zealander of our 1953 team) and, rather surprisingly, Kurt Diemberger and Sir Edmund Hillary. By late August, they had set up a Base Camp at 17,000ft (5,200m) and an Advance Base, 17,550ft (5,350m), or 'Buttress Camp' at the foot of the Main Buttress. They decided to tackle the Buttress head on, fixing 2,300ft (700m) of rope, and starting on snow ridges between sections of rock. Bad weather brought them down to Base for a conference on 10 September. Roskelley proposed moving to the North Face as they had a permit to try either Face. Hillary inspired the Americans to continue pioneering on the East rather than repeating a known route on the North. Unfortunately, he then developed cerebral oedema and had to be evacuated. So back to the Buttress they went, to Camp I, Snow Camp, at 18,800ft (5,730m), above which a long ice gully at 50–65° was also a natural chute for rocks and chunks of ice. The climbers felt like pins in a bowling alley, so that became its name, and the camp above appropriately called Pinsetter, at 20,100ft (6,130m). Above that was a serious headwall, tackled by Lowe, Reid and Perlman. Sue Giller, climbing with Lowe, said she had never been so frightened on a climb, with rocks breaking off and bouncing all around her as Lowe struggled with the extreme difficulty. After a number of climbers quit, only eight remained but Helmet Camp was established above the Buttress at 21,300ft (6,490m). On 5 October, Reichardt led through a crevasse system above to their highest point of 22,000ft (6,710m), but felt they were getting too extended in bad snow conditions and decided to call the expedition off before anyone got seriously injured.

The Americans returned in 1983 with many of the same team, this time led by Jim Morrisey. Their Liaison Officer, Wang Fu-chou, had been the first Chinese to summit Everest in 1960. Arriving at the end of August, they took a month to climb the Buttress again by the previous route. A major problem was how to get the necessary supplies up such steep cliffs, which were potentially dangerous and beyond the capability of normal teams of Sherpas. In late summer 1982, Morrisey had been sailing in the San Joaquin River in the boat of my friend John Boyle. Looking at the large winches used for line handling, he said: 'Boyle, you used to be an engineer, why don't you see if you can utilise these winches and help us get the supplies up the Buttress?' Boyle was hooked. They spoke to Kevin O'Connell, President of the Barient Winch Company, in the boat moored alongside. O'Connell said, 'If you guys are nuts enough to go climbing, I'm nuts enough to give you a winch or two.' Everything had to be capable of being carried into the mountains on the back of a yak.

They set up two systems. The first, powered by a 5hp engine, lifted loads of 80lb (36kg) 1,000ft (300m) up the Buttress. A rocket was initially used to carry the messenger line from Pinsetter Camp down to the glacier. The second hoist up the rock buttress between Pinsetter and Helmet was operated by a counterweight of snow packed in a canvas bag, and lifted the loads another 700ft (210m). Half a ton of gear was lifted in this way, saving a tremendous amount of manpower. Boyle wrote an interesting monograph describing his 'Aerial Tramway'. Pinsetter was established on 15 August. Carlos Buhler, jugging up with a winch load to Helmet, commented, 'I really felt the route was a unique and extraordinary one – very technical, unbelievably so for a big mountain route.' Much of this was due to George Lowe's aggressive climbing and positive attitude. Above Helmet, three more camps were set up on the upper snows at 23,400ft (7,100m), 24,900ft (7,590m) and 25,900ft (7,865m). Using oxygen, this would put them within striking distance of the summit – comparable with climbing directly from the South Col.

On 8 October, Buhler, Momb and Reichardt summitted, after nearly 11 hours of gruelling trail-breaking, having joined the normal South-East

Ridge route at about 27,500ft (8,380m). Buhler, never really expecting to be chosen for the first attempt, yet finding himself in the lead at the finish, said:

> The day was fantastic and the sun beat warmly on us even on those last few metres. Together the three of us cramponned up to the crest. It was all kind of a dream. The air around us was very calm and it seemed as though we could have lit a candle on the summit. Kim took a walkie-talkie and radioed down to Advance Base Camp. We could hear some Tibetan chanting – the local Yak herders who had stayed at Base Camp had begun to chant prayers for us at 5am that morning and hadn't stopped all day long. I was pretty moved by their voices.

They started down at 3.25pm, meeting five Japanese struggling up without oxygen at the bottleneck created by the Hillary Step. Then moments later, a lone Sherpa, Pasang Temba, who had started with the Japanese team but who had turned back, slipped on the hard-packed snow and slid past them out of control and tumbled off the ridge to his death. Two of the Japanese also died in falls the next day. With heavy hearts, they turned off down the East Face and reached their 25,900ft camp at 8pm. Six climbers squeezed into the single three-man tent for an uncomfortable night, but next day Lowe, Reid and Cassell also got to the top. 'Amazing activity, this mountain climbing,' concluded Buhler. 'Right from the start I knew it was for me.'

This epic American success still left the whole 5 miles of the gigantic East Face with only one route to the summit. On the far right of the Face a shapely subsidiary ridge descends to the east from a point just under 26,000ft, or 7,884m to be precise, on the very long North-East Ridge. It has been given the lovely name of the Fantasy Ridge, but cannot be a very rewarding one to try because you would still have to cross the infamous Pinnacles if you wished to continue to Everest's summit.

The first expedition to try it was a ten-member Japanese team from Meiji University Alpine Club, led by Shinichi Hirano. They set up Base

Camp on the Kangshung Glacier on 14 April 1991 and established two camps on the lower section of the ridge at 19,350ft (5,900m) and 20,000ft (6,100m). The route was threatened by ice and stonefall and they abandoned their attempt at 20,990ft (6,400m). It was altogether too ambitious an objective for the party, even though they had enough gear to employ 370 Tibetan porters for the 12-day trek from Kharta. The only other attempt was just recently in 2001, led by Santosh Yadav, the only Indian woman to have climbed Everest twice. She said the weather was the worst she had encountered in all her 15 years' climbing. Starting in mid-April and fixing ropes, her team finally gave up on 20 May after reaching 22,630ft (6,900m). But I am getting ahead of my story.

Climbing the Neverest Buttress

On the left of the Face, directly below the South Col, an optimistic American, Robert Anderson, already with considerable Everest experience, pondered a possible route. In late 1987, I had a letter from one of his helpers, Wendy Davis, asking whether I would become an honorary member of their expedition in spring 1988, to mark the 35th anniversary of our 1953 Everest climb. Rather bemused, I replied that they might be better off without me and encouraged them to get on with the climb. They had also asked John Hunt to be their honorary expedition leader and he, being rather more polite, felt it churlish to refuse this unusual accolade. To provide some logical link between 1953 and 1988, Hunt proposed they might consider including a leading British climber in their team and suggested the name of Stephen Venables. And so the team became Anderson, Ed Webster, Canadian Paul Teare and Venables. They were accompanied by photographer Joe Blackburn, Dr Mimi Zietman, two Nepalese cooks, and initially Tenzing Norgay's son, Norbu.

From photographs of the East Face, Anderson had zeroed in on a big rock buttress to the left of the American 1983 route, which they later coined the Neverest Buttress. He thought the serious technical difficulties might end at about 21,000ft (6,400m), followed by easier snow-climbing for 5,000ft (1,500m) to the South Col and then the normal South-East Ridge route to the top. They would have no porters or supplementary oxygen on the mountain, so it would have to be a fast lightweight attempt with no real back-up if anything went wrong.

They started on 3 April, from an Advance Base at 17,880ft (5,450m), fixing ropes on named sections of the rock buttress: the Snow Ledges; the Headwall; the Scottish Gully; the traverse leading to the Cauliflower Ridge. On 8 April, they found a site for Camp 1, partially up the Cauliflowers. On Day 5, Ed climbed the gently overhanging ice of Webster's Wall at 20,990ft (6,400m) and thought they had almost cracked the buttress, but the next day they were stopped dead by a huge crevasse spanning the entire slope. They retired to base for a rest. Refreshed, Ed and Robert spent three days at Camp I dealing with the crevasse. Ed abseiled into it and climbed the 100ft (30m) overhanging wall on the other side using ice-screws. It took another day to fix a Tyrolean traverse over these jaws of doom. Paul and Stephen then took over, breaking through a dangerous jumble of seracs to reach the easier undulating snow slopes. At 21,810ft (6,650m) they had cracked the technical crux and the way to the South Col was open. They took a week's rest at Base and to allow time for fresh snow to consolidate. They planned now to reconnoitre only as far as Camp 2 – to be set under a huge roof of ice, the Flying Wing, at 24,440ft (7,450m) – and not to sleep above Camp 1 until the summit push. It took them 11 hours from Camp 1 to 2 the first time, but a mere 1½ hours to descend. The journey to the South Col began on 8 May, leaving Advance Base at 4am, and Camp 2 at 8am on 10 May on a beautiful clear morning. Steve was enjoying himself despite carrying a 44lb (20kg) load but, as the day wore on, snow fell and elation gave way to despondency. To reach the Col it took 11 hours, where they emerged into a blasting wind which continued all night. They rested next day. Paul felt ill, possibly developing oedema, and wisely descended immediately, reaching Advance Base in just seven hours. The remaining three spent the day eating and drinking. By evening, the wind miraculously dropped so they started at 11pm, carrying the bare minimum of chocolate and a litre of juice, hoping to be on the summit in the early morning, Steve finally reached the South Summit alone at 1.30pm; Robert and Ed were falling behind. Four nights with little or no sleep were beginning to tell. Steve protected himself while he bridged up the Hillary Step, by tying his prussik loop onto the expected fixed ropes with a sliding Bachmann knot.

To his relief, the last 980ft (300m) were firmly crusted snow and at 3.40pm he stepped onto the summit, now adorned with three empty oxygen cylinders, prayer flags and discarded TV transmission equipment left by the Asian Friendship expedition on 5 May. He had become the first Briton to summit without oxygen – and by a new route – but was he going to survive the descent? He later wrote in the Alpine Journal:

So far instinct had served me well, but when I started down at 3.50pm the clouds, which had been building up steadily, enveloped the summit ridge completely. Suddenly I was struggling for my life, terrified of re-enacting Mick Burke's sad fate in 1975, as my glasses froze over and I groped my way through the mist, collapsing several times with oxygen deficiency, hyperventilating furiously to refill my lungs. I had always suspected that the problem would not be climbing Everest without oxygen, but getting down again, and now for the first time in my life I was having to draw on a whole new reserve of will and strength. I had grossly underestimated my level of exhaustion and the problems of orientation in the mist, so that when darkness fell I had still only just crossed back over the South Summit.

A bivouac in the open at about 28,210ft (8,600m) was inevitable. Luckily, it was a fine night. Ed and Robert had both turned back from the South Summit and sought refuge in an abandoned Japanese tent. They met up with Steve early next morning and symbolically tied to one rope for the remaining descent to the Col.

They knew they should descend immediately, but they were totally exhausted. When they finally left the Col on 14 May, they had spent 93 hours above 26,240ft (8,000m). Hunger and thirst reinforced their lethargy. They were lucky all to return safely, sustained by the close team spirit that had made the whole climb possible. They knew what they were letting themselves in for, and they paid a price in terms of frostbite: Robert lost half a big toe; Steve three and a half toes; Ed part of three toes and eight fingers.

Yugoslavs, Poles, Russians, Canadians and Brits

Here I propose to end my brief account of the most outstanding and innovative ascents of the post-1953 period. I have concentrated on those leading to success on the 15 principal different routes. There have, of course, been many more repeats and variations but frankly, like most of the climbers who return from the summit, I am exhausted! Let me just pay brief tribute to four major expeditions which, given more time and space, I might have included in greater detail.

13 May 1979

The Yugoslav ascent which 'straightened out' the West Ridge climb by Hornbein and Unsoeld in 1963. Instead of diverting onto the North Face, they followed the ridge all the way, doing some of the hardest rock climbing on Everest to that date. Andrej Štremfelj and Nejc Zaplotnik summitted with three more the next day.

17 February 1980

Arriving rather late on the Himalayan scene, the Poles made up with some astonishing first winter ascents mostly led by Andrzej Zawada. When I was President of The Alpine Club, it was my great pleasure to invest him as an honorary member. The first winter ascent of Everest was made by the South Col route by Leszak Cichy and Krysztof Wielicki. Three months later on 19 May, another Polish team climbed the South

Pillar on the right of the South-West Face. This was the shortest way to the top from the south side, achieved by Andrzej Czok and Jerzy Kukuczka (the second person to climb all 14 of the 8,000m peaks).

4 May 1982
This was the first Everest attempt by Soviet climbers on the South-West Face to the left of the original British route. Eleven climbers, including the leading pair, Eduard Myslovski and Volodya Balyberdin, reached the summit – the highest number on a new route.

20 May 1986
A Canadian expedition to the West Ridge reached it from the north side from the Rongbuk Glacier to the West Shoulder, and continued up the American 1963 route. Dwayne Congdon summitted with Sharon Wood, who became the first North American woman to climb Everest and the first woman to do so by a new route. On a more pleasurable note, I enjoyed serving with her on the jury at the Banff Mountain Film Festival in 2001.

Finally, a couple of Britons for whom I personally have a very high regard.

27 May 1993 by the North Ridge
Dawson Stelfox made the first Irish ascent of Everest and, because of his dual nationality, the first British ascent from the north. We served together on the board of the Mountain Training Trust when it was created in 1995 to take over the running of Plas y Brenin, the National Mountain Centre in North Wales, on behalf of the Sports Council. This has been judged a great success, largely due to the efforts of Iain Peter, whom we appointed as Chief Executive.

13 May 1995 by the North Ridge

Alison Hargreaves climbed without oxygen, the first British woman to do so. Hers was the third British woman's ascent after Rebecca Stephens, and Ginette Harrison in 1993. The first woman's ascent without oxygen was by a New Zealander, Lydia Bradey, in 1988, who was climbing without permission. All three of these were by the South-East Ridge. Alison was one of the most gifted and accomplished mountaineers of her generation. In a casual conversation at The Alpine Club, I had encouraged her to try to climb Everest, K2 and Kangchenjunga, the three highest peaks, all within a year. Nobody, man or woman, had done this and no woman had climbed Kangchenjunga. I felt such a feat was well within her capability. She succeeded brilliantly on Everest. Although formally part of an expedition led by Russell Brice, Alison climbed unsupported from the East Rongbuk Glacier to the summit, declining assistance – even a cup of tea – from any climber. Although she never claimed to have made a solo ascent, as there were other climbers on the mountain, others did so on her behalf. She then climbed K2 on 13 August, reaching the summit around 6pm with five other experienced climbers, but a thick layer of cloud to the north of the Karakoram, over China, was the harbinger of a violent storm which hit them on the descent with hurricane force; they all perished. Alison was literally blown off the mountain. 'It is not too much to hope,' concluded her biographer, Ed Douglas, 'that in the moments before the hurricane closed around her, as she started home from the summit of K2 with the world beneath her feet, Alison was happy.'

09

Climbing into the Millennium

'There are no true victors, only survivors.' Barry Bishop

With the main routes on Everest climbed, with or without oxygen, it is not surprising that interest now turned towards repeating them in unusual ways. For example, the Australian, Tim McCartney-Snape, had already climbed Everest by the Norton Couloir in 1984 without oxygen, but, on the north side, if you have driven up to the Base Camp you are already nearly two-thirds of the way up the mountain. The purest way must surely be to start from sea level and that is exactly what he did in 1990. He started on foot from the Bay of Bengal and solo, again without oxygen, reached the top of the world on 11 May by the South Col route. His journey involved a 2-mile swim across the Ganges!

At the other end of the scale, in 1988, the Asian Friendship Expedition was composed of 254 members from China, Nepal and Japan, including 36 from Japanese television. Nine climbers and a three-man TV crew reached the summit via the North and South Col routes on 5 May, which is Children's Day in Japan and a national holiday. The mountain was traversed in both directions and the pictures were beamed to 300 million viewers. I always wonder how they count them!

Almost equally spectacular was an expedition, assembled in 1990 by big Jim Whittaker, the Mount Rainier guide, who had made the first

American ascent in 1963. Now aged 61, he was determined to show that international expeditions could be successful if well managed.

It was called the Everest International Peace Climb, including members from the USA, Russia, Tibet, Kazakhstan and Ukraine, and cost over a million dollars. Whittaker had this to say:

> We succeeded far beyond our wildest dreams: no deaths; 20 to the summit, first Soviet woman to the summit, second Chinese-Tibetan woman to the summit; five ascents without bottled oxygen; two tons of garbage removed from the mountain.

It's in the Family

There are plenty of family relationships. Tenzing Norgay's son Jamling, by this third wife Daku, reached the summit as climbing leader of the 1996 IMAX Expedition on 23 May. His nephew Tashi Tenzing, grandson of Tenzing Norgay through his daughter Pem Pem, summitted on 23 May 1997, the third generation of his family to do so. Not to be outdone, Sir Edmund Hillary's son, Peter, had already summitted on 10 May 1990, and spoke to his father from the top by satellite telephone. Both Tashi and Peter have just climbed Everest again in May 2002 on separate expeditions by the South Col route, in connection with filming projects to mark the 50th Anniversary.

Another grandson of a famous grandfather, both named George Mallory, summitted on 14 May 1995 by the North Ridge with an American commercial expedition led by Paul Pfau – the route on which his grandfather perished in 1924.

To continue family ties: the first married couples to reach the summit were on an American commercial expedition on 7 October 1990. They were the Yugoslav pair Andrej and Marija Stremfelj and the American Cathy Gibson with her Russian husband, Aleksei Krasnokutsky. On the same day, with a French commercial expedition, Bertrand Roche, at 17 years 217 days, became the youngest person to climb Everest and, with

Jean-Noël Roche, the first father and son team. They descended from the South Col by paraglider!

Quite some years later, on 22 May 2001, Bertrand with his wife, Claire Bernier-Roche, summitted from the north side. Bernier, 28, only took up climbing in 1997, her main interest being in paragliding, a sport in which she was three times female world champion. They had carried a 13lb (6kg) double paraglider to the summit but were forced to descend 100m to a suitable snowy terrace from which to launch it. They spent just 10min on this first tandem paragliding descent to Advance Base at 20,990ft (6,400m) below the North Col. It was the first flight from near the summit since Jean Marc Boivin's descent in September 1988, which I mention later.

Bertrand's record for being the youngest was overtaken by Temba Chiri. After retreating in May 2000 from just below the Hillary Step with severely frostbitten hands, he returned in spring 2002 and succeeded on 23 May when he was just 16 years and 16 days old. The youngest female was the Indian Dicky Doma who was 19 when she summitted in May 1993.

From the youngest to the oldest: on the same busy day, 7 October 1990, on a British commercial expedition led by Stephen Bell, Ramón Blanco from Spain, at 60 years of age, became the oldest person to make the ascent. Of course, both the youngest and the oldest records will change progressively from the first ascent by Hillary at 33 years 313 days, and Tenzing at around 39 years of age. He was not sure of his exact birth date so after the climb adopted 29 May as being most appropriate! Before Ramón Blanco, Chris Bonington, 50, held the record briefly for nine days with his climb on 21 April 1985, overtaken by Dick Bass, 55, who became the first person to climb the highest mountain on each of the seven continents. But these achievements paled into insignificance in the spring season of 2003, the 50th Anniversary year. On 22 May, Yuichiro Miura, the Japanese who first tried skiing down Everest from the South Col in 1970, reached the top, aged 70 years and 222 days.

An extra camp above the South Col allowed a shorter summit day. He had spent the previous five years training and preparing for the ascent.

On the same day, on the north side, three siblings were involved in a Romanian expedition: Lhapka Sherpa, 30, her brother Mingma Gelu, 24, and sister Ming Kipa, just 15 years 18 days old. This created three records: three siblings together; Lhapka, the first woman to climb it three times; and Ming Kipa, the youngest ever. The Nepalese Government have sensibly now stipulated a minimum age of 16 for attempting it on their side.

By now, a number of people normally considered disabled have also climbed Everest to demonstrate their continuing zest for life. The first blind person was Erik Weihenmayer on 25 May 2001, who had lost his sight at the age of 13 due to a retinal disease. He took up climbing later in life and had summitted both Aconcagua and Mount McKinley (Denali). On Everest, he made excellent progress, reaching the top soon after 9.30am, climbing behind his partner, 28-year-old Luis Benitez, who wore bells on his rucksack. He found the most difficult part was negotiating the treacherous Khumbu Icefall.

The first amputee, Tom Whittaker, who has an artificial leg, reached the top in May 1998. He hails from Porthmadoc in North Wales.

Ski Extreme

Coming down on foot is not nearly as tiring as going uphill, but skiing downhill could be faster so, not surprisingly, there have been a number of attempts to ski down Everest, mostly by the normal South Col route. I have already mentioned the Japanese Yuichiro Miura in 1970, who started from the South Col and slowed himself down with a parachute before he lost his balance and fell the rest of the way. A more successful attempt was that of Pierre Tardivel on 28 September 1992. He skied from the South Summit thereby avoiding the notorious Hillary Step. However, the purest descent yet was made on 7 October 2000 by Davo Karnicar, from Slovenia and a member of the Yugoslav Alpine ski team from 1975–82. He chose to make his attempt during the early autumn to take advantage of the monsoon, which brought extra snow to the upper part of the mountain, covering the most hazardous rocks. He took less than five hours to go from the summit to the Base Camp at 17,600ft (5,360m) and said: 'I feel only absolute happiness and absolute fatigue. At some sections, I had to ski very fast to escape from breaking ice.' His descent was filmed by video cameras at intervals along the way and was broadcast on the Internet. Those three ski descents were on the south side.

On the north side in 1996, Hans Kammerlander had a spectacular success. He climbed through the night of 23 May from Base Camp to summit in 16 hours 45 mins without oxygen. He then skied down the same way, except for the short rock sections of the First and Second Steps, in 6 hours 45 mins, a total round trip time of 23½ hours.

When I was round the north side in Tibet on 8 September 1998, I met an American, Craig Colonica, who was planning to ski down but would have his work cut out to improve on Kammerlander. Colonica reached 22,960ft (7,000m), presumably on the North Col on 14 September, but then gave up because of sickness and dangerous snow conditions. At the same time, a French group led by Jerome Ruby hoped to snowboard down. They reached 26,570ft (8,100m) on 25 September and 4 October before giving up.

Vive La France!

French climbers had a relatively low-key presence on Everest in the early years, post-1953. It was not until 15 October 1978 that the first Frenchman reached the summit, the 49-year-old deputy leader Pierre Mazeaud, who was then the oldest climber to have done so. He had also been a member of Norman Dyhrenfurth's 1971 international expedition, but had made a rather stormy exit. Ten years later, they decided to celebrate the anniversary of Mazeaud's success by a strong expedition with enormous media backing. Five Frenchmen and three Sherpas reached the summit by the South Col route on 26 September; the average age of the French was 51 years. Jean Marc Boivin had kept his options open by taking up both skis and a parapente. He chose the latter, floating down from the summit in 11 minutes to Camp 2 in the Western Cwm. Marc Batard, a 37-year-old guide from Megève, preferred to see whether he could climb from base to the summit in a day, solo and without oxygen. He had trained for this speed attempt by making the first traverse of Makalu, 27,758ft (8,463m), and an 18-hour ascent of Cho Oyu, 26,899ft (8,201m), both earlier that year. He had two tries on Everest on 11 and 14 September but was driven back by strong winds and exhaustion. Undaunted, on 25 September he tried a third time. Climbing through the night, he arrived on the summit 22½ hours later, just an hour behind the other Frenchmen. This was well ahead of the astonishing partnership by the Swiss, Loretan and Troillet, on the North Face in 1986.

The first successful snowboard descent was finally achieved by a young Frenchman, Marco Siffredi, on 23 May 2001. It was also the first complete descent of the Tibetan side by either ski or snowboard. The previous night he had celebrated his 22nd birthday at Camp 4, 27,225ft (8,300m). Leaving at 2am, using oxygen, he was on the summit in 4½ hours waiting for his Sherpa, Lobsang Temba, to bring up his snowboard. He started at 8am, abandoning his oxygen set, but after only 490ft (150m) broke one of his bindings. Fortunately, Lobsang had a pair of pliers and they were able to repair it! There was so much snow that he was able to continue snowboarding instead of rappelling at the most awkward rocks, following the line of the Norton Couloir, and then cutting across to the North Col and down to Advanced Base in a total time of just over 2½ hours!

It was only when trying to secure a photograph of this epic descent for this book that I learned that Marco had sadly been killed on 9 September 2002, while attempting to snowboard down the adjacent Hornbein Couloir.

Sherpas Supreme

Marc Batard's 22½-hour speed record has now been well overtaken by indigenous Sherpas: first by Kaji Sherpa in 20 hours 24 mins in 1998 and then by Babu Chiri, in 16 hours 56 mins in May 2000.

Babu Chiri had become one of the best-known Sherpas in recent years. Sadly, he died on 29 April 2001 when at Camp II in the Western Cwm. He went out alone around 4pm to take some photos, wandered off the marked track and fell down a concealed crevasse. No one noticed his absence until after dark and when he was eventually located around midnight it was too late. Babu Chiri had made ten ascents of Everest, and also the highest bivouac by spending 21 hours on the summit, without oxygen, in 1999.

The 50th anniversary provided the impetus for speedier ascents. On 23 May Pemba Dorje, 25, from Beding in the Rowaling summitted in 12 hours 45 mins, after leaving Base Camp the previous day. Only three days later, Lhakpa Gelu, 36, from Jubing in Sola Kumbu, took 10 hours 56 mins from 5pm on 25 May to 3.56am on 26. He was back at base at 11.20am on the same day. The rivalry between these two Sherpas continued in 2004. On 21 May, Pemba Dorje reached the summit at 2.10am, having left Base Camp at 6pm the previous evening – a mere 8 hours 10 mins!

First Flight over Everest

The only way to go higher is to take to the air. Although it does not strictly count as climbing Everest, it is worth mentioning two historic events.

The first was the flight over Everest in 1933, which is a story in itself. The project was proposed by a Major Stewart Blacker in 1932 and the timing was just right. The 1933 climbing expedition was re-awakening public interest, the new Bristol Pegasus supercharged engine would enable a suitable aircraft to reach the required height and, in addition to the pilot, would be able to carry equipment and an observer with sufficient photographic equipment to record the flight for posterity. Blacker created a prestigious committee but they were very short of funds until the society hostess Lady Houston came up with £10,000. She was a friend of Lord Clydesdale, MP, who was a squadron leader and was nominated as one of the pilots. Air Commodore P.R.M. Fellowes, a wartime flying hero, took over organisation of the project and with dashing efficiency in sharp contrast, in the writer Walt Unsworth's opinion, to the bumbling efforts of the Mount Everest Committee, who considered it an undesirable distraction, particularly if it were to upset the Tibetans. While the climbers had to combat the wind and dust of the Tibetan plateau, the aviators were most comfortably accommodated in a country club atmosphere in a bungalow belonging to the Maharaja of Darbhanga close to the selected airfield at Lalbalu, some 300 miles (480km) north of Calcutta.

Westland provided the aircraft, a prototype PV3 of which there was just one, which was renamed the Houston Westland in honour of their sponsor. A second aircraft was a Westland Wallace. Both were biplanes and most carefully modified for the conditions, including electrical heating for the pilots' suits, the oxygen supply and the all-important cameras for survey, still and ciné photography.

Fair weather was just as important for the fliers as it was for the climbers. On 3 April, the forecast was favourable and the two aircraft took off at 8.25am. Clydesdale piloted the Houston Westland with Blacker as observer and stills photographer; Flight Lieutenant D.F. McIntyre flew the second with S.R. Bonnett, a professional ciné cameraman fromn Gaumont British Films.

Once they had risen above the haze, Everest was sighted, some 50 miles (80km) away, with its characteristic plume. Because of the haze, they had difficulty locating their landmarks and judging their drift, so instead of approaching from the south-west over Namche Bazar, they came in from the south. Here is Blacker's account:

> I was just able to see an infinite tangle of the brown mountains of Nepal, seamed with black forests, and caught occasional glimpses of the swift Arun river in its gradually steepening valley as now and then I opened the hatchway of the floor and looked down through thousands of feet of purple space. We crossed the frontier of this forbidden kingdom at 13,000 feet. Then, suddenly, a little after our craft sprang clear of the haze into the wonderful translucent air of the upper heights, and away to our right an amazing view of Kangchenjunga in all its gleaming whiteness opened out against the blue.
>
> Fumbling with the catches in my thick gloves, I threw up the cockpit roof, put my head out into the icy slip-stream and there over the pulsating rocker arms of the Pegasus, showing level with us, was the naked majesty of Everest itself.

Climbing steeply so as to cross the summit by a safe margin of some 2,000ft (610m), Clydesdale was suddenly caught in a strong downdraught and as a result he barely skimmed the ridge of Lhotse, but was then able to climb again to clear Everest by a mere 100ft (30m), which was later revised to 500ft (150m). It was 10.05am. Flying through the 'plume', he discovered it was not just cloud but a barrage of ice crystals which cracked the windows of the rear cockpit. Blacker continues:

> Thus almost, and indeed before I expected it, we swooped over the summit and a savage period of toil began. The pilot swung the machine skilfully again towards the westward into the huge wind force sweeping downwards over the crest; so great was its strength that, as the machine battled with it and struggled to climb upwards against the downfall, we seemed scarcely to make headway in spite of our 120 mile an hour air speed. I crammed plate-holder after plate-holder into the camera, releasing the shutter as fast as I could, to line it on one wonderful scene after another. We were now for a few moments in the very plume itself, and as we swung round fragments of ice rattled violently into the cockpit.

Meanwhile, McIntyre had his own difficulties; carrying the heavier ciné equipment he could not match Clydesdale's rate of climb, so he came in between Makalu and Everest, just scraping over the frontier ridge. He had to make three tight circuits before he had gained enough height to clear Everest. Glancing back, he noticed Bonnett was in trouble; he had fractured an oxygen feed pipe and nearly passed out before making a temporary repair. Then, struggling with the heavy camera against the icy slipstream, he collapsed unconscious on the floor of the cockpit. In turning around, McIntyre's own oxygen mask had come apart, and he had to hold it in place with one hand for all the return flight. Halfway back, to his intense relief, he saw Bonnett struggling up from the floor – still alive. Both aircraft touched down at 11.25am. It was all over in just three hours.

Nowadays, flying routinely in pressurised air-conditioned comfort in jet aircraft over 30,000ft (9,150m), it is difficult to imagine the magnitude of this achievement that was organised and executed in little over a year.

Ballooning over Everest

The second historic flight was that of a hot air balloon over Everest which took less than an hour in the air from 6.40 to 7.30am on 21 October 1991.

Leo Dickinson's description in *Ballooning Over Everest* could hardly be more different from the official account of the Houston Westland flight of 1933, but styles do change over nearly 60 years. Dickinson's group of rugged individuals fought, co-operated, quarrelled, laughed and occasionally cried, but they pulled it off. In fact, they had two balloons with the intention of being able to film each other and the mountain as they floated over it together at some 60mph (95km/h). Unfortunately, as the two pilots were barely on speaking terms, quite apart from some problems with the intercom, they did not take off within 20 seconds of each other as intended, but crossed Everest eight miles apart. So they were never really in touch, and a unique filming opportunity was lost.

These days, however, with the aid of computers and a Quantel Graphic Paint-box, you can now manipulate your photographs to make it all seem nearly as dramatic as it really was. The pictures are truly magnificent.

The fairy godmother or sponsor was Star Micronics UK Ltd, a computer printer manufacturer. In the early days of the project, well-known characters such as Per Lindstrand and Chris Bonington were briefly involved, but then Peter Mason became the project manager – 'a cuddly and argumentative sod,' says Leo, who had the impossible job of organising this daunting task.

In a hot air balloon one is, of course, entirely at the mercy of the wind, so meteorologist Martin Hutchins was a key member of the team, bringing an impressive array of equipment. They planned to fly from west to east over the mountain from Nepal to Tibet where Russell Brice was to wait 23 days to retrieve them. I was, therefore, intrigued that they were nearly beaten by a Japanese team in spring 1990 attempting to fly in the opposite direction from Tibet to Nepal, starting from the village of Yaleb, 40 miles north-east of Everest. They were becalmed over the mountain and were caught in a terrible downdraught, descending 12,000ft (3,660m) in minutes, and crashed near the North Face. The pilot failed to extinguish their pilot lights and the envelope caught fire, leading to a dramatic explosion witnessed by the journalist flying above in their chartered Chinese jet. Miraculously, no one was killed, although the co-pilot's femur was broken and it was 36 hours before they were rescued.

Leo's team made their take-off from the hamlet of Gokyo at 15,700ft (4,790m), 16 miles (26km) just south-west from Everest. It is a popular trekking destination as the summit of nearby Gokyo Ri at 17,990ft (5,483m) is one of the finest viewpoints in the Himalayas with a clear view of Everest. The two balloons were of identical size, 240,000cu²ft (6,792cu²m). The pilot of the first was Chris Dewhirst from Australia, accompanied by Leo Dickinson, a cameraman who has an established reputation for 'filming the impossible'. The pilot of the second was Andy

Elson with Eric Jones as cameraman. Eric is better known as a climber for soloing the Bonatti Pillar on the Dru in 1969 and the North Face of the Eiger in 1970. Leo and Eric also filmed Messner and Habeler on the first ascent of Everest without supplementary oxygen in 1978.

The team arrived in Gokyo on 23 September, with the balloon envelopes rolled up like a long thin saucisson so that they could each be transported along the narrow, undulating mountain trails on the shoulders of a team of nine porters, looking like extraordinary giant caterpillars. Now they just had to wait until a weather forecast could promise light winds for take-off and stronger ones at altitude that would take them directly over the summit. It was a frustrating period; one forecast predicted a flight 5–7 miles (8–11km) south of Everest, but this was rejected. If the right day did not come before the onset of winter then their near one million pounds of effort would be wasted. One diversion occurred when Lisa Young contracted pulmonary oedema – excess fluid in the lungs – after climbing Gokyo Ri. If this occurs, the patient has to be moved to lower altitude without delay or they may die, but at Gokyo this just isn't feasible, so they popped her into a special airtight Gamow bag pumped up to a pressure equivalent to an altitude 5,000ft (1,520m) lower, and kept her there for four hours. It did the trick. Her pulse went down from 160 to 118.

At last the right day came, 21 October. Quoting Leo:

> As the huge nylon envelopes swelled against the deep blue sky, illuminated by our bright filming lights, three Brahmini ducks were startled into flight across the lake. The yaks stopped chewing their cud to gaze at us disdainfully. The loads they had carried up on their backs were preparing to fly . . . In a balloon going from 16,000ft to 29,000ft and over, there is only one knob to turn and that is up. Once past Everest, we would have a choice – either continue or go down!

They had agreed to lift off 20 seconds apart with Andy going first. But the ambient temperature was 59°F/15°C above what they had expected, and

Chris was concerned that the top of his balloon was overheating and might fall to pieces (in fact they established later that the temperature gauge, or thermistor, was faulty), so he wouldn't wait and took off at 6.40am, Andy following some two minutes later.

For all the times Leo had been trekking and climbing in the Himalayas, nothing had prepared him for the immensity of the view from their basket.

> The highest mountains on earth massed around me. The soft breeze rocked the basket gently. I felt as if I had left my body behind, allowing my mind to float unencumbered through space. If it wasn't an out of body experience, it was certainly an out of basket one.
>
> Nuptse, at just under 26,000 feet, loomed up, but we cleared it easily. I looked straight down into the Western Cwm, with the summit of Everest rising up ahead of us, Nuptse now to my left. If I leant back a little, I could also get Lhotse in the viewfinder. The balloon was at 33,000 feet, the South-West Face stretched down for 6,000 feet, and Base Camp lay a further 6,000 feet below that – altogether 16,000 feet below our basket. I wondered if anyone down there was looking up at us!

Chris narrated later:

> As we flashed over the summit at 60 miles an hour, I looked back to the Hillary Step, on to the summit itself, and it became a totally different mountain. All was white and crystalline. It was like rowing across the River Styx, coming from the underworld to the real world. We had floated from the dark, black forbidding area of the western side to this beautiful illuminated summit of a fluted mountain. It was a phenomenal feeling.

Through his 300mm lens, Leo could just make out the tiny speck of the second balloon containing Andy and Eric. They were over the Khumbu Valley when suddenly the burners failed; their deafening roar gave way to a discomforting silence. Andy grabbed one of the strikers and managed to relight them, but the balloon was plunging downward and the radio tracking sonde enclosed in a 'Kermit frog', which should be hanging 20ft (6m) below the basket, was now bobbing up above their heads. Eric was getting ready to jump with his parachute, but Andy concentrated on relighting. With all five burners blazing, they limped towards the South-East Ridge. Suddenly, there was a loud twang followed by another and another. Seven of the 28 steel wires anchoring basket to balloon had parted, six of them at one corner, which now relied on one solitary strand. If that went it would be 'curtains'. Andy directed the burners away from the damaged wires into the side of the envelope. Molten nylon swirled round their heads as the bottom of the envelope melted. Slowly they gained precious height, clearing the mountain by 2,000ft (610m) before they hit turbulence. The great Kangshung Face with its ice-flutings and huge seracs drifted into view. Andy throttled back a little as they floated over the Arun Valley. Suddenly, the radio burst into life for the only time in the entire flight: 'Running short of fuel – landing shortly' was the terse message from Chris.

On the far side of Ama Drime, about 50 miles (80km) from Everest, Chris and Leo hit a moraine ridge at about 20mph (33km/h), balloon and basket dragging horizontally across the boulders. One hit Leo in the chest and snapped a rib. He was trapped under the basket, his left boot caught in a line. Panicking, he wrenched hard until his foot came free of the boot and he fell away. Chris tried to grab him and then fell out himself. They had had enough! Ironically, Andy and Eric still had half their fuel, and had a relatively gentle landing, a few miles away, bouncing three times but coming to a halt, upright in zero wind. Returning from Lhasa to Kathmandu by a scheduled flight, they saw Everest from 36,000ft (10,975m). One passenger said to his wife, 'Somebody flew a balloon over Everest last week.' Leo sat back in his seat and said nothing.

A Change of Style

Over time, the style of conventional Everest expeditions was changing. Whereas originally only one expedition was allowed each year in Nepal, the governments both in India and China realised that expeditions were a ready source of income, and started imposing substantial royalties and allowing more expeditions simultaneously on the mountain. In 1991, the fee for trying Everest from Nepal was $2,300. By 2000, this had risen to $70,000 for a party of up to seven, with a further $10,000 for every climber above seven. Smaller parties of competent climbers would, therefore, tend to link up informally under a single permit so that they could share the fee. They still, of course, had to pay all the costs associated with the expedition. It then became convenient to have a professional 'manager' or nominal leader of the combined group who could provide some of the infrastructure, such as Base Camp tent and messing, oxygen equipment and spare cylinders, and, not least, teams of skilled Sherpas.

The next stage was the development of fully commercial expeditions run by a recognised company. Any individual who was hooked on the idea of climbing Everest merely has to apply and, if accepted, write out a cheque for somewhere between $30,000–65,000 depending on the company. The climbing leader, his assistant guides and leading Sherpas would then undertake – at considerable personal risk and responsibility – to get you as high up the mountain as your condition and the state of the weather would permit, allowing a reasonable margin for safety which would depend on their judgement. A reputable company would not accept you for Everest unless you already had some experience of mountaineering and of conditions at high altitude gained on peaks over 19,680ft (6,000m) and preferably over 22,960ft (7,000m) as well. The astonishing thing was that so many people seemed to be able to find the money to burn for this ego trip – such is the attraction and fascination of the highest summit on earth. Many people would apply with totally inadequate qualifications and either be rejected or helped to acquire sufficient experience first. However, with so much money at stake, there was a considerable temptation for some companies to accept inadequately prepared and totally unsuitable clients. The crunch would come when they got above 26,240ft (8,000m), for the final day's climb to the summit – if they ever got that far.

On the most popular South-East Ridge route they would start before midnight from Camp 4 on the South Col at just under 8,000m. Then, in good conditions, they should summit before midday and return safely to Camp 4 before dark. If the client had not reached the top by 2pm, then his leading guide or mentor had the difficult decision to tell his client to turn back. Nowadays, with so many people trying for the summit on a good day, there can be considerable congestion and waiting time at the Hillary Step where ideally only one person should be climbing up or descending the fixed ropes at one time. It only needs high winds or a sudden storm to blow up and severe frostbite, or death from hypothermia or an accidental slip can occur in no time. The steeper, more difficult and exposed sections of the route will have been protected by fixed ropes and steps cut in the ice. The inexperienced client merely has to clip on to the rope with their jumar, which is a metal clamp attached to their climbing harness that can be pushed up but will not slide down, and stagger up the icy staircase as long as their breath holds out. It is all a far cry from 1953, but the mountain is still the same. Some clients are lucky – the climb goes very smoothly; other clients are not and they pay the ultimate price. I do not propose to describe the shambles of May 1996, when 11 expeditions were assembled on the south side alone. There were a total of 11 deaths, eight occurring in just two days, 10 and 11 May, five on the south side and three on the north side, including those of the expedition leaders Rob Hall and Scott Fischer. Although there had been comparable Himalayan disasters, on this occasion three websites at the Base Camp helped to create unprecedented massive publicity and worldwide interest in mountaineering. They spawned a spate of books, notably Jon Krakauer's Into Thin Air, for those who wish to read the full tragic story. I would echo the comments of Barry Bishop, who was on the American expedition of 1963:

> Everest is a harsh and hostile immensity. Whoever challenges it declares war. He must mount his assault with the skill and ruthlessness of a military operation. And when the battle ends, the mountain remains unvanquished. There are no true victors, only survivors.

The World's Highest Garbage Dump

It is not surprising that with so many expeditions milling around Everest a considerable mountain of rubbish has accumulated which needs to be removed. There have been a number of Everest clean-up expeditions. For example, Bob Hoffman's American environmental expedition put 13 climbers, including ten Sherpas, on the summit on 24 May 2000, but is reported to have brought down 509 oxygen cylinders left on the South Col, as well as 122 of their own. They also collected 26lb (12kg) of batteries, 370lb (168kg) of burnable and 77lb (35kg) of non-biodegradable rubbish from all over the mountain, much of it being taken back to Kathmandu or the USA for proper disposal. They also arranged to transport 1,830lb (832kg) of human excrement and 1,650lb (750kg) of waste food in plastic barrels to Gorak Shep for burial. Base Camp, at least, is now much cleaner and better maintained than many other public places. (I am not particularly proud of our most popular English seaside resorts after an August bank holiday!) However, I question whether it is worth risking the lives of Sherpas to make special journeys through the unpredictable Khumbu Icefall in order to bring down dead bodies and empty oxygen bottles from the South Col and above, particularly if it does not make economic sense to do so. Why not stack the cylinders into a great pyramid on the South Col like a Buddhist chorten as a reminder and memorial to those 170 or more who have died on the mountain? When I met Tashi Tenzing again after his second ascent in May 2002, he told me the latest clean-up expedition had been very successful. There were no longer any oxygen cylinders left on the South Col.

Whereas in the early days, deaths in the Khumbu Icefall predominated (50 per cent of fatalities up until 1969), now a high proportion occur above 26,240ft (8,000m), and there are surprisingly few in the Icefall (only 4.3 per cent during the 1990s). The reason is not entirely clear; perhaps the movement of ice is slowing down and it is marginally more stable. Also there is now co-operation in making the initial route through the Icefall each season, to avoid a proliferation of routes which cannot all be the safest. When it was agreed which party would take on the responsibility, then the others would be asked to contribute towards the cost. This has now progressed further. Since 2000, the locally staffed Sagarmartha Pollution Control Committee (SPCC) has been charged with equipping the Icefall, subcontracting to the trekking agency Arun Treks. The cost to expeditions for this service was $2,100 per expedition of up to seven members, plus $275 for each additional member.

The Madding Crowd

The number of climbers coming to Everest and successfully reaching the summit continues to rise as shown by the graph. For example, the number of ascents in 2000 was more than five times greater than in 1978, and was greater than the total number achieved for the years 1953 to 1981.

The statistics from 1953 to the end of 2001 were as follows:

Number of ascents	1,501
Number of individuals	1,114
Number of deaths	171
Number of women ascents	73
Number of women: individuals	69
Number of ascents without oxygen	107
Number of ascents without oxygen: individuals	85

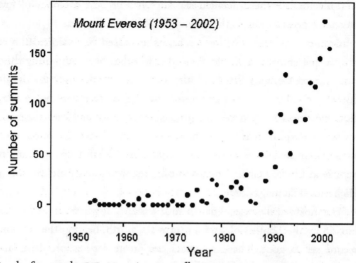

Graph of ascents by R.B. Huey (provisionally 267 ascents in 2003)

In round figures, only 1 in 14 ascents is made without supplementary oxygen, and 1 in 21 ascents by a woman. The statistics for the year 2001 were impressive. There were nearly 50 separate teams on the mountain. All were on the standard southern or northern route except one. Counting Sherpas and Base Camp staff, probably over 1,000 people were involved. There were 183 successful ascents in just five days: 19, 22, 23, 24 and 25 May. Of these, 101 were from Nepal and 82 from Tibet. On 23 May alone, 47 climbers reached the summit from Nepal and 42 from Tibet: a grand total of 89! In 2002 there were another 159 ascents. In spring 2003, commemorating the 50th Anniversary, there were thought to be a further 267 ascents by 260 people. High winds during the first half of May prevented serious attempts, but patience was rewarded and all the ascents were between 20 and 31 May. In contrast, the autumn season 2003 was very quiet, with no ascents at all! So to the end of 2003, according to the latest estimate by Eberhard Jurgalski, there have probably been some 1,925 ascents.

Collecting all these detailed statistics has become a labour of love by many people. Elizabeth Hawley in Kathmandu used to interview returning expeditions. More recently she passed her information to the Basque chronicler Xavier Eguskitza who has been compiling them since 1974. A German, Eberhard Jurgalski, started independently in 1981 but as the volume of data increased they began co-operating in 1997. Now Eguskitza has retired and Jurgalski has continued with the backing of the Explorers Internet company and the data may be found on www.AdventureStats.com. I am most grateful to all these people, and to my friend Lindsay Griffin, who compiles the 'Mountain Info' section of High Mountain magazine.

The most popular ascent day in 2003 was 22 May when 117 reached the top; 68 by the South Col, and 49 from the north, beating the previous record set in 2001. These numbers can create serious problems and congestion at places like the Hillary Step where you can really only move one at a time up or down the fixed ropes. Guides have to act like high-altitude traffic wardens! The previous record was a mere 40, on 10 May 1993. If William Wordsworth had been there what would he have had to say? Hardly:

> I wander'd lonely as a cloud
> That floats on high o'er vales and hills

I think he would have been very glad to get back to Dove Cottage!

The Last Great Problem

What is there left to do on Everest? Not very much.

A bright red frisbee was skimmed from the summit down the East Face by Chris Pizzo on 24 October 1981 in conjunction with serious sampling of alveolar air, as part of Dr John West's medical expedition. Then in May 2003, an Irishman struck the highest hurling shot in history. Zaid Aasa Al

Refa'l from Kuwait became the first Arab on 22nd, and 33-year-old Sibusiso Vilane became the first black African on 26th. Finally on 30th, the Alaskan guide Vernon Tejas took up his guitar to strum a few chords on the summit before descending.

There is still the unclimbed but seemingly rather dangerous Fantasy Ridge on the East Face. Nobody has traversed the mountain, up the West Ridge and down the East or vice versa. The truly gargantuan challenge is the complete Everest horseshoe from the Nepalese Base Camp: up the West Ridge, down the South-East to the South Col, then up the North Ridge of Lhotse and continuing the traverse along the ridge to Nuptse, and descending its North-West Ridge towards the Khumbu Icefall. It's the sort of challenge the Russians like to accept, with their experience of the Bezingi Wall in the Caucasus and their magnificent traverse of all four summits of Kangchenjunga in 1989, led by Eduard Myslovski. I am sure it will be done some day.

Meanwhile, as a different sort of challenge to mark the 50th anniversary in 2003, we were approached in 2001 by a television production company to consider an expedition to Everest 'in the style of 1953', which could be broadcast live to television audiences in the UK and around the world. The idea was to use the same route, resources, organisation and equipment as our original 1953 expedition as far as possible. A team of young climbers would be chosen who were highly experienced but who had not previously been to Everest. It was an intriguing concept to see how they would cope using long, old-fashioned ice axes and cutting hundreds of steps on the Lhotse Face, while having to climb alongside the caravans of commercial clients staggering up their icy staircase, or perching on the front points of their fitted crampons while clients jumar up the fixed ropes. We got as far as interviewing potential leaders, selecting one and several core members of the team. All we lacked was sponsorship. I had actually been in the TV production company's offices on 11 September 2001 when the World Trade Center was demolished in New York. We stood transfixed watching the live action as the second aircraft flew into the second tower. After that shattering world changing event, the chance of finding sponsors for our project seemed to fade away and the idea was abandoned, but all was not lost.

On his way home after interview, one of the potential leaders, Lt Col. Nick Arding of the Royal Marines, realised that a British Navy team had never yet climbed Everest, although the Army and the Royal Air Force had already done so. He was able to persuade his top level command that this was a worthy objective, and could be combined with three support treks, as part of the Navy's adventurous training.

Despite high winds earlier in the month, on 22 May 2003 the climbing leader, Dave Pearce, and Chering Dorje Sherpa reached the summit by the North Ridge. The team then became involved in a dramatic rescue. Conan Harrod, a British climber from another team, suffered a broken leg at around 27,880ft (8,500m), just below the Second Step, when a climber from yet another party, using the same fixed rope, slipped and fell just above him. 'I thought I was dead,' said Harrod, 'and there was no chance I was going to get off the mountain.' His companions Abuhaider and Madew were able to help him down over the First Step and, with the assistance of others, to reach the High Camp at 26,900ft (8,200m) for the night. Continuing down to 24,930ft (7,600m), the larger Navy team, renouncing any further summit attempts, were able to help Harrod down to the North Col using a rope stretcher and eventually to the safety of Advance Base. Madew was also now suffering from snow-blindness and frostbite. Marine Darren Swift accompanied him down to Advance Base, at times carrying him on his back. So happily this time, fatalities were avoided and the rescue brought to a successful conclusion by the selfless act of those climbers who generously went to their aid.

The incident came to the notice of the Royal Humane Society which gives bravery awards to people who have put their own lives at risk in order to save someone else. In May 2004, the Society awarded Marine Darren Swift its most prestigious Gold Medal for the most outstanding rescue of the year.

Our Debt to the Sherpas

Finally, how far would any of us have got up the mountain without the porters and the high altitude Sherpas of Nepal and their counterparts on the Tibetan side? We owe them an immense debt. For many of the Sherpas, it was just a job that paid rather better than tending yaks and supporting treks, although not without its risks. But for a fair proportion it was a challenge that they gladly accepted and they showed tremendous loyalty and often great affection for their employers, which was reciprocated. Many have now become competent mountaineers in their own right, drawing upon the strength, stamina and speed that comes naturally to them at high altitude. Of the 1,318 Everest ascents to the end of the year 2000, 489 were made by Sherpas, or Nepalis acting in a 'Sherpa' role. With the increase in commercial expeditions, some Sherpas have climbed Everest again and again in support of their clients. Several of the outstanding ones have come from the village of Thame where Tenzing was brought up, and are quiet, unassuming and modest men. Ang Rita has become a legend, climbing Everest ten times without supplementary oxygen. His record has been overtaken by 42-year-old Apa Sherpa with 13 ascents, using oxygen on occasions but generally without it. Apa Sherpa's first ascent was in 1990 and he has summitted almost every year since. I had the pleasure of meeting him at the Kendal Film Festival in November 2003 and he assured us that he had not finished yet! The popular Babu Chiri, already mentioned, had made ten ascents until his tragic crevasse accident in April 2001. These men were proud to maintain the traditions established by the earlier great Sherpas: men such as Angtharkay, forever associated with the names of Shipton and Tilman; our own Tenzing Norgay of 1953; his nephew Nawang Gombu; Dawa Tensing, our sirdar on Kangchenjunga; and Chris Bonington's favourite sirdar, Pertemba, of whom Chris would later write:

> Highly intelligent, good-looking, charismatic, he seemed at home in any situation in the West, and yet he hadn't lost the traditional values of Sherpa society. He had that combination of twinkling humour, dignity and warmth that is one of the enduring qualities of so many Sherpas.

I had an unusual and heart-warming experience in Darjeeling only last April 2002, on my way to lead a trek in northern Sikkim. It was triggered by George Lowe who had been there the previous year trying to contact any Sherpas still living from our 1953 Everest expedition, in addition to Nawang Gombu, who is still hale and hearty. George met another Sherpa, Dawa Temba, who said: 'Would you like to meet my father, Ang Tsering, aged 97 years, who has been on 14 major Himalayan expeditions?' That is an incredible age for a Sherpa; they rarely live much beyond 70 years. George had a memorable meeting and I was able to repeat the experience on 30 April. Ang Tsering was the only surviving member of the 1924 Everest Expedition which was led by Colonel Norton. A remarkable co-incidence was that a member of my trekking party was Bill Norton, one of Colonel Norton's sons, and Bill came with me to meet Ang Tsering.

Gombu led us to Ang Tsering's modest but beautifully kept house and garden in the Sherpa quarter of Darjeeling called Toong Soong. Ang Tsering stood to meet us, still firm and upright, although he complained he was now a little deaf. The softly spoken Dorje Lhatoo, who had succeeded Gombu as director of field training at the Himalayan Mountaineering Institute, kindly came with us and helped to interpret. Ang Tsering was born in 1904, so he would have been 20 on the 1924 Expedition. He had earned his Tiger badge by carrying a load to Camp V at 25,500ft (7,620m), well above the North Col. His name is recorded as Angtenjin in the expedition book. Subsequently, he was on Kangchenjunga with Bauer in 1929 and with Dyhrenfurth in 1930, and again on Everest in Ruttledge's Expedition of 1933. Then with Willi Merkl on Nanga Parbat in 1934, he narrowly escaped disaster when three Sahibs and six Sherpas were killed. He survived seven days without food, but got frostbitten feet and several toes had to be amputated. He was hospitalised for most of a year, and had not recovered sufficiently to climb Everest again in the 1930s, but his name cropped up as a cook with the Swiss on Everest in 1952. His last expedition was to Abi Gamin in Garhwal in 1964 when he was 60. We looked through various old photo albums, and at an impressive display of medals, among them the Tiger's badge, but in the centre was an unusual white cross. This had been presented by Adolf Hitler for his outstanding performance on the Nanga Parbat expedition.

Ang Tsering intrigued us with one story about Everest in 1924. When Colonel Norton and the expedition members went to the Head Lama of Rongbuk to receive his blessing, the Lama wished the Sahibs success in their climb, but he spoke separately to the Sherpas in their own tongue. 'Do what the Sahibs ask of you,' said the Lama, 'but not so that they reach the summit, because this would be a bad omen for your families, for the monks here at Rongbuk and for the local people.' The Head Lama was a wily old bird! So ended this remarkable meeting. We came outside for photographs in the sunshine and to bid Ang Tsering farewell feeling that he would have no trouble in reaching his century. Sadly it was not to be. When I returned home to England an e-mail was waiting for me. 'On 22 May Ang Tsering passed away at his home in Darjeeling. He suffered a stroke three weeks ago and never regained consciousness.' We were privileged to be his last foreign visitors. Bill Norton and I felt that the Everest story had come full circle.

Although Ang Tsering might not be able to express his motive for going to Everest any better than I can, I think in our hearts we would both agree with the words of Wilfrid Noyce:

> But if adventure has a final and all-embracing motive it is surely this: We go out because it is in our nature to go out, to climb the mountains and sail the seas, to fly to the planets and plunge into the depths of the oceans. By doing these things we make touch with something outside or behind, which strangely seems to approve

our doing them. We extend our horizon, we expand our being, we revel in a mastery of ourselves which gives an impression, mainly illusory, that we are masters of our world. In a word, we are men, and when man ceases to do these things, he is no longer man.

The Supporters of Everest Expeditions

Mount Everest Foundation

PATRON: HRH THE DUKE OF EDINBURGH, KG, KT

The Mount Everest Foundation (MEF), a UK-based charity, was an imaginative and far-sighted initiative set up after the first ascent of Everest in 1953, and financed from the proceeds of the British 1953 Everest Expedition. Its principal aim is to encourage exploration and science in the world's mountain regions – to continue the superb endeavour of 1953.

The MEF has now supported about 1,400 expeditions from Britain and New Zealand. Most grants are now awarded to lightweight expeditions attempting innovative ascents and exploration in remote, often little-known ranges. Scientific objectives span many disciplines in high mountains. Many of the British and New Zealand first ascents of the last 50 years have been supported by MEF grants, enabling climbers from these countries to maintain a high profile in international mountaineering. No other nation has a similar resource dedicated to these ends. The MEF also aims to protect mountain peoples and wildlife. All projects must conform to strict environmental criteria.

Between 1954 and 2002, over £750,000 in grants has been awarded, and at minimal administrative cost. The foundation is keen to attract additional funds. Further information can be found on the MEF website www.mef.org.uk or by writing to the MEF, c/o the Royal Geographical Society, 1 Kensington Gore, London SW7 2AR.

The Alpine Club

The Alpine Club is a club for experienced mountaineers who climb in the Alps and other mountain ranges around the world, and has a current membership of around 1,200. It was founded in 1857, when it was the first and only climbing club in the world, and as such its early members more or less invented the sport and made many of the first ascents at the time. Since then it has remained at the forefront of world mountaineering and has included most of the leading British mountaineers of each generation, from Whymper to the climbers in the early Everest expeditions from 1921 to 1953, and later outstanding performers such as Chris Bonington, Doug Scott, Stephen Venables and Alison Hargreaves.

In addition to its vigorous climbing activities, with many first ascents made every year in mountain regions all around the world, The Alpine Club promotes a code of climbing ethics that seeks to protect mountains, mountain regions and their people.

The Alpine Club also has an extensive collection of photographs and paintings on mountaineering subjects, which it can supply through its Picture Library, and a world-renowned collection of mountaineering literature with over 25,000 books, journals, guide books and expedition reports. Further information, including its unique computerised Himalayan Index, is available on The Alpine Club website, www.alpine-club.org.uk or by writing to The Alpine Club, 55 Charlotte Road, London EC2A 3QF.

Royal Geographical Society
(with the Institute of British Geographers)

The Royal Geographical Society (with the IBG) was founded in 1830 and given a Royal Charter in 1859 for 'the advancement of geographical science'. It was pivotal in establishing geography as a teaching and research discipline in British universities, and has played a key role in geographical and environmental education ever since. Today the Society is a leading world centre for geographical learning, supporting education, teaching, research and expeditions, as well as promoting public understanding and enjoyment of the subject. The Society holds historical collections of national and international importance, much of which relate to the Society's association and support for scientific exploration and research from the 19th century onwards. The Society is proud to hold the 'Everest Archive', a collection of some 20,000 images taken on the nine British Mount Everest expeditions between 1921 and 1953, of which a selection are featured in this book.

The Society would like to thank Rolex for its generous support of the Everest Archive Project 2001–3. This support has allowed photographs to be catalogued and electronically databased. This information will be available on-line and widely accessible. The Society welcomes those interested in geography and its collections. For further information please visit the website, www.rgs.org, or write to the Royal Geographical Society (with the IBG) at 1 Kensington Gore, London SW7 2AR.

Selected Bibliography

This is only a selected Bibliography, relating mostly to British attempts and ascents, or to notable ascents by climbers from other nations. For a more comprehensive Bibliography consult Walt Unsworth's *Everest* (1981, 2000), and for the definitive work consult *Climbing Mount Everest, The Bibliography*, compiled by Audrey Salkeld and John Boyle (1993). Even this work is not complete. When John Boyle visited my library, I was delighted to show him a paperback he had not seen called *Het Geheim van de Mount Everest*, the lurid fictional adventures of Frank, The Flying Dutchman, which I had picked up from a bookstall in the Netherlands. He was later able to track down a second cartoon edition for himself but I never dared ask how much he had to pay for it!

There are, of course, numerous articles about climbing Everest in magazines, periodicals and newspapers. The two best historical sources to consult are *The Alpine Journal* (now published annually by The Alpine Club) and the *Geographical Journal*, published by the Royal Geographical Society or the more popular *Geographical Magazine*. The Times newspaper prints exclusive reports, dispatches and occasional special supplements reporting the successive British expeditions in return for helping to fund them.

For summaries of contemporary activity on Everest, I regularly consult the 'Mountain Info' section of *High Mountain Sports magazine*, published monthly by Greenshires of Kettering, NN16 8UN, UK (www.greenshires. com).

Journals

Alpine Club, The, *The Alpine Journal*. Continuous record since 1863, now published annually.

American Alpine Club, *American Alpine Journal*. Continuous record of all mountain activity, published annually.

Royal Geographical Society, *Geographical Journal*. Regular periodical of the Society, of particular interest to the Everest story from the first reconnaissance expedition of 1921 to the successful climb of 1953 (the period of the Mount Everest Committee on which the RGS was represented).

Books

Barnes, M., *After Everest: An Autobiography* (of Sherpa Tenzing), London, 1977.

Bass, D. and Wells, F. (with Ridgeway, R.), *Seven Summits*, New York, 1986.

Bonington, C.J.S., *Everest, South-West Face*, London, 1973.

Bonington, C.J.S., *Everest, The Hard Way*, London, 1976.

Bonington, C.J.S. and Clarke, C., *Everest, The Unclimbed Ridge*, London, 1983.

Boyle, J., *Everest 83, An Aerial Tramway*, privately printed, San Francisco, 1988.

Breashears, D. and Salkeld, A., *Last Climb, The Legendary Everest Expeditions of George Mallory*, Washington, 1999.

Bruce, Brig. Gen. The Hon. C.G., *The Assault on Mount Everest, 1922*, London, 1923.

Bruce, Brig. Gen. The Hon. C.G., *Himalayan Wanderer*, London, 1934.

French, P., Younghusband, The Last Great Imperial Adventurer, London, 1994.

Gillman, P. and L., The Wildest Dream, Mallory, His Life and Conflicting Passions, London, 2000.

Gillman, P. (ed.), Everest, The Best Writing and Pictures from Seventy Years of Human Endeavour, Great Britain and USA, 1993, updated as Everest, Eighty Years of Triumph and Tragedy, 2001.

Goswami, S.M., Everest, Is it Conquered? Calcutta, 1954.

Greene, R., Moments of Being, London, 1974.

Gregory, A., The Picture of Everest, London, 1954.

Gregory, A., Alfred Gregory's Everest, London, 1993.

Gulatee, B.L., Mount Everest, Its Name and Height, Dehra Dun, 1950.

Habeler, P. (transl. by Heald, D.), Everest, Impossible Victory, London, 1979.

Haston, D., In High Places, London, 1972.

Hemmlab, J., Johnson, L.A. and Simonson, E.R., Ghosts of Everest, The Authorised Story of the Search for Mallory and Irvine, Seattle, London, 1999.

Hillary, Sir E.P., High Adventure, London, 1955.

Hillary, Sir E.P., View from the Summit, London, 1999.

Himalayan Club, The, The Himalayan Journal, continuous record of the Club, founded in 1928.

Holzel, T. and Salkeld, A., The Mystery of Mallory and Irvine, London, 1986.

Hornbein, T.F., Everest, The West Ridge, San Francisco, 1965; London, 1971.

Howard-Bury, Lt. Col. C.K. (and others), Mount Everest: The Reconnaissance, 1921,. London 1922.

Hunt, J. (Brigadier Sir John Hunt, later Lord Hunt), The Ascent of Everest, London, 1953.

Hunt, J., Our Everest Adventure, Leicester, 1954.

Hunt, J., Life is Meeting, London, 1978.

Izzard, R., The Innocent on Everest, London, 1955.

Bryant, L.V., *New Zealanders and Everest*, Wellington, NZ, 1953.

Burrard, Col. (Sir) S.G., *The Geography and Geology of The Himalayan Mountains and Tibet*, Dehra Dun, 1933–34 (with Heron, A.M.).

Burrard, Col. (Sir) S.G., *Mount Everest and its Tibetan Names*, Dehra Dun, 1931.

Carr, H. (ed.), *The Irvine Diaries, Andrew Irvine and the Enigma of Everest*, Reading, 1979.

Coburn, B., *Everest, Mountain without Mercy*, MacGillivray Freeman Films, USA, 1997.

Cranfield, I. (ed.), *Inspiring Achievement, the Life and Work of John Hunt*, Penrith, 2002.

Curran, J., *High Achiever, The Life and Climbs of Chris Bonington*, London, 1999.

Denman, E., *Alone to Everest*, London, 1954.

Dickinson, L., *Ballooning over Everest*, London, 1993.

Dittert, R., Chevalley, G. and Lambert, R., *Forerunners to Everest, The Story of the Two Swiss Expeditions of 1952*, London, 1954.

Dolbier, M., *Nowhere near Everest*, USA, 1955.

Douglas & Clydesdale, Sq. Ldr, the Marquess of, and McIntyre, Flt Lt D.F., *The Pilot's Book of Everest*, Edinburgh, 1936.

Douglas, E., *Tenzing, Hero of Everest*, National Geographic Adventure Press, Washington DC, 2003.

Douglas-Hamilton, J., *Roof of the World, Man's First Flight over Everest*, Edinburgh, 1983.

Eggler, A., *The Everest-Lhotse Adventure*, London, 1957.

Evans, C., *Eye on Everest, A Sketch Book from the Great Everest Expedition*, London, 1955.

Fellowes, Air Commodore P.F.M. (and others), *First Over Everest, The Houston Mount Everest Expedition*, London, 1933.

Finch, G.I., *The Making of a Mountaineer*, London, 1924; 1989.

Finch, G.I., *Climbing Mount Everest*, London, 1930.

Fleming, J. and Faux, R., *Soldiers on Everest*, London, 1977.

Japan Everest Skiing Expedition, Mount Everest: Yuichiro Miura and The Japanese Everest Skiing Expedition, Tokyo, 1970.

Jefferies, M. and Clarkbrough, M., Sagarmatha, Mother of the Universe; The Story of Mount Everest National Park, Auckland, 1985.

Keiser, A.B. (photographs) and Ramsay, C.R. (text), Sir Edmund Hillary and The People of Everest, Kansas City, 2002.

Kohli, M.S., Nine Atop Everest: Story of the Indian Ascent, Bombay, 1969.

Krakauer, J., Into Thin Air, New York, 1997.

Lowe, G., Because it is There, London, 1959.

Lunn, A., A Century of Mountaineering 1857–1957, London, 1957.

Mason, K., Abode of Snow: A History of Himalayan Exploration and Mountaineering, London, 1955.

Messner, R. (transl. by Salkeld, A.), Everest: Expedition to the Ultimate, London, 1977.

Messner, R., The Crystal Horizon: Everest – The First Solo Ascent, Marlborough/Seattle, 1989.

Miura, Y., The Man Who Skied Down Everest, Tokyo, 1974; and San Francisco/New York, 1978 (with Perlman, E.).

Morin, M., Everest: From the First Attempt to Final Victory, London, 1955.

Morris, James, Coronation Everest, London, 1958.

Morrow, P., Beyond Everest: Quest for the Seven Summits, Camden, Ontario, 1986.

Murray, W.H., The Story of Everest, London, 1953.

Murray, W.H., The Evidence of Things Not Seen – A Mountaineer's Tale, Baton Wicks, 2002.

Neate, W.R. (Jill), Mountaineering and its Literature, Milnthorpe, 1978.

Noel, Captain J.B.L., Through Tibet to Everest, London, 1927; 1989.

Norton, Lt. Col. E.F. (and others), The Fight for Everest: 1924, London, 1925.

Noyce, C.W.F., South Col, One Man's Adventure on the Ascent of Everest 1953, London, 1954.

Pye, D., George Leigh Mallory: A Memoir, London, 1927.

Roberts, D., I'll Climb Mount Everest Alone; The Story of Maurice Wilson, London, 1957.

Robertson, D., George Mallory, London, 1969.

Rose, D. and Douglas, E., Regions of the Heart, The Triumph and Tragedy of Alison Hargreaves, London, 1999.

Rowell, G., Mountains of the Middle Kingdom, San Francisco, 1983.

Ruttledge, H. (and others), Everest 1933, London, 1934.

Ruttledge, H. (and others), Everest, The Unfinished Adventure, London, 1937.

Salkeld, A. and Boyle, J., Climbing Mount Everest, The Bibliography, Clevedon, 1993.

Seaver, G., Francis Younghusband 1863–1942, Explorer and Mystic, London, 1952.

Shipton, E.E., 'The Mount Everest Reconnaissance, 1935' (articles in Geographical Journal, February 1936 and The Alpine Journal, May, 1936).

Shipton, E.E., The Mount Everest Reconnaissance Expedition 1951, London, 1952.

Shipton, E.E., That Untravelled World, London, 1969.

Smythe, F.S., Camp Six, London, 1937.

Somervell, T.H., After Everest, The Experiences of a Mountaineer and Medical Missionary, London, 1936.

Steele, P., Doctor on Everest, London, 1972.

Steele, P., Eric Shipton, Everest and Beyond, London, 1998.

Stephens, R., On Top of the World, London, 1994.

Stobart, T., Adventurer's Eye, London, 1958.

Summerhayes, D. and Thomas, J., Christopher Summerhayes, Soldier, Levant Consul and Diplomat, Chichester, 1998.

Summers, J., Fearless on Everest, The Quest for Sandy Irvine, London, 2000.

Tasker, J., Everest, The Cruel Way, London, 1981.

Tasker, J., The Savage Arena, London, 1982.

Tenzing Norgay, J., Touching my Father's Soul, In the Footsteps of Sherpa Tenzing, Great Britain and USA, 2001.

Tenzing, J. and T., Tenzing and the Sherpas of Everest, Sydney, 2001.

Tilman, H.W., Mount Everest 1938, Cambridge, 1948.

Tilman, H.W., Nepal Himalaya, Cambridge, 1952.

Ullman, J.R., Americans on Everest, USA, 1964.

Ullman, J.R., Tiger of the Snows: The Autobiography of Tenzing of Everest, Philadelphia, 1964.

Unsworth, W., Everest: A Mountaineering History, London, 1981, Third Edition, 2000.

Venables, S., Everest Kangshung Face, London, 1989.

Ward, M.P., In this Short Span, A Mountaineering Memoir, London, 1972.

Ward, M.P., Everest: a Thousand Years of Exploration, Glasgow, 2003.

Ward, M.P. and Clark, P.K., 'Everest, 1951: Cartographic and photographic evidence of a new route from Nepal', Geographical Journal, Vol. 158, No. 1, March 1992, pp. 47–56.

Ward, M.P., Milledge, J.S. and West, J.P., High Altitude Medicine and Physiology, London, 1989.

Webster, E., Snow in the Kingdom, My Storm Years on Everest, Colorado, 2000.

Wells, C., A Brief History of British Mountaineering, Manchester, 2001.

West, John B., Everest, The Testing Place, McGraw Hill Book Company, 1985.

Younghusband, Sir F.E., The Epic of Everest, London, 1926.

Younghusband, Sir F.E., Everest, The Challenge, London, 1936.

Index